Contemporary Fused Glass

A guide to fusing, slumping, and kilnforming glass

by Brad Walker

Four Corners International, Inc.   Clemmons, North Carolina, USA

Contemporary Fused Glass

A Guide to Fusing, Slumping, and Kilnforming Glass
by Brad Walker

Published by:

Four Corners International, Inc.
4140 Clemmons Road, #320
Clemmons, NC 27012

Front cover artwork by Samantha Allen and Jody Danner Walker

Library of Congress Control Number: 2010923806

ISBN Number: 0-9700933-1-4
ISBN 13: 978-0-9700933-1-8

Printed in the United States of America

http://www.warmglass.com

Acknowledgements

When *Contemporary Warm Glass*, the forerunner of the book you now hold in your hands, was written over a decade ago, it was meant to serve as an introduction to the basics of working with glass in a kiln. My goal was to write a readable, informative, and up-to-date overview of the state of the art of kilnforming.

The goal of this book is the same. It begins with an extensive update of the information contained in my earlier book, then expands with new material, processes, and techniques. *Contemporary Fused Glass* is 30% larger than *Contemporary Warm Glass*. My hope is that the revised and additional information proves valuable to both the novice and the experienced glass artist.

As with my first book, the online community at warmglass.com has been an invaluable source of information, inspiration, and enjoyment. Many of the posters on the bulletin board started as strangers, but have since become friends and confidants. The willingness and generosity of people I've met on the internet will never cease to amaze me.

Thanks to the sponsors of warmglass.com for their support, with special mention to Bullseye, Spectrum, and Uroboros, who have been there from the start. Thanks also to all of the artists who contributed photos of their work to this edition. A melancholy tip of the hat to Brock Craig, for sharing his extensive knowledge of kilnforming. And special thanks to Carol Beckett and Jace Allen, who should have been around to help with my first book.

Finally, thanks most of all to my wife, Jody, and to our daughter, Samantha. They have been invaluable partners in both business and life. Their assistance, guidance, and patience can not be overstated.

Table of Contents

Chapter 1

Introduction

Kiln-formed glass • A condensed history • Basic equipment

Kiln-formed glass

The discipline of kiln-formed glass goes by several names, including kilnforming, fused glass, kiln glass, and warm glass, but whatever name is used it involves using a kiln to heat and shape glass. The kiln, which is basically a very hot oven, can be a especially made for firing glass, or it can be a pottery kiln that has been adapted for glass.

To better understand this process, let's look at what happens if we want to make a basic glass bowl like the one shown below.

Making a bowl involves several firings in the kiln. The first is a "fuse" firing, where previously cut pieces of glass are assembled together, placed on a flat shelf in a kiln, and then heated

to a temperature approaching 1500 Fahrenheit (815 Celsius). At this temperature the individual pieces of glass "fuse" together to form a single, solid piece. This process is called "glass fusing."

Because fused pieces are generally flat, fusing is often used to form coasters, tiles, or flat wall hangings. But if you want a piece to take on a shape like a bowl, then fusing is not enough. A second firing, called a "slump" firing, is also needed.

Slumping requires a "mold," a specially prepared piece of clay or stainless steel the shape of the final piece. A previously fused glass piece is placed on top of the mold and re-fired. This second firing isn't as hot as the first, generally going only to a temperature between 1100 and 1300F

"Smiley's Bowl" by Karuna Santoro. Fused and slumped bowl. (Photo courtesy of the artist.)

(670 to 700C). At that temperature gravity and heat combine to help the glass move down (or "slump") into the mold. After the piece is shaped, it is carefully cooled, then removed from the mold and cleaned, ready to admire and use.

That's the kilnforming process in a nutshell. Some pieces are more complicated than others, and some require more than one or two firings to achieve their unique appearance, but the basic idea is to fuse together individual pieces of glass and then slump them if you want your finished piece to be shaped rather than flat.

A third type of kilnforming activity, called kiln casting, is used to make more complicated shapes. Casting involves constructing a more elaborate mold that's designed to hold individual pieces (or a large chunk) of glass. The mold-making process can be quite extensive, but once the mold is created, it is filled and then fired in the kiln, so that pieces melt together and take on the shape of the mold.

So, to summarize, the three major kinds of kilnforming activities are:

- **Glass fusing** - joining individual pieces of glass together by melting them in a kiln. This takes place at around 1400 to 1500F (760 to 815C).

- **Glass slumping** - shaping glass by heating it over or into a simple mold inside a kiln. This takes place from 1100 to 1300F (670 to 700C).

- **Kiln casting** - using a kiln to melt and shape glass pieces that have been placed inside a specially constructed mold.

This book will cover the first two of these activities in detail and will also offer a general description of the more complicated kiln casting process.

A condensed history

Although glass is inherently fragile, and only fragments and isolated vessels survive from the distant past, most scholars agree that the first glass was created in the Bronze Age, about 3000 years BC. Early glass processes evolved from ceramics and metalworking techniques, with glass taking its place alongside gold and silver as a precious material.

By the time of the first millennium BC, many of the basic glass fusing and slumping techniques had been developed. Although the details of their construction are doubtless different than bowls made today, slumped and cast bowls were created in ancient Syria, Persia, Egypt, and Rome. In addition, artisans during this time developed other glass techniques, such as working with glass rods (now called flameworking or lampworking), grinding and polishing, and creating vessels with sophisticated patterns.

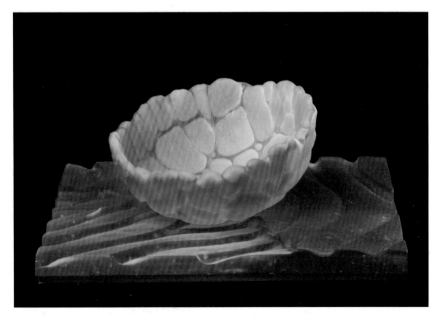

Bob Leatherbarrow, "Swept Away." Kiln-formed glass powders, slumped to bowl shape. Kiln cast base, using shell as model. (Photo courtesy of the artist.)

Above: Assorted fused and slumped glass plates by Dorothy Hafner. Each plate is 8" square. (Photo by Magin Schantz, courtesy of the artist.)

Right: Avery Anderson, "Spirit of the Wolf." Kilnformed glass, laminated and sandblasted. (Photo courtesy of the artist.)

Below: Terri Stanley, "Paradox." Kiln cast glass. (Photo by William Stanley, courtesy of the artist.)

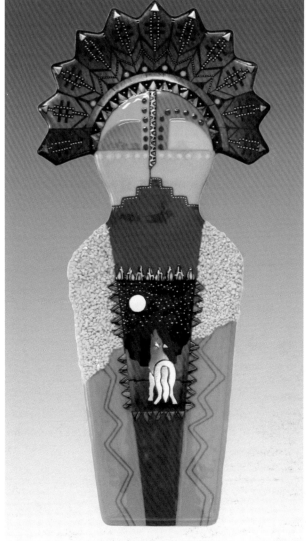

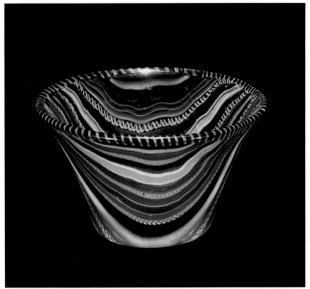

Ribbon Glass Cup. Roman Empire, probably Italy, late 1st B.C.–mid 1st A.D. Preformed canes; fused, slumped in mold, fire-polished, lathe-turned. Collection of The Corning Museum of Glass, Corning, NY (72.1.11).

Ribbed Bowl. Roman Empire, about 50–75 A.D. Translucent deep blue; cast. Collection of The Corning Museum of Glass, Corning, NY (67.1.21).

The development of these techniques, which tended to produce glass pieces one at a time (not unlike contemporary fusing and slumping), led to a period during the latter part of the first millennium BC when glass was consider very rare and precious.

This flowering was short-lived, however, due to the emergence of the new technique of "glass-blowing." This approach, which involved using a long rod (called a "blowpipe") to manipulate glass that had been heated in a furnace, was invented by the Syrians and developed by the Romans. Compared to kilnforming, glassblowing had the advantage of greater efficiency, repeatability, and lower cost. It became the technique of choice and rapidly spread throughout the Roman Empire.

By the second or third century AD, many kilnforming techniques were overshadowed by the emergence of glassblowing. Although cast and slumped items were still being made, they were dwarfed in quantity and influence by glassblown items, which were less expensive and more easily produced in quantity.

In the 19th century in Europe, the growth of the craft arena as a vehicle for artistic expression, coupled with discoveries of ancient glass by archaeologists, led to attempts to recreate the

kilnforming methods used by the ancients. These efforts led to the rebirth of kilnforming and the second flowering of the discipline.

One of the first centers for the rebirth of warm glass was the pate de verre movement which began during the late 19th century in France. This movement, whose major proponents included Henri Cros, Albert Dammouse, and Gabriel Argy-Rousseau, developed techniques for casting with a paste made from small glass particles..

In the United States in the first half of the twentieth century, pioneering work in kilnforming was done by Edris Eckhart, Maurice Heaton, and Michael and Francis Higgins. The Higginses, in particular, were instrumental in developing many fusing and slumping techniques that are now commonplace.

The studio glass movement, which was led by Harvey Littleton and centered mostly on glassblowing, brought respectability to the new discipline of working with glass.

The Bullseye Glass Company, formed by three glassblowers in 1974 in Oregon, played an important role in the development of the kiln-formed glass discipline. Bullseye led the first major effort to research and develop a line of "tested compatible" glass made specifically for

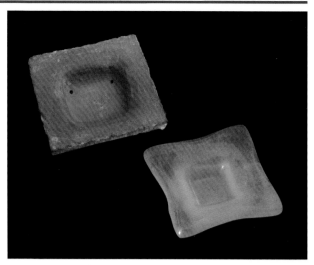

Left: "Upward Unulation," Harvey Littleton, 1974. Kiln-formed sheet glass; aluminum base. Collection of The Corning Museum of Glass, Corning, NY (79.4.145).

Above: "Dish and Mold," Frances and Michael Higgins, 1948. The first glass object made by the Higgenses. The ceramic mold is the original mold. Collection of the Corning Museum of Glass, Corning, NY (2007.4.25)

use in fusing. Other manufacturers, including Uroboros and Spectrum, followed suit, expanding the options and color palette available to the glass artist.

The availability of glass made specifically for use in the kiln led to a new generation of glass artists who explored the possibilities of the medium. Most notable of these was Klaus Moje. In addition to working with Bullseye to develop tested compatible glass, Moje was instrumental in spreading the knowledge of fusing and slumping throughout Europe and Australia.

Today, after nearly two centuries of rediscovery and enhancement, kiln-formed glass continues to develop and grow as a viable artistic discipline. The increasing availability of better materials, coupled with the widespread availability of information in books and on the internet and the widespread adoption of kilns with computer controllers, have greatly expanded the opportunities for artists and hobbyists alike. Add to that a relatively low cost of entry and it's no wonder that the kilnforming discipline is well positioned for continuing growth in the twenty-first century and beyond.

Klaus Moje: "Untitled 9-1989-#45." Kiln-formed glass, ground. Collection of the Corning Museum of Glass, Corning, NY (2007.6.10).

Basic equipment

Aside from the glass, the most important item needed for fusing and slumping glass is a kiln. Glass kilns are electric and are capable of reaching temperatures of approximately 1800F/982C. Kilns are available in sizes ranging from less than a cubic foot to big enough to fill a room. Kilns made for ceramics can be used for fusing and slumping glass, but it's better to have one that's specifically engineered for firing glass.

Kilns must be capable of accurately monitoring and displaying the temperature inside the kiln. This requires a pyrometer, a precise thermometer that is often coupled with a controller, a computerized device that helps manage the firing of the kiln. A controller greatly simplifies the task of precisely directing and monitoring temperature changes inside the kiln. It's possible to fire glass without a controller, but it requires keeping a close watch on the kiln as it fires.

In addition to the kiln, fusing glass requires a shelf to set the glass on and (if you want to slump) a mold to help shape the glass. Shelves are generally made of clay or a lightweight refractory material, while molds can be made of clay, stainless steel, or various kinds of cements and plaster mixtures. The key is that both the shelf and the mold must have the ability to withstand heating and then cooling back to room temperature.

Top loading kiln with controller. (Photo by the author.)

Keeping glass from sticking to the kiln shelf requires a separator between the shelf and the glass. This can be a special kind of paper that glass won't stick to at high temperatures (called fiber paper or shelf paper) or it can be an emulsion that you apply to the shelf, then allow to dry (commonly called a shelf primer or kiln wash). Without this separator, glass will stick to the shelf or mold when it gets hot and your piece of artwork will be ruined.

That's it. If you have some glass, a kiln, a shelf or mold, and something to keep the glass from sticking, you have the basic ingredients to begin fusing and slumping. Add some tools to help cut the glass and a few essential pieces of safety equipment, and you're ready to begin.

An assortment of molds for slumping. (Photo by the author.)

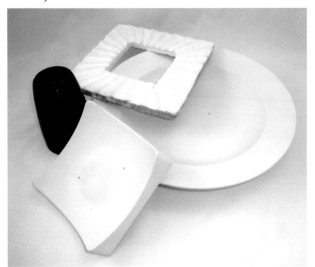

Essential safety equipment: gloves, mask, and glasses. (Photo by the author.)

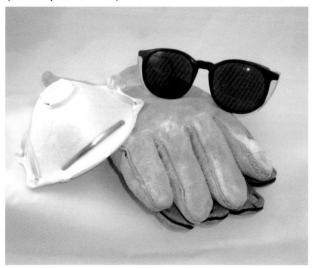

Chapter 2

Glass types and forms

Compatibility and coefficient of expansion • Compatibility testing • Tested compatible glass • Stained glass • Float glass • Recycled glass and bottle glass • Iridescent glass • Dichroic glass • Glass shapes and sizes • Sheet glass • Striking • Frit and powder • Stringers and noodles • Rods • Cullet, billets, patties, and dalle • Confetti

There are many different production methods and recipes for making glass. As a result, there are almost as many different types of glass as there are glass artists who want to use them. Types of glass range from basic window glass (called "float glass") to brightly colored stained glass (often called "art glass"), and many of the types of glass come in numerous sub-types and categories.

In addition, there are many types of glass coatings, such as iridescent and dichroic, which have unique properties when applied to glass. New types of glass and glass coatings are constantly being developed.

> *Because different pieces of glass expand and contract at different rates, care must be taken to only fuse glass that is "compatible."*

Compatibility and coefficient of expansion

All of these different glass types are candidates for fusing, slumping, and other kilnforming processes. Some can be used off the shelf, but others require testing to make sure they will work in the kiln. That's because it's likely that you will want to combine more than one different sheet of glass in your projects. If so, then you'll need to make sure the glass you select is "compatible."

Using incompatible glass may cause cracking or even shattering of the piece when it cools.

To better understand compatibility, let's consider what happens when glass gets heated in a kiln. Like many other substances, glass expands when it gets hot and contracts when it cools. This change in density, which occurs at the molecular level, can be measured in a laboratory. A typical one inch piece of Bullseye brand glass, for example, will expand 0.0000090 inches for each 1 degree Centigrade (about 1.8 degrees Fahrenheit) increase in temperature. That's nine-millionths of an inch!

This rate, which is commonly known as the coefficient of expansion (COE), is usually expressed as a whole number, rather than as a long decimal figure. Most Bullseye glass, for example, is said to have a coefficient of expansion of 90, and you will often hear glass artists refer to it as COE90 glass. System 96, another popular fusing glass, has a COE of 96, while Corning's Pyrex glassware has a 32 COE. Standard window glass, referred to as "float" glass by the glassmaking community, has a COE that is usually around 84-87, while Effetre (Moretti) glass, commonly used for lampworking, has a 104 COE.

These differences in expansion and contraction may not sound like much, but they are very significant on the molecular level. A 10 inch (25.4 cm) length of Bullseye glass, for example, will shrink about 0.046 inches (about 1 mm) in cooling from around 950 degrees Fahrenheit to room temperature. By contrast, a 10-inch piece of System 96 glass will shrink about 0.049 inches over the same temperature range. That difference (.003, or three thousandths of an inch) sounds trivial, but it's enough to make it likely that Bullseye and System 96 glass will eventually crack if they are fused together.

Two glasses with considerably different COEs are said to be incompatible. Take care not to fuse them together. Keep glasses with different COEs in separate areas in the studio to prevent their accidentally becoming intermingled.

This is especially critical because you can't always tell incompatible glasses just by sight. In the example below, Bullseye glass has been fused with Spectrum System 96 glass. All looks fine to the naked eye, but when the glass is viewed with a polarized film the underlying stress appears as bright "halos" around the edges of the fused glass. Even though the glass hasn't cracked yet,

the lack of compatibility suggests it will at some point in the future.

You can sometimes get away with using two different glasses where the COE is only slightly different (say, a 90 with a 91), but not always. Sometimes even two glasses with the same COE can not be successfully fused together. That's because the laboratory test that determines COE takes place at a much lower temperature than typical fusing temperatures. In addition, compatibility can be impacted by viscosity, a measure of how much the glass flows when heated.

There are really only two ways to know if your glass is compatible:

• Use glass that has already been certified as "Tested Compatible" by the manufacturer.

• Conduct compatibility testing on your own.

Since most manufacturers charge a premium for "Tested Compatible" glass, it's generally less expensive to use glass that has not been tested. Testing for compatitbility helps determine if other glasses (such as regular stained glass) can be used for your fusing projects.

How to Conduct a Compatibility Test

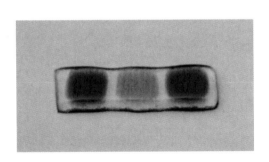
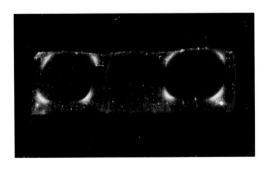

To conduct a compatibility test, simply fuse small squares of the glass you want to test on a known base glass using a standard fusing schedule. Then examine the glass by sandwiching it between two pieces of polarized film that have been crossed to block all of the light. Hold the sandwiched glass up to a light source and look for the halo at the corners of the glass.

Top: Base clear glass with three fused squares: the dark blue are 96 COE Spectrum, while the middle square and the base glass are both 90 COE Bullseye. To the naked eye, the glass appears to have successfully fused. (Photo by the author.)

Bottom: The same glass sandwiched between two sheets of polarized film and viewed on a light table. Note the bright halos around the Spectrum squares, indicating stress due to lack of compatibility. The Bullseye square in the middle has no halo, demonstrating compatibility with the base glass, which is also Bullseye. (Photo by the author.)

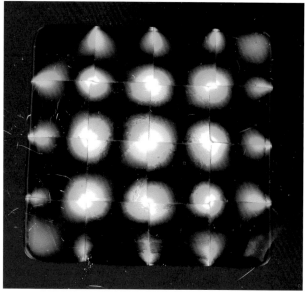

A fused piece made with incompatible glass can remain intact for many days (or even years) before cracking. The piece on the left, for instance, is made with Spectrum System 96 yellow and Bullseye green glass. It appears *perfect to the naked eye, but looking at the piece between polarized film, as illustrated above, makes the internal stress visible. Eventually, this stress can lead to visible cracks. (Photos by the author.)*

Tested compatible glass

Several different companies offer lines of tested compatible glass, with the largest and most popular being Bullseye and Spectrum. In addition, tested compatible glass is made by Uroboros, Wasser, Gaffer, Effetre (Moretti), and several other, generally smaller, manufacturers.

Of the companies that manufacture tested compatible glass, Bullseye currently offers the broadest range. Shapes available include traditional sheets, rods and stringers of various thickness, and frits (glass pieces) of several different sizes. A wide range of colors, as well as iridescent and dichroic coatings, is also available.

Spectrum's tested compatible program, initially launched in Spring 2000, has offerings from Spectrum and a number of other manufacturers, all marketed under the "System 96" name. This line includes sheet glass, iridescent glass, frit, stringers, and a range of other products specifically designed for kilnforming.

As the "System 96" name suggests, Spectrum's glass has a coefficient of expansion of 96. Bullseye, by contrast, has a 90 COE, making the two incompatible.

Uroboros, another glass manufacturer, makes both 90 COE glass that is made to be compatible with Bullseye and 96 COE glass that is part of the System 96 line. Although Uroboros's product line is not as extensive as either Bullseye's or Spectrum's, it does offer several colors, textures, variations, and unique sizes not manufactured by the larger firms.

Effetre, an Italian company formerly known as Moretti, manufactures a line of glass that is frequently used for lampworking and beadmaking. The company offers an extensive line of glass rods and also makes some glass sheets. Most of these are in the range of 104 COE, but there does appear to be considerable variation across the product line. If you use the glass for fusing, testing is highly recommended.

Wasser glass, which was created by Robert Wasser in 1975, has been offered by a variety of different manufacturing firms. It was unavailable from 1997 to 2000, but is now being produced and marketed by Diamond Tech International, a firm which is also known for making glass saws, grinders, and other tools. Wasser has the unique property that its fusing and slumping temperatures are very close together; as a result, it is sometimes possible to fuse and slump pieces made with Wasser in a single firing. Wasser is claimed to be 90 COE, but should still be tested for compatibility when used with Bullseye and other 90 COE glasses.

Another brand of glass for kiln glass work is Gaffer glass, made by a company of the same name, is located in New Zealand. Gaffer's casting glass, which has a high lead content, is notable for its brilliant colors, which maintain their clarity and intensity when used for casting. In addition to the casting glass, which has a 92 COE, Gaffer also makes glass rods with a COE of around 88.

In recent years several other manufacturers have launched tested compatible lines. Sometimes these new product lines are made to be compatible with existing product lines (most often, with Bullseye), but sometimes they are manufactured to a different COE. If trying new varieties of tested compatible glass, it's usually a good idea to test first until you build up some degree of confidence in the new product.

Stained glass

Many of the companies that manufacture tested compatible glass also manufacture stained glass that is not guaranteed compatible. In addition to those already discussed, a more complete listing would include Armstrong, Desag, Freemont, GNA, Kokomo, Wissmach, and Youghiogheny. If you wish to use any of glasses from these companies for fused glass projects involving more than one sheet of glass, you will need to test for compatibility.

Other art glasses can sometimes be used for fusing. Many Armstrong cathedrals and wispies work well together, for example. Also, it is sometimes possible to find compatibility from manufacturer to manufacturer. Some colors of Wissmach, for instance, fit well with Desag. Don't be afraid to test any combination for compatibility; in many cases, that's the only way you know for sure what will work and what will not.

Float glass

Made by "floating" molten glass on a bath of molten tin, float glass is better known as common window glass. It is inexpensive and widely available. It can be fired in the kiln, but care should be taken to test for compatibility if different brands and types of float glass are mixed together. If at all possible, cut pieces to be fused together from the same glass sheet.

Float glass, available predominately in a clear (often slightly greenish) formulation, tends to slump and fuse at slightly higher temperatures than most art glass. Some formulas can be prone to devitrification, a crystallization of the glass that appears whitish and dirty to the eye. The COE of float glass depends on the specific formulation used and can be as low as 83 or as high as 90, but it generally ranges from 85 to 87.

A sheet glass assortment, showing the wide range of colors available. (Photo by the author.)

Recycled glass and bottle glass

It's also possible to fuse and slump with recycled glass, including glass bottles and other castoff glass items. However, since most glass is not made with a specific coefficient of expansion in mind, extreme care should be taken to make certain that the glass being used is compatible. If using recycled glass for fusing, testing is essential to avoid potential disasters and unwanted cracks.

Glass wine, beer, and soft drink bottles can be fairly easily slumped or otherwise shaped in the kiln. Since most of these kinds of firings do not combine more than one bottle, compatibility is not usually an issue. Still, it is essential to heat and cool properly in order to achieve the best results.

Iridescent glass

Virtually any stained glass, whether tested compatible or not, can be treated with an iridescent coating that causes the treated side of the glass to take on a metallic sheen. Some liken this effect to a shimmering rainbow. The shimmer goes away when the piece is lit from behind, allowing the normal color of the glass to shine through.

There are two basic processes for manufacturing iridescent glass. Both involve spraying a solution on the glass while it is hot, but they are applied at different temperatures and have different characteristics during fusing. Some iridescent coat-

ings starts to burn off at 1300F (704C), so it's best to use glass that has a coating that has been specifically formulated not to burn off at fusing temperatures.

You can lessen the likelihood of iridescent burn-off by fusing with the coated side facing down on the kiln shelf and minimizing the time spent above 1300 F/704 C. This is a good practice to follow for all varieties of iridescent glass, not just those that burn off more easily. Fusing with the iridescent side down also makes it much less likely that kiln wash and fiber paper will stick to the glass.

It is possible to make your own iridescent glass, but the procedure can be quite hazardous. In addition to the appropriate chemicals, iridizing glass requires excellent ventilation, a respirator that can handle acid fumes, and protective goggles and clothing.

Dichroic glass

Dichroic, which means "two colors," is a particular kind of glass that has the unusual property of reflecting one color while it transmits another. This means that the different colors can be viewed by examining the glass at different angles.

This unique glass is manufactured by spraying a thin chemical film on the glass. This must be done in a controlled environment in a vacuum chamber, making dichroic glass one of the most expensive glasses made. Because of this expense,

Dichroic pendant by Geri Comstock. Pendant from Geri's "Asian Memories" series, large cabochon from her "Shibori" glass series. (Photo by David Comstock, courtesy of the artist.)

dichroic glass is more commonly used in jewelry and similar items, or to bring a flash of bright color to larger scale fusing projects.

The coating on dichroic glass can be fragile and some varieties can be scratched before firing, but after firing, the dichroic coating is usually stable and unlikely to be removed by scratching or normal handling.

Glass shapes and sizes

Glass is available in several different shapes and sizes, the most common of which are:

- **Sheet glass** - relatively flat, up to 30" (76 cm) wide and generally 1/8" (3 mm) thick

- **Frit** - small, irregularly shaped glass pieces, generally less than 1/2" (12.7 mm) in width and sometimes in powder form

- **Stringer** - long, thin threads of glass, generally either 1 or 2 mm in diameter and up to around 18 inches (46 cm) in length

- **Rods** - round cylinders of glass, about 4-5 mm in diameter and up to 18 inches in length

- **Cullet, billets, patties, and dalle** - various sizes and shapes of glass "chunks" used primarily for casting

- **Shards and confetti** - paper-thin slices of glass

Sheet glass

The most common type of glass is "sheet glass," a flat expanse of glass that's manufactured in various widths and thickness.

Sheets of glass for fusing are generally made in 24" (61 cm) and 17" (43 cm) widths. For fusing and slumping, the most common thickness (sometimes called one "layer") is 1/8" (3 mm). One-sixteenth inch thick (1.6 mm) glass, marketed under varients of the "thin" label by Bullseye, Uroboros, and Spectrum, is also available, as is a double thickness (1/4" / 6 mm) glass useful as the base for fusing projects or for thicker pieces.

The surface of a sheet of glass can be smooth, but quite often it is textured on one or both sides. Textures range from slight waves in the surface of the glass to pronounced ridges or patterns. Many fusers prefer their glass as smooth as possible because it it easier to cut and may reduce the chance of bubbles being trapped between fused layers. However, textured glass can also yield interesting and varied pieces.

Striking

It's possible for some glasses to change color significantly during a firing. This is called "striking" and is related to how the coloring substance used by the manufacturer precipitates in the glass as it cools.

To understand striking, consider what happens when a sheet of glass is made. The manufacturer rolls the glass into a sheet, then allows it to cool, capturing the coloring substance in the glass as it cools. This gives the glass its original color.

Because the sheets of rolled glass cool very fast, some of the coloring material is trapped in the glass -- it doesn't precipate as a visible color, it's just there. Later, when you reheat the glass in your kiln, the coloring material fully precipitates, causing the color of the glass to change to its final, mature, color. This means that unfired sheets of glass will not always appear the same color as they'll appear after firing in the kiln. This can be confusing, especially if scraps of glass are unmarked.

Reds, oranges, and yellows are more likely to be srikers, but many other colors, such as pinks and purples, can have this characteristic. Striking can't be avoided, but firing more quickly above 1100F/593C can sometimes reduce the intensity of the color change.

The related phenomenon of some transparent glasses becoming opaque during high temperature firings is discussed in Chapter 15.

Lee Brady's "Verdant Seed" achieves it's unique look from the combination of iridized glass (in the rim and base) and a precise arrangement of stringers. Fused and slumped bowl above, detail to right. (Photos courtesy of the artist.)

Depending on the manufacturer and the retailer, sheet glass may be sold by either the square foot (or square meter) or by weight.

Frit and powder

Frit, which is nothing more than small pieces of glass, is often used in kiln casting and related techniques. It's also used to add decorative splashes of color in fusing projects.

Frit is available in many different sizes and colors, ranging from powder to pieces as large as half an inch (13mm) or more. Generally sold by the pound or kilogram, frit comes presorted by the size of the grain.

In addition to purchasing frit, it's also possible to make your own from sheet and scrap glass. The ways to do this range from using a hammer to break the glass into pieces to more elaborate processes involving heating the glass in the kiln.

Stringers and noodles

Stringers are long thin threads of glass made from melted and extruded pieces of glass. They're generally available in both 1 mm and 2 mm two thicknesses. One mm stringers, which are about the thickness of thin spaghetti or vermicelli, can be bent with the heat of a candle. Two mm stringers, which are about the thickness of regular spaghetti, require more than the heat of a candle to bend.

Stringers are often used as decorative elements on fused glass pieces. They can be used to create air bubble patterns or they can be stacked and fused to create a vessel or design with a woven, fabric-like appearance. If you have access to a flameworking torch, you can make your own stringers by heating small pieces of glass in the flame and using pliers or flameworking techniques to "pull" the stringers. Stringers can also be made with a vitrograph kiln, discussed in Chapter 15.

Noodles, like the name suggests, are thin strips of glass, not unlike linguini noodles. Like stringers, these are extruded from sheet glass and are particularly appropriate for use in strip constructions or as decorative surface elements. Uroboros is the largest manufacturer of noodles in both System 96 and 90 COE formulations.

Rods

Glass rods are available in various thicknesses, ranging from slightly thicker than stringers up to around 1/2" (12.7 mm) in thickness. They are commonly used in flameworking, but may also be used in fusing. Effetre (Moretti) has the largest selections of rods, but they're also available from Bullseye and other manufacturers.

In addition to using rods by arranging them as you would stringers or regular cut glass, they can be sliced into narrow sections and fused. Rods may also be broken into frit or worked in a flame to make design elements for fusing.

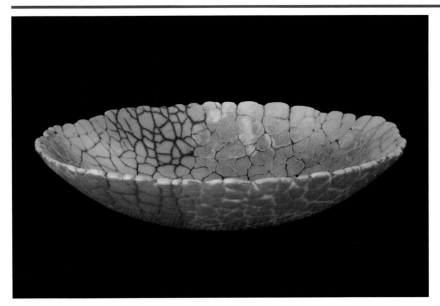

Bob Leatherbarrow's fused and slumped "Crazed Mustard Bowl" uses glass powders to achieve its distinctive crackled appearance. (Photo courtesy of the artist.)

Cullet, billets, patties, and dalle

Cullet is broken or scrap glass. Often, it is glass that is leftover from use in a glass furnace or similar manufacturing operation. For the kiln glass artist, cullet provides a relatively inexpensive source of chunks of glass for casting or fusing. Cullet tends to be irregularly shaped, but the pieces are generally larger and thicker than frit.

Billets and patties are also large and thick, but they're generally available in precise shapes, either rectangular (billets) or round (patties). Like cullet, billets and patties are most frequently used for kiln casting items that require the increased clarity associated with using large chunks of glass.

Dalle is short for dalle de verre, thick slabs of stained glass that can sometimes be adapted for use in fusing and casting. Dalle de verre slabs can be prone to devitrification or incompatibility, so make sure to test them to determine their suitability for using in the kiln.

Confetti

Confetti are delicate, extremely thin, pieces of glass that can be overlaid on other glasses and used as design elements. They are frequently used to shade, accent, or blend colors, but because they're not tested for compatibility they're usually not appropriate for heavy layering.

Traditionally, confetti is made by blowing glass until the walls of the glass bubble become extremely thin and the bubble bursts into shards. It's also possible to make small quantities of confetti in the kiln or with flameworking techniques.

An assortment of casting molds, filled with chunks of glass and ready to be fired. These pieces use uniformly shaped casting crystal made by Gaffer Glass in New Zealand. (Photo courtesy of Terri Stanley.)

Chapter 3

Supplies and equipment

Kilns • Kiln furniture • Kiln wash • Refractory materials • Fiber paper • Thinfire shelf paper • Fiber blanket and fiber board • Ceramaguard and vermiculite board • Oversprays • Adhesives • Glass cutters and pliers • Grinders • Glass saws • Gloves • Respirators and masks • Safety glasses • Coldworking equipment

Although it is possible to fuse and slump with little more than some glass, a kiln, and some kiln wash, many other pieces of equipment are available. In addition, there are numerous kinds of kilns, glass-shaping tools, and chemicals formulated to help the warm glass artist. The most important of these are discussed in this chapter.

Kilns

Aside from the glass, the most important piece of equipment for doing kiln-formed glass work is the kiln. The essential characteristics of a kiln are the ability to reach at least 1700F/926C, a large enough size to hold the particular piece being fired, and a way to accurately measure the temperature of the inside of the kiln.

Most kilns for glass work are powered by electricity, rather than by gas. Electric kilns are less expensive to purchase and easier to use than gas kilns. They also do a better job of maintaining even heat throughout the kiln. For this reason, gas powered kilns are only used for specialized kinds of kiln activities, such as rapidly firing painted work.

Electric kilns can be designed for ceramics or glass. Kilns that are designed for ceramics may

Top loading electric kiln with controller. Note the elements in both the top and the sides of the kiln, as well as the computer controller in front. (Photo by the author.)

Larger kilns, such as this one, are often lined with fiber board, rather than kiln brick. Fiber kilns generally require less power than brick kilns. (Photo by the author.)

be used for glass, but there are a few drawbacks. First, ceramic kilns tend to be taller than glass kilns. While this means that it may be possible to fire more than one shelf of glass at a time, it also means that these kilns are less efficient than glass kilns in a typical, single layer firing.

Because ceramic kilns tend to have heating elements only on the sides, rather than on both the sides and top of the kiln, they can lead to uneven heating. This increases the possibility of cracking the glass piece and requires that kilns with only side elements be fired more slowly than kilns with elements on both the sides and the top.

The most significant decision to be made when purchasing a glass kiln revolves around the size of the kiln. Very small kilns, generally about the size of a microwave oven, are relatively inexpensive and work well for someone who is just learning to fuse, but their small size limits them to equally small projects. They do, however, have the advantage of reaching full temperature very quickly, and are ideal for small items (like jewelry) and quick compatibility or other tests.

Larger kilns use more electricity and cost more to operate, but of course they can fire larger projects. Most large kilns are multi-sided (eight sides are common) or rectangular. In general, the size is given in inches or centimeters across. Keep in mind that the kiln shelf that holds the glass for firing will be smaller than the stated size of the kiln. An 18 inch kiln, for example, will generally hold a 16 inch (40 cm) shelf. An inch (2.5 cm) or so of clearance space is required for each side of the item being fired.

In the United States, kilns are also differentiated by voltage, with small kilns tending to be 120 volt and large ones tending to be 240 volt. This means that small kilns can operate using standard household electric outlets, while large ones require specialized "dryer," "electric range," or other outlets. Large kilns, which are also available in other voltages (such as 3-phase 208), must sometimes be installed using a single dedicated electric circuit.

Once the kiln size has been determined, the next major consideration is whether to rely on manual controls or a full featured electronic controller. Manual controls are less expensive, but they require that the kiln be constantly monitored during the firing. Nevertheless, if the kiln is equipped with a pyrometer, a special kind of thermometer that displays the temperature inside the kiln, it's possible to fire using only manual controls.

However, most glass artists prefer kilns that are equipped with a computer controller. The advantage of a controller is that it can be programmed very precisely, so that a desired firing cycle can proceed relatively unattended. Controllers won't eliminate the need to learn the idiosyncrasies of a particular kiln, nor will they totally eliminate checking on the work as it fires, but they will greatly simplify the firing process. They can also easily replicate firing cycles, so you can be certain that similar projects are fired the same way. A controller makes firing glass easier and more consistent and is highly recommended.

Another important consideration is whether the kiln should be top loading, front loading, or clamshell loading. Kilns that load from the top are generally less expensive than front loading or clamshell kilns. Front loading kilns retain heat very well if opened during a firing. Clamshell kilns, which as the name suggests open like a clam, also hold the heat well and the easiest type to load and unload.

Kiln furniture

The term "kiln furniture" is used to refer to various posts and shelves that are required to support the glass during firing. These items are usually made from either "cordierite" or "mullite," very dense clays that are made to be fired over and over again.

Generally, kiln shelves are flat surfaces slightly smaller than the inside of the kiln and about 5/8" (16 mm) to 1" (25 mm) thick. It's preferable to fire your projects on kiln shelves, rather than directly on the floor of the kiln. This will give the underside of your glass piece a smoother finish and will also allow for more even heat circulation during kiln firings.

To use the shelves, they are placed on top of small posts, rather than directly on the kiln floor. Three or four of these posts are usually used, each at least 1/2" (12.7 mm) high. Kiln posts allow for ventilation below the shelf and promote more even temperature flow, allowing for better annealing and control. Posts of other heights are also available and can be used for different projects.

Shelves and posts should last a long time, but they won't last forever. Using shelves that haven't been dried properly or firing at extreme rates or with wet molds can cause shelves to crack and even split into two pieces. Products do exist for repairing these cracks, but they generally do not do a very good job of restoring the shelf to full usefulness.

Because heated glass will stick to kiln shelves and related kiln furniture, it is essential that before a firing you protect the shelves by coating them with a shelf primer (commonly called "kiln wash") or by covering them with refractory fiber paper or a product such as thinfire fiber paper.

Kiln wash

Kiln shelves can be protected in one of two main ways: either by applying a shelf primer, or kiln wash, to the top of the shelf or by placing a sheet of specially made paper between the shelf and the glass. Although some molds are heat resistant and do not require kiln wash, most molds need to be coated with kiln wash prior to use.

Kiln wash, which is the least expensive way of protecting the kiln shelf, is usually purchased in the form of a powder that is mixed with water to form a thin liquid. Most formulations require four or five parts water to one part powder. This mixture is applied to the shelf with a sprayer or a brush. In most cases a brush that minimizes brush strokes is used, such as a bamboo handled haike brush or a foam paint brush. Four or five layers are usually applied, with each layer brushed on in a different direction than the previous one. Using fewer layers risks the glass sticking to the shelf during the firing. Using more than four or five layers is not necessarily

The small kiln shown below is controlled with an infinite switch, a dial like the knob on an electric range. Small kilns such as this one are best for quick tests or for firing small pieces such as jewelry. (Photo by the author.)

An assortment of kiln furniture, including kiln shelf, posts, fire bricks, and a mullite strip for damming. (Photo by the author.)

better, since the thicker application can cause the kiln wash to crack prematurely.

Once the kiln wash has been applied, it should be dried before the shelf is used. The prepared shelf can be left alone to dry naturally, placed in the sun to speed up the process, or even heated in the kiln to around 500F/260C. If the shelf is heated in the kiln, it can be heated and cooled as quickly as the kiln allows. Once the kiln wash is dry, it forms a thin coating that prevents the glass from sticking.

The dry particles of the kiln wash are generally not harmful if they are inhaled, but some people are sensitive to the chemicals. If you are concerned, it's a good idea to wear a mask when mixing and applying kiln wash. With or without a mask, good ventilation is absolutely essential.

Kiln wash will generally last several firings before it needs to be reapplied. The exact number of firings depends on the type of glass (opaques glasses such as white tend to stick more than transparent colors) and the temperature of your firings (the higher the temperature, the shorter the life of the kiln wash). Before reapplying new kiln wash, the old wash must be scraped from the shelf.

Because of the hassle of applying kiln wash and removing the old kiln wash, some people prefer to use specially made papers between the kiln shelf and the glass. These tend to be more expensive than kiln wash, but they're also easier to use. The most commonly used products are fiber paper and thinfire shelf paper.

Refractory materials

A refractory material is one that doesn't burn in the kiln. If necessary, it should also retain its strength in the kiln. Fiber paper and thinfire shelf paper, which are used instead of kiln wash, are refractory materials, as are various rigid boards such as Ceramaguard and vermiculite board. These products are summarized in the chart on the right and are discussed more fully in the sections that follow.

Fiber paper

Fiber paper is made of very fine alumina and silica threads that have been bound together. This paper is sometimes called Fiberfrax (a brand name owned by Unifrax, a major manufacturer of fiber products). Fiber paper is available in various thicknesses, ranging from as thin as 1/32" (less than 1 mm) to 1/4" (6 mm) or more.

Fiber paper is textured, with the top surface being relatively smooth (but not as smooth as a kiln shelf) and the bottom surface usually having more texture than the top. After a fuse firing, the glass takes on the texture of the paper.

Before using fiber paper, it is normally cut to the desired shape using scissors or a craft knife. If a large quantity of the paper is being used, it is often pre-fired to remove a binder created during the manufacturing process. To pre-fire, fiber paper should be placed in the kiln and fired to about 1300F/700C. The firing can be as quickly as desired and the kiln can be turned off after a few moments at temperature. The kiln should be vented during this procedure, as it will smell (like burning sugar) and may give off a black smoke. Although this smoke is generally not harmful, good ventilation is essential.

Most types of fiber paper work best in the kiln up to about 1700F/927C. As the temperature increases, paper has a tendency to stick to the glass being fired, but with care you can usually remove the paper in one piece. Paper will also remove more easily if the glass is allowed to cool completely. Loose fibers from the paper can be harmful to the lungs -- a good way to prevent this is to wash off residual fiber paper in a container of water, rather than in the open air.

Typically, fiber paper will last up to about half a dozen firings in the kiln before it will need to be replaced. This makes it more expensive to use than kiln wash.

One kind of fiber paper which has the advantage of lasting longer than most ordinary papers, is a rigidized paper called "110 paper." This paper, which is made by Unifrax, is rigid, rather than

An assortment of fiber and shelf papers, including (from left to right), thinfire paper, 1/32" fiber paper, rigid 110 fiber paper, and flexible fiber paper. (Photo by the author.)

Several rigid refractory products, including (from left to right) fiber blanket, Ceramaguard, and vermiculite board, all resting on a strip of cordierite. (Photo by the author.)

TABLE OF COMMON REFRACTORY MATERIALS

Refractory Product	Common Thicknesses	Common Uses	Major Characteristics
Fiber paper	1/32" to 1/4" .75 to 6 mm	• Shelf liner • Kiln carving	• Flexible • May require pre-firing • Useable half a dozen times, more or less
110 fiber paper	1/8" 3 mm	• Shelf liner • Kiln carving	• Rigid • May require pre-firing • Useable 25 or more times
Thinfire shelf paper	Paper thin	• Shelf liner	• Flexible • No pre-firing • Single use
Fiber blanket	1/2" to 2" 12 to 50 mm	• Mold material • Decrease cooling rate	• Flexible, but may be rigidized • Requires pre-firing • Long lasting
Fiber board	1/2" to 2" 12 to 50 mm	• Kiln shelf • Mold material • Dam material	• Rigid • Requires pre-firing • Long lasting
Ceramaguard	5/8" 16 mm	• Mold material, especially drop rings	• Rigid • Requires pre-firing • Long lasting, inexpensive
Vermiculite board	1" to 2" 25 to 50 mm	• Kiln shelf • Dam material	• Rigid • May require pre-firing • Long lasting
Mullite or cordierite	1/2" to 1" 12 to 25 mm	• Kiln shelf • Dam material	• Rigid, very heavy • Long lasting

flexible. It's particularly useful because it deteriorates less than ordinary paper during firings, and is less likely to stick to the glass. 110 paper can last 25 to 50 firings or more.

Some types of fiber paper are carcinogenic, so should be handled only as necessary and with the proper safety precautions. Isofrax is the major brand of non-carcinogenic paper.

Thinfire shelf paper

Thinfire shelf paper, which looks and feels like a sheet of paper, was originally developed by Bullseye Glass. It is more expensive to use than either kiln wash or regular fiber paper, but its ease of use makes it very popular.

Thinfire imparts a slightly smoother than normal sheen to the underside of fused glass, making it an ideal candidate for many fusing projects. However, the thinness of the paper means that it's normally a single use product. It should never be pre-fired, since this will destroy the paper.

Thinfire can be easily cut to size with scissors. After firing, it should be removed from the kiln shelf with a damp cloth or paper towel or by vacuuming. The fired particles are generally not considered harmful, but a HEPA filter is best if using a vacuum cleaner.

One of the limitations of thinfire paper is that it shouldn't be used with iridescent coatings fired down against the paper. This can cause the irid to pit or stretch unattractively. Thinfire can also mar the top surface of the piece if it touches it during a firing.

Fiber blanket and fiber board

Two other kinds of products that are often useful when kilnforming are fiber blanket and fiber board. Fiber blanket is similar to fiber paper, except much thicker. It is commonly available in thicknesses up to three inches (75mm).

Fiber blanket is sometimes used to insulate kilns or is wrapped around a piece of glass, so that the glass cools more slowly. Fiber blanket's flexibility allows it to be stuffed in or around a mold to keep the glass flowing in a particular area. It can also be cut to a specific shape and can be used to impart unique textures to the bottom of a piece of glass.

It's also possible to make a slumping mold with fiber blanket. To do this, saturate the material with a rigidizing solution, shape it as desired, and allow it to dry. This mold making process is discussed in greater detail in Chapter 9, "Molds for Slumping."

Fiber board is commonly used to line large kilns or as a kiln shelf in large kilns. It can also be carved and used as a mold or to impart textures to fused glass.

Since many varieties of fiber blanket and fiber board are carcinogenic, it's often a good idea to use a mask or respirator if you will be in contact with the material for any significant length of time.

Ceramaguard and vermiculite board

There are numerous other kinds of refractory materials. Two of the most common, are Ceramaguard and vermiculite board.

Ceramaguard is a commercial ceiling tile which is manufactured by Armstrong. It has the advantage of being much less expensive than most fiber boards. It is also non-carcinogenic and can be cut with a craft knife or worked with common woodworking tools and sandpaper. Ceramaguard is a rigid material that needs to be pre-fired to remove paint from one side. It can be used as a small kiln shelf or as supports beneath a shelf, but its best use is as a drop ring mold.

Vermiculite board is another refractory product that works well in the kiln. It is rigid enough to serve as a kiln shelf and may also be worked with woodworking tools. Like Ceramaguard, vermiculite board needs to be pre-fired, then coated with kiln wash or with a shelf paper to keep the glass from sticking. Skamol is a leading brand of vermiculite board.

Oversprays

Oversprays are solutions which are applied to the surface of the glass prior to firing. Commonly called "devit sprays," they are used to prevent devitrification, the scummy white layer that can crystallize on the top surface fused glass. Oversprays are available under several different brand names (Spray "A", Clear Coat Overglaze, Super Spray). Chapter 20 contains a formula for mixing your own version. Some oversprays contain lead and are not safe for food-bearing surfaces.

Applying oversprays can be done with a brush or by spray. In either case, it's important to apply the spray evenly to minimize "puddling." Applying too much may result in a dull appearance, while not applying enough will keep the spray from doing its job. Be sure to allow the overspray to dry thoroughly before firing. Only apply the spray to glass surfaces that will be exposed to the air; if it is applied to the bottom side of the glass, it can stick to the shelf when fired.

To work properly, oversprays must be fired high enough to mature and shine up the top surface of the glass. In most cases this is 1350F/730C or higher. Firing to too low a temperature will leave the top surface of the glass cloudy or dull.

Adhesives

Adhesives are used in two different situations: to secure one piece of glass to another prior to fusing and to permanently attach one piece of glass to another surface (either glass or something else) after fusing.

When used before firing, the purpose of the glue is to make sure individual pieces of glass stay in place until the glass heats enough for fusing to take place. Aside from its adhesive quality, the main characteristic desired of glues used for this purpose is to burn out, without leaving a trace.

The best glues to use for fusing are either "fusing glues" that are especially made for securing one piece of glass to another prior to fusing or glues that are forumlated without carbon.

Although they're not the first choice, standard white glues (such as Elmer's brand in the US) can work in some situations. Because these glues can sometimes leave a carbon residue, it's best to mix the glue with water (about a 50-50 mixture) and use them sparingly. Or even better, use a glue that has been formulated without carbon, such as hair spray, Elmer's Gel, or a "fusing glue" such as Thompson's Klyr-fire. Glues such as super glue, which give off a potentially hazardous fume when fired, should be avoided.

But whichever kind of glue you use, it's essential to remember that the purpose of the glue is only to hold two pieces of glass together until the piece is placed in the kiln. The glue will burn off before the glass fuses together.

A totally different kind of adhesive is used to permanently attach one piece of glass to another. This is done outside the kiln, after all firings are complete, and may also be useful for creating shapes and sculptures that would be impossible to create in the kiln.

The strongest adhesive in this class is an epoxy called Hxtal. Quite expensive, and requiring precise measurement to use, this epoxy must be thoroughly mixed and applied to scrupulously clean surfaces. It takes up to a week to cure completely, but is nevertheless favored for its strength and clarity.

A second kind of permanent adhesive is ultra-violet (UV) glue, which cures under ultraviolet light (sometimes the sun can be used). It dries clear in a relatively short time, resists yellowing, and forms a strong bond. Unfortunately, since it relies on light to activate and cure the glue, it can only be used on transparent glass. Also, UV glues have a relatively short lifespan and should be protected from sunlight once the container is opened.

Another type of glue is more commonly used for jewelry and similar applications. These are most often used to glue metal bails to the back of glass cabochons. Typical glues in this category are E-6000 and Loctite.

One final type of commonly used glass adhesives are the silicones. This glue, which was one of

Basic glass cutting tools, including (from left to right) running pliers, pistol grip glass cutter, and groziers. (Photo by the author.)

the first strong glues developed for glass, bonds firmly but flexibly. The slight movement it allows helps keep the glass from cracking as the glass expands and contracts. Some silicones have a tendency to yellow, however, so test the variety you use before doing extensive gluing.

See chapter 18 for more on glues and adhesives.

Glass cutters and pliers

When it comes to manual glass cutters, the first rule is to purchase one that is made for cutting stained glass. Glass cutters from the local hardware store don't work very well on stained glass and they won't last as long as a purpose-built cutter. Glass cutters come in two basic shapes: pencil grip and pistol grip. The difference is more a matter of preference than anything else, but a pistol grip cutter generally requires a bit less hand strength. Ideally, you should try both types and select the one that feels best to you.

After the glass cutter, the next most important piece of glass cutting equipment is a pair of glass running pliers. Running pliers are used to help break glass once a score has been made. There are many other different types of pliers, ranging from grozing pliers to glass nippers, both of which are used to snip off small pieces of glass. All cutters are designed to make cutting glass easier. As with glass cutters, you should try out a few different pliers to see which ones work best

for you. Some people own half a dozen or more different pliers, but many get along just fine with a single pair of running pliers.

Chapter 4 contains suggestions and tips for successfully cutting glass.

Grinders for shaping

It's possible to do virtually the entire glass cutting task with nothing more than a glass cutter and a pair of pliers, but most people eventually opt to purchase a grinder. Grinders, which consist of a motorized shaft with an abrasive head attached, are used to make certain the edges of the glass are smooth and precisely shaped. This aids in fitting the pieces of a pattern together and also makes for a better fitting final appearance.

Grinders can also be used to shape the outside edges of a piece of glass. With the right grinding head, they can quickly and safely remove unwanted glass projections and compensate for most errors in cutting and fusing. The two major grinder manufacturers, Glastar and Inland, both carry broad ranges of grinder and abrasive head types and sizes. Each manufacturer also offers a five-year guarantee, so your grinder purchase should last for a while.

The grinding head should always be kept wet. This keeps the glass from overheating and cracking. It also prevents ground glass (silica) dust from becoming airborne. This is important because inhaling ground silica can harm the lungs and cause a lung disease called silicosis.

It is also highly recommended that you wear a pair of safety glasses when using a grinder. This is to prevent glass particles from accidentally lodging in the eye.

Please note that while a grinder can remove glass and smooth out edges, it can not polish them. That must be done in a separate fire polishing firing or with polishing equipment.

In addition to tabletop glass grinders, which are relatively inexpensive, more elaborate and efficient glassworking equipment is also available.

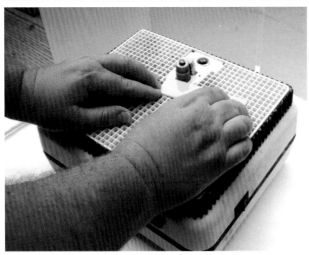

View of a grinder being used to smooth the edges of a small piece of yellow glass. (Photo by Jody Danner Walker, courtesy of the author.)

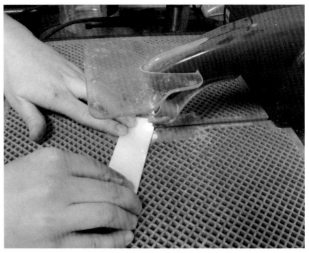

Close-up of a Taurus ring saw cutting an intricate shape out of a piece of glass. These saws are best for cutting shapes, rather than straight lines. (Photo by the author.)

Lap wheels, lathes, and welt belt sanders, all discussed in Chapter 18, can all be used to grind and shape glass.

Glass saws

The concept of using a saw to cut glass is intriguing (it works for wood, doesn't it?), but there are a number of drawbacks. Glass saws are much more expensive to purchase than glass cutters and grinders. They are also very expensive to operate, with blades costing as much as a hundred dollars each. Because they require a steady flow of water to operate, they can be messy to operate and clean. Moreover, they cut much more slowly than cutting by hand.

So why use a glass saw? The answer is simple: they can cut things that are impossible to cut by hand. Once glass has been fused, for example, it's often too thick for a normal glass cutter to work. Some glass, fused and otherwise, also has a texture that makes it difficult to cut by hand. In these cases, only a glass saw has the strength and precision to get the difficult job done.

Glass saws are also capable of making intricate cuts that would be impossible to make by hand. Elaborate designs incorporating sharp inside curves and abrupt changes of direction can only be cut with a saw. These pieces, which may be too flimsy to provide adequate strength when used in a work of stained glass, can easily be fused to a base sheet of glass, yielding a fused piece that is both unique and solid.

For cutting thicker items, the best kind of saw to use is a tile saw. These saws, which are widely available in hardware and similar stores, have the virture of being fairly inexpensive. In order to prevent the glass from overheating and cracking, they must be used wet, and are best for cutting straight lines. They will perform much better if the standard blades are replaced by a blade made specifically for glass.

Cutting intricate shapes in glass requires a different kind of saw. Band saws, for instance, use a thin blade with diamonds on one edge. Glass is cut by pushing it into the blade, which is flexible enough to permit maneuvering the glass to cut intricate patterns. To keep the glass from overheating and cracking, the blade requires a constant flow of water.

The ring saw is another type of saw used for cutting intricate shapes. It uses a a round, diamond-coated blade that's capable of cutting in any direction, rather than the single direction of the band saw. The major drawback of the ring saw is that the blade is relatively thick; as a result, as it cuts it removes more glass than the band saw.

If you purchase a glass saw, realize that it will supplement, not replace your manual glass cutter and pliers. While saws can make intricate cuts and can safely cut through thick or heavily textured glass, they are noisy and messy. A manual glass cutter is still the best tool for straight lines or quick cutting in single thicknesses of glass.

Gloves

When working with kiln-formed glass, there are two main situations that call for the use of gloves: protecting the hands from heat and protecting the hands from caustic chemicals.

Many of the processes involved in the kiln glass field involve the use of chemicals that may damage the skin. For this reason it's a good idea to keep on hand a supply of thin latex gloves and thicker plastic gloves. These are relatively inexpensive and should be used anytime you are dealing with potentially dangerous chemicals.

Several types of gloves are available for protecting the hands from the heat. The least expensive are welder's gloves, which are made of leather. Available at most hardware stores for less than ten dollars (US), they will protect the hands for temperatures up to about 500F/260C.

Since leather has a tendency to hold heat (rather than dispel it), welding gloves will quickly become very hot if you hold on to an item for too long. Despite this shortcoming, they're ideal for tasks such as grasping a hot handle to open the kiln or protecting your hands during combing.

For most people inexpensive leather welding gloves are sufficient, but if you plan to be exposed to the heat for longer periods of time, you may want to consider investing in a pair of Kevlar or Zetex gloves. These products can resist higher temperatures and will not transfer the heat as quickly as leather gloves. In general, gloves that are lined with wool or cotton are preferable to ones that are not.

Respirators and masks

Good ventilation is essential in your work area, but situations sometimes arise where ventilation alone can't keep potentially harmful fumes and contaminants away. In these situations it's essential to use an appropriate mask or respirator.

Paper masks are the least expensive option. While they don't provide as thorough a protection as respirators, they're easy to find and fairly comfortable to wear. Look for a respirator that contains the N95 designation. This provides for better filtration than the common dust mask and will work well in most situations.

For even better protection, consider investing in a half-face respirator, such as those made by 3M Corporation. These products have a rubber mask that fits over the lower part of the face and disposable cartridges that catch potential irritants. In most cases you should opt for a P100 cartridge, which provides excellent protection against most vapors and chemicals.

Respirators aren't necessary for every potential problem, nor do they need to be worn continuously. It's even possible (though not exactly an act of genius) to get along without one or to just use a flimsy paper mask. But if you intend to work frequently with chemicals or if you're susceptible to dust and fumes, money spent on a good respirator is money well spent.

Safety glasses

It is essential that you own two different types of safety glasses. Clear glasses, generally with plastic lenses, are used for protection when cutting glass, grinding, polishing, or using other tools or machines that have the potential to throw off small particles that could damage the eye.

Dark glasses are useful for looking into the kiln at high temperatures. You need glasses that will protect your eyes from infrared rays. Welder's glasses (use #2 to #3) are inexpensive and work well. Didymium glasses made for lampworking are not sufficient for kiln work.

For both kinds of glasses, make certain you select ones that fit well. Most kinds available will easily fit over a second pair of prescription glasses if necessary. For those who wear safety glasses

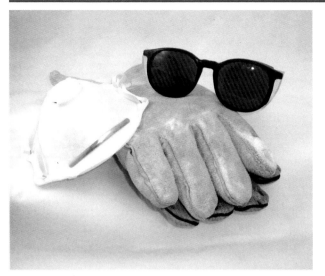

Essential safety equipment: mask, gloves, and glasses. (Photo by the author.)

Diamond hand pads are available in various grits and sizes. (Photo by the author.)

frequently, it's also possible to have them made to a prescription.

Coldworking equipment

Coldworking is the process of shaping and finishing glass at room temperature. While tools such as grinders and saws are coldworking tools, there are many more tools that can be used for finishing and polishing glass.

In its simplest form, coldworking can be done by manually rubbing an abrasive compound on the glass. This can be done with loose abrasives (usually silicon carbide), with abrasive papers (usually wet/dry sandpaper), or with faster working diamond hand pads.

Abrasive and polishing pads and discs are also available to fit many common mechanical devices. A range of products in various shapes, sizes, and degrees of roughness can be purchased for traditional stained glass grinders, Dremel-type tools, variable speed drills, and more. These pads are often diamond-coated, but can be made of cork, felt, or various synthetic materials.

Moving up the scale in terms of sophistication (and expense), coldworking can be done with wet belt sanders or more specialized tools, such as rociprolaps. All of these approaches require a steady stream of water and an appropriate pad

or disc. Polishing may require additional compounds. In all situations, a steady flow of water is required is to keep the glass from overheating and cracking.

By using a series of finer and finer abrasive surfaces to wear away the surface of the glass, it is possible to achieve a high degree of polish. The artist generally starts with a coarser grit, abrades for a while, then switches to finer and finer grits until the surface of the glass is sufficiently polished. In essence, you just keep scratching the surface until the scratches get so small they can't be seen.

This approach, as well as other ways to achieve a smoother or polished finish on glass, is discussed in greater detail in Chapter 18.

"Autumn Colors" by Emily Brock. Fused, slumped, cast, and lampworked glass. Asssembled with silicone adhesive. (Photo by Terry Brock, courtesy of the artist.)

Chapter 4

Glass cutting

Basic tools • Cutting fundamentals • Strip cutting • Circle cutting • Cutting systems

One of the pleasures of working with fused glass is that it's possible to create satisfying pieces with only rudimentary cutting skills. So long as you can learn to cut a straight line, you can easily make tiles, coasters, and similar square or rectangular shapes. Fused glass can make cutting errors less noticeable, and adding glass frit or powder to a piece can allow you to achieve great detail with minimal time spent cutting glass.

As enjoyable as that can be, your enjoyment will increase significantly if you spend a little time developing your cutting skills. It's not difficult to cut glass well, it just takes a little time spent with the proper tools. Once your cutting skills improve, fusing gets even better. New design possibilities appear and projects with narrow strips or circles won't seem so intimidating.

A variety of glass cutters, including both pistol grip and barrel type. (Photo by the author.)

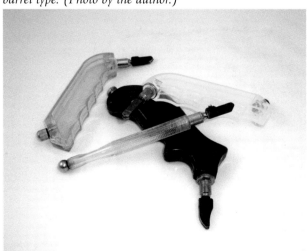

Basic tools

There are several different types of glass cutters, but most fall into one of two different categories. Barrel (or pencil) cutters are six to eight inches (15 to 20 cm) long and are held between the fingers like a marking pen or pencil. Pistol grip cutters are curved, rather than straight. They fit in the palm and are gripped by the full hand, rather than just the fingers. It's possible to cut well with either type, but consider using a pistol grip cutter if hand strength or fatigue is an issue; they're a bit easier to hold and control and won't strain the hand as much as a pencil type cutter.

In addition to the glass cutter, good cutting requires one or more different kinds of pliers. By far the most useful is the running pliers, which

Two types of pliers. Groziers (on the left) are used for nibbling off small pieces of glass. Running pliers (on the right) are used to help run and break a glass score. (Photo by the author.)

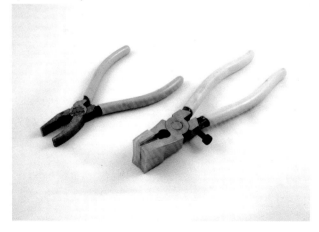

Scoring with a pistol grip cutter. The purple L-square helps the cutter follow a straight line. (Photo by the author.)

To use running pliers, line the mark on top of the pliers up with the score, then gently squeeze. (Photo by the author.)

is used to apply pressure to a score and break the glass more easily. Running pliers come in both plastic and metal varieties; the two types are priced similarly, but the metal type is much more durable. They have a plastic cover which can be easily replaced once it becomes worn.

The jaws of the running pliers have a slight curve and a line marking the top of the pliers. To use them, first score the glass, then hold the running pliers so that the mark on top lines up with the score. Squeeze the pliers gently, so that the score will run, breaking the glass in two. Running pliers work best if they're properly adjusted, so that the gap between their jaws is slightly less than the thickness of the glass being cut.

There are other kinds of pliers for glass cutting, with groziers being the most common. These are used for nipping small pieces of glass or for breaking scores that are too small or sharply curved for running pliers to work.

Cutting fundamentals

The problem with glass cutting is that it has the wrong name. It should be called glass scratching. What you want to do is scratch the surface of the glass to create a weak spot that will break (or "run") in the direction you want it to. So to get the best results, don't think of the process as cutting through paper or a piece of steak; instead, think of firmly scratching the surface of the glass to get the results you want.

Start your cutting with scrap glass -- no need to waste expensive glass on practice. It's better to cut standing up than sitting down. And make certain you have a level, firm cutting surface and that you're cutting on the smoother side of the glass.

As you cut, keep the following in mind:

- **Steady and even is best**. Avoid jerky starts and stops. And try not to allow the cutter to wobble or drift to the right or left. If the cutting wheel is tilted or if your strokes aren't smooth, then you won't be able to get a good score.

- **Try both forward and backward.** It doesn't matter if you score from bottom to top of the piece or vice versa. Some prefer starting closer to the body and pushing the cutter away, while others prefer to start far away and bring the cutter closer. Try both ways and use whichever stroke you find most comfortable.

- **Listen to the glass.** When the cutter scratches the surface of the glass, you should hear a clean scratching sound, like paper being smoothly ripped. With experience, you can tell a good score just by listening for this sound.

- **Examine the score.** Obviously you're not pressing hard enough if the score line is barely visible. Also, if you see flaking slivers on the score line, then you're pressing too hard.

- **Only cut once.** Never correct a mistake by going over the scored line a second time. Not only will that fail to cut the glass, it also can dull your cutter. Instead, cut in another spot or turn the glass over and cut on the other side.

- **Use just a touch of lubricant.** Some people cut without oil, others lubricate their cutters generously. For fusing, use the least amount you can use and still keep the cutting wheel turning smoothly. Excess lubricant means more time cleaning the glass. Also, use a lighter oil such as mineral spirits that cleans quickly and won't leave a residue. Some prefer to use no oil at all, just a few drops of mineral spirits from time to time to keep the cutting wheel moving freely.

Once you've scored the glass, it's time to break it. Larger pieces can be cut using the edge of a table, but smaller pieces require a different approach. Here's where a good pair of running pliers comes in handy.

To use running pliers, hold the tool with its sight line on top of the score and about 1/2" (13 mm) from the outer edge of the glass. Squeeze gently, allowing the tool to do the work. If the glass doesn't want to run, try the other end of your score. Sometimes one end of the score is easier to run than the other.

The key to good breaking, just like good cutting, is practice. Use scrap window glass until you feel comfortable with how to use your cutter. If you have a grinder, you can use it to trim up your mistakes, but with practice and time you'll find that your cutting skills will get good enough that you'll hardly need the grinder at all.

Finally, be careful when disposing of glass. Use a Morton surface or similar system to collect small shards of glass as you cut. Or line your work area with newspapers to collect small glass slivers and scraps as you work. When you're done, simply roll up and then discard the paper, slivers and all. This quickly tidies up the workplace and also avoids accidental cuts.

Strip cutting

It's been said that if you give a glass artist a sheet of glass, that sooner or later he or she will try to cut the glass into strips. That's probably true; certainly it's true that some of the most common designs revolve around strips of glass cut to various lengths and thicknesses. The ability to quickly and precisely cut strips can be one of the most important skills for the fused glass artist to develop.

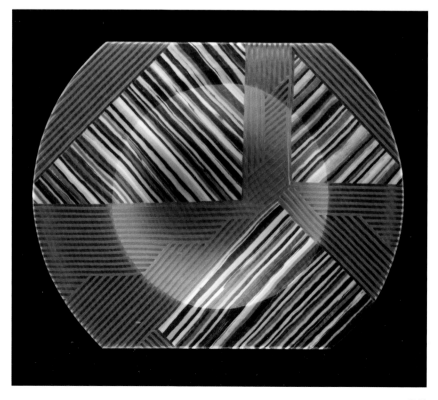

Klaus Moje: "Untitled 3-1988-#15." Kiln-formed glass, ground. Collection of the Corning Museum of Glass, Corning, NY (2007.6.8).

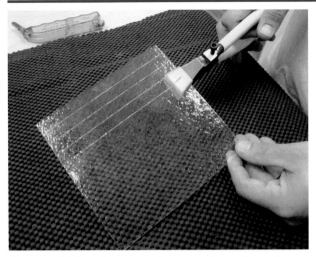

To cut multiple strips at one time, start by scoring at least four strips at once. It's easier to break off a group of strips than to break one at a time. (Photo by the author.)

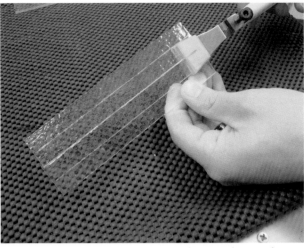

Use your running pliers to separate the scored strips from the main piece, then break in half, then in half again. (Photo by the author.)

Devices and larger cutters designed specifically for strip cutting can speed up the strip cutting process, but it's also possible to strip cut using a glass cutter, running pliers, and a straightedge. A common T-square makes a handy straightedge. Or seek out an L-square, designed specifically for cutting precise 90 degree angles in glass.

The key to cutting strips successfully is not to make the strips too thin. 1/4″ (6 mm) is about as thin as strips can be comfortably cut in standard single layer (3mm) glass. Cutting 3/8″ (9 mm) strips is preferable; not only are they easier to cut than narrower strips, they work well when turned on edge to make strip pieces.

Also, it's good practice to cut strips in multiples, rather than one at a time. Cutting a single nar-

row strip off the edge of a sheet of glass is much more difficult than cutting strips in multiples.

To do this, start by making several scores at once, rather than scoring one at a time. For example, suppose you want to create four 3/8″ wide strips. Starting at one edge of the larger piece of glass, use a glass cutter to score all four strips, each next to the other. Then use running pliers to break off the entire group of four strips from the main body of the glass. Cut that piece in half with your pliers, then cut each of the remaining halves in half again. Using this method is much more likely to yield four perfect strips than trying to cut the strips one at a time.

Above all, keep the head of the cutter straight and listen to the sound of the score. Strips can

Detail from Steve Immerman's "Maris," showing precise strip cutting. The full piece is on page 145. (Photo courtesy of the artist.)

be cut by either pulling the cutter toward you or pushing it away, so try both and do whichever feels more comfortable.

Note that textured glass is harder to cut than smooth glass and opalescent glasses are harder to cut into strips than transparent ones. If you're having trouble, try practicing first using inexpensive float glass.

Circle cutting

In addition to more elaborate cutting systems, it's possible to cut a circle both by hand with an ordinary glass cutter and a pair of running pliers or with a special circle cutting tool. Both approaches are fairly straightforward, but like all cutting activities they require some practice to develop proficiency.

- **Cutting circles by hand**

Start by cutting a square of glass slightly larger than the diameter of the circle you wish to cut. For an eight inch circle, for instance, cut approximately a nine inch square. This will give you some working space on the edges of the circle and will also help minimize wasted glass should you make a mistake when cutting.

Once the square has been cut, use a marking pen to draw the circle onto the glass. This can be done with a compass, with a template, or by

1. To cut a circle by hand, first cut the glass to size, then use a marking pen to draw a circle of the desired size. (Photos in this series by Jace Allen.)

2. Begin the cutting process by using your glass cutter to score from an edge of the square of glass to about a quarter of the way around the circle.

3. Use running pliers to run the score. Repeat this four or five times, until the entire circle has been scored and run.

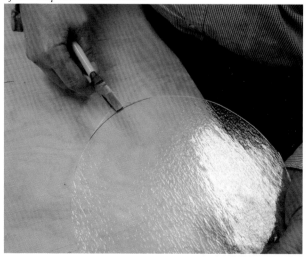

4. It may be necessary to use groziers or a grinder to remove the last bits of glass.

37

drawing around the edges of the upturned slump mold you plan to use for your project.

Don't attempt to cut the entire circle at one time. Instead, divide the task into four or five separate cuts, each following along one arc of the circle. Start at the edge of the glass square and score from there along an arc of the circle. Follow the curve of the circle about one quarter around, then finish the score at another edge. Use running pliers to carefully break the score.

Once you've cut the first arc, cut a second one that runs another quarter or so of the circle. For this second cut, start on the arc, then continue around the circle and off the glass to finish. After scoring, break this second arc, and then repeat the process until you've completed the trip around the drawn circle. It should take four or five cuts.

You may need to use a grinder to smooth out a few rough spots, but with practice you can cut circles by hand quickly and efficiently. For smaller circles (under 4 inches / 10 cm in diameter) cutting by hand will often work better than using a circle cutting tool.

• **Cutting circles with a circle cutting tool**

Purpose-built circle cutters range in price from a few dollars to several hundred. Generally, the really inexpensive circle cutters don't work that well -- they have a tendency to "walk" while scoring -- so consider spending a few extra dollars for a better quality cutter.

Prepare the glass for cutting as you would if you were using an ordinary glass cutter. Cut a square slightly larger than the diameter of the circle being cut. But there's no need to draw the outline of the circle on the glass; instead, most circle cutters have an adjustment screw that can be set to the appropriate diameter.

Once adjusted to size, place the circle cutter so that the suction cup is in the center of the glass. You'll have better success if you place the glass on a piece of carpet or cloth in order to cushion it as you cut. A dark surface will make the score easier to see. Cleaning the glass before cutting

will help the glass cut smoother and will also help the cutting head last longer.

Secure the suction cup so that it attaches firmly to the glass. Before starting the score, it's important to double check to make certain the suction cup is properly placed. It's also good practice to lubricate the area being scored to make the cut go more smoothly.

Fortunately, it's possible to perform both of these tasks at the same time. Start by dipping a small square of paper towel into odorless mineral spirits. Mineral spirits work well because they're inexpensive and they burn off cleanly in the kiln. Place the damp paper towel under the cutting head of the cutter, so that it lies on the glass and keeps the cutting head from scoring the glass. Now rotate the cutter in place, checking to ensure that the suction cup is secure and that the cutting head rotates without hitting any objects or running off the cut glass square. While rotating, keep the paper towel under the cutting head so that the glass isn't being scored as the cutter rotates. You should see a thin layer of lubricant being applied to the area to be scored.

Once you're confident that the cutter is secure and the glass has been lubricated, it's time to score. Remove the paper towel and rotate the cutting head the entire perimeter of the circle. Try to rotate in one motion, rather than in stops and starts. Don't go over any area twice. Listen to the score and stop scoring when you've completed the circle -- the sound will change and become rougher when you reach the starting point.

Next, carefully flip the glass over, so that the scores are on the bottom side. Then firmly run the tip of your finger along the underside of the main score around the circle. Don't force the glass; instead, follow the score to see if it will start to run. The larger the circle, the less pressure required. Go all the way around the score, watching for the score to run as you apply pressure. It may be necessary to go around the score several times. Don't worry about cutting your finger as you do this; since you're on the backside of the glass, cutting isn't really possible.

After you've run the score as best you can, flip the glass back over, making certain to support

Cutting Circles with a Circle Cutter

1. *Start with a square of glass slightly larger than the diameter of the circle to be cut. Allowing an extra inch or two in each direction is generally sufficient.*

2. *Position the glass cutter in the center of the square and pivot it without scoring the glass to make sure it can move freely and stay on the glass.*

3. *Dip a small piece of paper towel into mineral spirits or glass cutting oil, place it under the cutter head, and rotate it around the glass to lubricate the area to be scored.*

4. *Once the glass has been lubricated, remove the paper towel and score the glass. Hold the cutter firmly and score evenly and completely all the way around the circle.*

5. *Once the score has been made, flip the glass over and press the back side of the score to help it begin to run. Carefully work your way all the way around the glass.*

6. *Flip the glass back over, use your glass cutter to cut a small relief score, then use running pliers to cause the score to run.* *(Continued on next page...)*

Cutting a circle using a circle cutter
(continued from previous page)

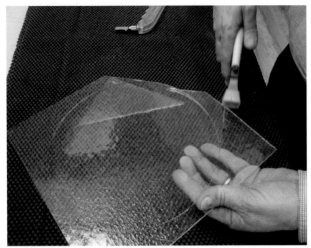

7. *After running the first relief score, move on to a second and run it as well. Don't force the glass; if one spot is difficult, simply move on to another one.*

8. *It may help to use the running pliers to run the score around the circle. In many cases the glass will almost fall apart from just a little pressure with the pliers.*

9. *The finished circle. Clean it well before firing in the kiln. (All photos in this series by Jace Allen.)*

the circle as you flip. It's possible for the circle to pop out onto the table as you flip the glass.

Use your regular glass cutter to create four relief scores around the edge of the glass. These scores should begin on the outer edge of the circle and go at a tangent from the circle to the edge of the original cut glass square.

After making the relief scores, use your running pliers to begin breaking the glass away from the circle. Take care when doing this; the circle can be very flimsy. Continue running the relief scores to break the glass away from the edges of the circle. It should only take a few moments to completely run the perimeter of the circle and obtain your completed piece. Most often, the edges of the circle will be clean and ready for use, but don't hesitate to use a grinder, if minor cleanup is necessary.

Cutting systems

The most common cutting system is the Morton system, which consists of a white grid designed to support the glass during cutting. The grid can be used by itself, simplifying cleanup after cutting, or it can be used with any of a vast array of attachments and additions. The Morton system has a number of different attachments designed for cutting strips, circles, and more unusual shapes.

Alternatives to the Morton system are offered by a number of different companies, including Creator's Stained Glass, Bohle/Silberschnitt, and Glastar. Creator's Cutter's Mate, for example, uses a weighted handle and hinged arm to simplify cutting and reduce fatigue.

These systems vary greatly in price and quality; if at all possible, get a hands-on demonstration before making the purchase.

Chapter 5

The basic fusing process

What happens when glass is fused • Six stages of fusing • Initial heating phase • Thermal shock • Bubble squeeze phase • Fusing phase • Rapid cooling phase • What is devitrification • Annealing phase • Cooling to room temperature phase

What happens when glass is fused

"Glass wants to be two layers thick."

That's a phrase that's spoken so often in fused glass circles that it's almost a mantra. Some people go so far as to declare it the most important principle of working with glass in a kiln. And it might be.

But if you think about it, it's a fairly strange phrase. What's a layer? How thick are two of them? And how does glass want to be anything at all?

To better understand the concept, let's do a small experiment to find out what happens when a piece of glass is placed in the kiln and fired. The answer depends, of course, on many variables, including the kind of glass and the temperature in the kiln. But let's use a typical fusing glass and a typical full fuse firing in a glass kiln.

Start with a single sheet of glass, which is typically around 1/8" (3 mm) thick. Any color or texture of glass can be used for this experiment, but a standard clear glass is easy to cut and least expensive. Using your glass cutter, cut a square of glass from the sheet. Make it around 3" by 3".

Place the square inside the kiln on a kiln shelf that has been prepared for fusing. Place just a single piece of glass on the shelf. This is commonly called a one "layer" firing.

Start the kiln and let it fire as quickly as you would like to a typical full fuse temperature of 1480F/805C. Hold the temperature there for around ten minutes and then turn the kiln off and allow it to cool back to room temperature.

When the fired glass emerges, you'll notice that it still looks and feels like glass. But there are several significant changes.

First, the fired square of glass is slightly smaller than it was when it entered the kiln. Second, any texture on the original square of glass will have

Firing a single 1/8" (3 mm) layer of glass in the kiln will round the edges, change the texture, and cause the glass to draw up slightly. (Photo by the author.)

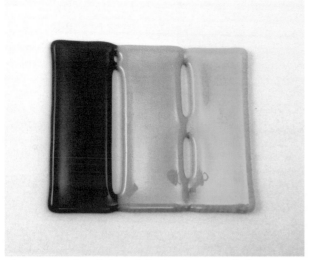

Three rectangles of glass, fully fused as a single layer. (Photo by the author.)

changed. The bottom of the glass will now have the texture of the kiln shelf it was fired upon. The top surface of the glass will be smooth, the bottom will not be as shiny as the top, and the edges will have rounded. If you look closely, you'll also notice that the edges are slightly thicker than the middle of the glass. It's as though the piece was drawing up slightly, trying to become thicker than it was when it was originally placed in the kiln.

And that's more or less what has happened. When a single layer of glass is fired to 1480F/805C in a kiln, it draws up slightly. The edges round and it takes on the texture of the shelf.

So imagine you want to make a small glass tile or coaster. But rather than make it with a single color, you decide to make a multi-colored tile. To do this, we cut three rectangles of glass, each 1″ by 3″ (2.5 x 7.5 cm) and arrange them to form a small square, with each piece fitting edge to edge

to form a square. After moving to the kiln shelf, fire the glass to 1480F/805C in the kiln.

Surprise! What happens is that each of the three rectangles draws up slightly, just as the large square did when it was fired. And as the photo at the left illustrates, what we get is not what we expected.

To get around this problem, most glass artists build their basic fused pieces in two layers, each 1/8″ (3 mm) thick. (Now you know where the term "layer" comes from!) So the basic process for making a simple three-colored tile is to cut three rectangles as we did before, but also add a fourth piece of glass – a clear square the size of our full piece.

Once we cut the pieces, we have two choices of how to arrange them. We can place the square on the kiln shelf, with the three rectangles on top. Or we can do the opposite, place the three rectangles on the shelf and cap them with the large clear square.

Either way will work. But – and here's another surprise – after firing, each method results in a slightly different finished piece. In both cases, the edges will be round, the top will be shiny, and the bottom will take on the texture of the kiln shelf. And both methods create the desired shape: three colored rectangles side by side.

But the version with the clear square on top will look different from the version with the clear on bottom. The clear on top will give the piece a depth that is lacking in the piece with the clear on bottom. Having clear on top will also hold the seams between the glass together better,

Three rectangles of glass and one clear square, fused with the square on bottom (far left) and the square on top (near left). (Photo by the author.)

42

leaving sharper lines between individual pieces. On the other hand, a large piece of clear on top may trap air bubbles between the clear and the three rectangles. These bubbles, which some try to avoid and others accept as part of the beauty of fused glass, can be minimized but they're very hard to eliminate entirely. They're what happens when one piece of glass is placed on top of another and then fired in a kiln.

To summarize, a full fuse firing in a kiln requires a thickness of around two layers – about 1/4″ (6 mm) – in order for the piece to fully fuse properly and still maintain its shape. And putting a layer of clear on top of the piece gives depth but also risks capturing air bubbles inside the glass. The other option – putting the clear on bottom – gives the necessary thickness. It also sometimes leaves a slight bit of texture on the top of the piece where the three rectangles come together.

Taken together, these two variations are the most common ways to fuse glass in a kiln. They're at the heart of making tiles, coasters, bowls, or even fused glass jewelry. Neither of the two variations – clear on top, or clear on bottom – is better than the other, they're just two different ways of arranging the glass before you fuse.

Often, glass designs are made more interesting by sprinkling glass frit or placing stringers on top of the glass. The full fuse firing will cause the additional items to melt into the layer below. And the amount of glass used is small enough that it doesn't have to count as an additional layer.

But what if we did add another layer of glass? Suppose we make a piece with the three rectangles sandwiched between two layers of clear

– one on top and one on bottom. Firing that piece to our full fuse temperature of around 1480F/805C will result in a finished piece that's different from any other we've made. The top will be shiny, the edges rounded, and bottom will take on the texture of the kiln shelf. But the piece will be larger than it was when it started. It will have spread out, shrinking in thickness from three layers (3/8″/9 mm) -- to close to two (1/4″/6 mm). While one fully fused layer becomes smaller, three layers becomes larger!

This phenomenon – the fact that fully fused glass in a kiln wants to be around 1/4″ (6 mm) thick – is probably the most important law of fusing glass. It's why "glass wants to be two layers thick." Putting a single 1/8″ (3 mm) layer of glass in a kiln and firing to full fuse won't usually yield satisfactory results. And fully fusing three layers – a thickness of 3/8″ (9 mm) – on a kiln shelf will result in a piece that's less than three layers thick.

The two layer rule, which is related to surface tension and the viscosity (or "runniness") of glass in a kiln, can't be broken. But if you understand it fully, you can still create pieces that are thicker or thinner than two layers.

One way is to fire to a different temperature. Full fusing, where the edges of the glass round, top of the glass becomes smooth, and the piece evens out at two layers thick, takes place at around 1480F/805C. The exact temperature may be slightly higher or lower – it depends on the type of glass, the kiln being used, and the details of the firing schedule – but in most situations a full fuse is in the range of 1450F/788C to 1500F/815C.

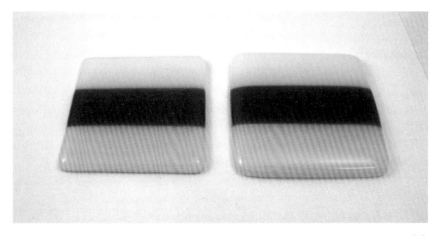

Two layers on the left piece, three layers on the right. Both pieces started the same size, but the extra layer on the piece to the right causes it to spread out at full fuse temperatures. (Photo by the author.)

Ten 1" (2.5 cm) square layers of glass, stacked and fused together at 1500F/815C. (Photo by the author.)

Firing to a lower temperature changes what happens. If we fire three layers of glass to around 1400F/760C, for instance, the edges will still round and the layers will still fuse together, but the piece won't have time and heat enough to thin out to only two layers thick. Instead, it will be "tack" (sometimes called "contour") fused – stuck together by the heat, but not fully joined. The individual pieces will still be permanently fused together -- if you drop the glass on cement it will break completely rather than coming apart at the seams between the colors. Still, tack fused pieces are not quite as fully joined together as pieces that have been fully fused.

If you had placed loose frit on top of the layers, you'd see that the lower temperature didn't give the frit time to melt down into the top layer. The piece would still be shiny on top, but it would have a definite texture where the loose glass had been placed. This is called "tack fusing" – which is just a fancy way of saying that the glass was fused at a high enough temperature for the pieces to join, but not so high that the top surface totally flattened out.

Tack fusing generally takes place between around 1350F/732C and 1450F/788C, while full fusing takes place above 1450F. These temperatures can vary slightly from glass to glass and kiln to kiln, but they're good rules of thumb for fusing glass. If you want a totally smooth surface on the top of your glass, fire to a full fuse temperature. To get more texture or to prevent three layers of glass from spreading out to two layers thick, fire to a temperature in the tack fuse range.

As you would expect, firing to temperatures at the low end of the tack fuse range will give you a different look than firing to temperatures at the high end or firing to a full fuse temperature. The higher the temperature, the more rounded the edges of the piece and the closer it gets to being fully flat on top. An experienced fuser can usually guess the firing temperature just by examining the degree to which the piece is fused together.

This concept – adjusting the temperature to achieve a particular thickness – is at the heart of what glass artists refer to as "volume control."

There's one other common way to control volume that's frequently used with thicker pieces. This is to dam the piece by placing material around the edges of the piece before it is fired in the kiln. By doing this the glass is not allowed to flow and will remain as thick as it was when it was placed in the kiln. Chapter 14 discusses damming in greater detail.

Six stages of fusing

Now that we have an basic understanding of what happens when glass is fused in a kiln, let's take a closer look at the details of the actual kiln firing. Generally, a basic fuse firing has six steps (or phases):

- **Initial heating phase** - from room temperature to around 1100F/600C. If glass is fired too quickly in this range, it will crack.

- **Bubble soaking phase** - from 1100F/600C to around 1240F/670C. This is the range where air bubbles can be trapped between layers of glass. Going slowly during this phase helps minimize ugly bubbles.

- **Fusing phase** - from roughly 1375 to 1500F (750 to 815C), this is the phase where layers or particles of glass fuse together. The higher the temperature, the more rounded the edges of the glass become and the more fully the glass will be fused together.

An example of thermal shock. The glass can break with enough force to split into pieces and even be knocked off the kiln shelf. (Photo by the author.)

- **Rapid cooling phase** - when the temperature is quickly dropped from its highest point to the annealing range for the glass.

- **Annealing** - the critical step that relieves the stress in the glass so that it won't crack when it returns to room temperature. This varies by type and brand of glass, but takes place from roughly 1000F/540C down to roughly 800F/425C.

- **Cooling to room temperature phase** - where the glass gradually becomes cool enough to touch. Final cooling is sometimes controlled by the kiln's controller, but more often the kiln is simply allowed to cool on its own.

"Thermal shock" refers to the cracking of the glass that occurs when the temperature changes too quickly.

Initial heating phase

During the "initial heating" phase of the firing, which begins at room temperature and continues to approximately 1100F/600C, glass behaves as a solid. It expands slowly as it heats, but still remains rigid and brittle. Any glue, moisture, or surface contaminants burn off the glass during this phase; most are gone by the time the temperature reaches 1000F/540C.

Although a small ventilation port hole is appropriate (especially when venting fumes from glue

or paint), it's a very good idea to keep the kiln closed during the initial heating phase; opening it will may cause the glass to break. The glass can also break if it is heated too quickly or if the heat is uneven. This kind of temperature related fracture is called "thermal shock."

Thermal shock

How rapid a temperature change is rapid enough to cause thermal shock? The answer depends on several factors, but the most important is the thickness of the glass being fired. Small items such as jewelry can be fired very fast (even as fast as 1000 degrees Fahrenheit per hour), but large items such as thick castings may need to be fired at 100 F per hour (56C) or slower. A good rule of thumb for typical two layer pieces is to fire at around 400F per hour (222C) on the initial fuse firing and 300F (167C) for any additional firings. Go slower than this if using a kiln that only has side elements.

When thermal shock occurs, the glass can break with such force that it can actually be moved across (or even off!) the kiln shelf. Typically, the glass breaks into two to four pieces.

By the time the temperature of the glass gets above 1000F/540C, the glass begins to soften slightly and the surface of the glass will look glossy. Thermal shock will not normally occur above this temperature.

Bubble squeeze phase

As the temperature of the glass passes 1100F/600C, it begins its transition from solid to liquid, a journey that isn't complete until the temperature of the glass is well above 2300F/1260C. This transition phase, in which glass behaves differently depending on the exact temperature, is what makes working with glass in a kiln possible.

From 1100F/600C to 1300F/700C, glass gradually becomes soft enough to move slightly in the heat. It may start to glow a bright yellowish-red. The edges may soften and round and two pieces of glass that are touching will begin to stick together. This is the temperature range where slumping takes place.

More importantly for fusing, this is the temperature range where trapped air bubbles can be minimized. If a glass piece is constructed with one piece or layer of glass on top of another, then it's very likely that air bubbles will be trapped between the layers. A certain amount of trapped bubbles is inevitable, but large unsightly bubbles are seldom desireable.

By firing slowly from 1100F/600C to around 1240F/670C, and then holding the temperature at 1240F, air bubbles are given the opportunity to escape from between layers of glass.

Fusing phase

As heating continues above 1300F/700C and moves toward 1500F/820C), the color of the glass deepens and becomes redder and brighter. It may look slightly liquidy in the kiln. Glass in this range has relaxed completely and starts to stretch out of shape.

Full fusing, the complete merging of two or more pieces of glass into one, takes place at around 1450 to 1500F (785 to 820C). At temperatures below full fuse, from around 1375F/750C to 1450F/785C, layers of glass will permanently stick together, but will retain some texture, rather than being totally smooth. This is known as a "tack" fuse (sometimes called a "contour" fuse).

Once the desired fusing temperature is reached, the kiln is generally held at that temperature for five to ten minutes. This is called "holding" (or "soaking") and allows the temperature of the glass to equalize and give the glass time to fuse evenly and fully.

Rapid cooling phase

After fusing, the firing enters the "rapid cooling" phase. This involves cooling the glass as quickly as possible until the red color goes away and the natural color starts to come back.

Traditionally, rapid cooling was accomplished by lifting the lid of the kiln for a few seconds and allowing hot air to escape. However, opening the kiln isn't usually necessary. It's also a risky maneuver, so it's a good idea to wear gloves, safety glasses, and other protective gear if you must open the kiln while it's very hot.

The major reason for the rapid cooling phase (as well as for the rapid temperature increase at the end of the heating phase) is to reduce the amount of time the glass spends above 1300F/700C. Glass left too long in this zone has a tendency to devitrify, or take on a scummy, generally unattractive surface appearance that is difficult to reverse.

Traditionally, fusers tended to vent their kilns after fusing to allow hot air to escape and more quickly cool the glass to the annealing range. Current thinking is that this is not needed. Not only does opening the kiln at high temperatures run the risk of injury, it also can cause the kiln brick to develop microfractures which can dislodge small particles of brick dust onto the glass when the kiln is closed. Also, today's fusing glass is less likely to devitrify than glasses commonly used twenty or thirty years ago. So most people would argue that simply allowing the kiln to cool naturally is best.

What is devitrification?

Devitrification is when glass molecules start to crystallize. It usually takes the appearance of a whitish scum on the top edge of the glass being fired. Most glass artists consider it to be a nuisance to be avoided, but some like the effect and use it in their glass projects. It is most likely to occur above 1300F/700C; for this reason, it's a good idea to minimize the time glass spends around that temperature.

Some glasses are more prone to devitrification than others and some, such as the "tested compatible" glass manufactured by Bullseye, Uroboros, and Spectrum, have been especially formulated to resist devitrification. Note that even these formulated glasses will devitrify under certain conditions, such as numerous firings or prolonged temperatures above 1300F/700C. Also, note that opaque glasses are more likely to devitrify than transparents.

You can minimize devitrification by spraying or brushing on a "devit spray" prior to firing. This spray is available commercially under several different names (Spray "A", Clear Coat Overglaze, Super Spray). Chapter 20 has information about mixing up your own devit spray.

Annealing phase

Once the rapid cooling phase is complete and color has started to return to the glass, the kiln has cooled to approximately 1050F/566C and the "annealing" phase begins. Annealing is a process by which the stress in the glass is relieved and the molecules in the glass are allowed to cool and arrange themselves into a solid, stable form. Successful annealing is the key to creating glasswork that will remain stable once it cools to room temperature.

Unlike many substances, glass does not harden at a single temperature. Instead, it gradually solidifies as the temperature changes. The phase during which this transition from liquid to solid occurs is called the "annealing zone." There are three critical points within this zone.

- **The upper annealing point** - this is the upper end of the annealing zone where the glass begins to return to solid form.

- **The annealing temperature** - this is the temperature where the molecules in the glass optimally realign themselves evenly throughout the glass. It's always between the upper annealing point and the strain point.

- **The strain point** - this is the lower end of the annealing zone. It's the place where the glass solidifies. The stress (or strain) remaining in the glass at this point is unlikely to be changed or relieved unless the glass is heated up again and annealed again.

The concept of annealing glass centers on the notion that soaking the glass at a point in the annealing zone can relieve stress. In theory, you can relieve the glass of strain and anneal at any temperature in the annealing zone, but the closer you are to the annealing temperature, the more efficiently annealing will take place.

After soaking at the annealing temperature, you should slowly reduce the temperature until it is below the strain point. The purpose of the initial soak is to allow the glass molecules time to adjust as the glass moves from liquid to solid. Slowly dropping from the annealing point to the strain point helps ensure that stress is not reintroduced before the strain point is reached.

Every type of glass has a different annealing temperature and a different annealing zone. Tests can be performed to determine these points, but even for the same type of glass they will differ slightly depending on the color or other variables in the glass. If your fused item uses many different types of glass, it may have many different annealing points and annealing zones, making the annealing zone soaking and cooling process extremely complicated.

An alternative approach to annealing does not require you to know the annealing point of the glass. In this approach, you simply allow the temperature to drop very slowly over a range that is large enough to encompass many different annealing zones. The idea is that you will be able to anneal at a number of different annealing points as the temperature drops through the range. This method works well for situations where you do not know the precise annealing point or do not have a controller that can precisely control your kiln's temperature, but it can take longer than annealing schedules that use an anneal soak.

Cooling to room temperature phase

Once annealing is complete, the cooling to room temperature phase begins. Often this is no more complicated than simply allowing the kiln to cool naturally, but thicker pieces of glass and kilns that cool rapidly require a bit more attention. The key is to slow down the rate of cooling, so that thermal shock is prevented and the glass cools without cracking.

Probably the most important factor in how quickly you can cool the glass is the overall size and thickness of the glass being cooled. Very small pieces can generally be cooled as rapidly as desired, but larger pieces need more time to cool. For example, a 12″ (30 cm) diameter, 1/8″ (3 mm) thick piece of glass, can safely cool from 750F/400C to room temperature in 40 minutes. Doubling the thickness to 1/4″ (6 mm) doubles the time required to 80 minutes and 3/8″ thick glass requires at least two hours to cool to room temperature.

For almost any kiln, the natural cooling rate of the kiln is probably slower than this. In some cases, however, you may need to intermittently fire the kiln to slow down the rate of cooling. It's a good idea to keep records so you learn how quickly your kiln cools.

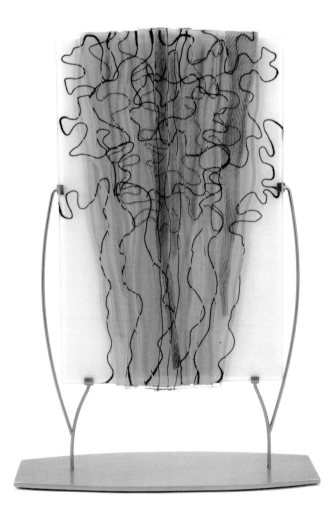

Nina Falk, "Japanese Maple." Copper wire fused between layers of glass. (Photo by Larry Berman, courtesy of the artist.)

Right: Marcia Newren, "Work in Progress." Fused, slumped, sandblasted, airbrushed, handpainted, torchworked, and hot manipulated. (Photo by Margot Geist, courtesy of the artist.)

Below: Delores Taylor, "Life in the Forest." Pate de verre. (Photo courtesy of the artist.)

Chapter 6

Preparing the kiln for firing

Protecting the kiln floor • Mixing kiln wash • Applying kiln wash with a brush • Applying kiln wash with a sprayer • When to reapply kiln wash • Using fiber paper • Using thinfire shelf paper • Placing the kiln shelf into the kiln

If you've never used your kiln before, then you'll need to prepare it for the first firing. Both the kiln floor and the top surface of the kiln shelf will need to be protected so that your glass project doesn't stick to them.

Protecting the kiln floor

Let's start with the floor of the kiln. The first thing you'll need to do is to vacuum (or "hoover") the floor. Using a vacuum cleaner with a HEPA filter is the best way to remove any dust or other unwanted particles from the bottom of the kiln. When vacuuming, take care not to hit the kiln elements or dig the nozzle of the vacuum into the soft fire brick that usually makes up the walls and floor of the kiln.

Once the kiln is vacuumed, you'll need to protect the floor. This is so that stray pieces of glass that fall off the kiln shelf will not eat into the kiln floor. The best thing to use to protect the floor is kiln wash, a solution that when applied properly will prevent glass from sticking to the kiln floor.

Mixing kiln wash

There's nothing magic about using kiln wash. Compared to cutting glass, it doesn't even require much practice. You do, however, need three major ingredients.

- **Kiln wash.** This usually comes in a powder that needs to be mixed with water. You can buy it or make it on your own if you prefer.

- **A container to hold the kiln wash.** Any container that will hold liquid will work. An opening that allows easy access for the brush works best.

- **A brush or sprayer to apply the kiln wash.** Applying with a brush requires less preparation, but spray application leaves a smoother, more even, finished surface.

Note that kiln wash is also known as "shelf primer." There are a number of different formulations; although ceramic kiln wash will work, it has a greater tendency to stick to glass, so it's best to get a formulation that's specifically made for glass.

It's a good idea to be cautious when mixing and using kiln wash. Although the dry powder isn't normally harmful, it can be an irritant if accidentally inhaled. If you are using a sprayer to apply the kiln wash, you should be especially careful and might consider wearing a respirator to avoid breathing in airborne particles.

Using a haike brush to apply kiln wash to the shelf. Note the angle of brush, positioned to lay down a thin, even layer of the wash without leaving pronounced brush strokes. Kiln wash powder should be mixed with four to five parts water to a smooth, thin consistency. A container with an opening large enough to accommodate the brush being used is preferable. (Photo by Jace Allen.)

Mixing kiln wash is straightforward. Just put the desired amount of the powder into a container and then add the amount of water recommended by the manufacturer. Most formulations call for four to five parts water for each part kiln wash. Shake or stir the container gently to mix the powder and water together. The final mixture should be relatively thin, like skim milk.

Applying kiln wash with a brush

Most people use a Japanese or Chinese "haike" brush to apply kiln wash. This kind of brush has very fine bristles that allow the kiln wash to go on more smoothly. A regular paintbrush can be used in a pinch, but it will have a tendency to leave visible brush strokes on the shelf. Wide, soft bristles are best. Foam paintbrushes also work well for kiln washing cool surfaces, but don't use them with hot shelves or molds.

To apply the kiln wash, it's often best to pour a bit of it into a bowl or similar container to allow easier brush access. Make sure you shake or stir the kiln wash mixture before pouring, as it settles very quickly. You should also stir the mixture several times while applying to keep the particles from settling to the bottom.

To brush on the kiln wash, first dip the brush into the mixture, then glide it over the item you want to coat, usually a kiln shelf, slump mold, or the floor of the kiln. Glide in one direction,

allowing only the tip of the brush to touch the surface. Don't drag the brush or draw it back and forth as though you were painting. Apply a thin coat, rather than a thick one.

You should apply at least four coats, each in a different compass direction (right to left, top to bottom, then once more in each of the two diagonal directions). There's no benefit from drying the wash between coats, but it won't hurt if you do. Once you've applied four or five coats, allow the kiln wash to dry. If you want this to happen more quickly (air drying can take a day or longer), speed up the drying process by placing the shelf in the kiln, then heating to about 500F/260C and then letting it cool naturally. When you fire to dry the shelf, leave the kiln door propped open slightly or the port hole unplugged to allow the moisture to escape.

Once the kiln wash is dry, inspect the shelf to make sure it is covered with a smooth layer. If you want, you can smooth the kiln wash slightly with a soft lint-free cloth. An old pair of pantyhose works well for this purpose. If the item is a mold that will be slumped into, check to make sure that the air holes at the bottom have not been filled by the kiln wash. If they have, just re-poke them using a bent paper clip or similar thin wire.

If you want your shelf to be as smooth as possible, try rinsing your brush in clean, warm water and applying two or three additional coats of warm water over a kiln washed shelf. When the water dries, it will leave an exceptionally fine and smooth surface.

Applying kiln wash with a sprayer

The procedure for using a sprayer to apply kiln wash can vary slightly depending on the type of sprayer used. For airbrushes and similar equipment, follow the manufacturer's recommendations in terms of sprayer preparation and use.

When using a sprayer, the kiln wash should be mixed just as for using a brush -- about four to five parts of water for each part kiln wash. Take care not to mix the wash too thick or it may clog the sprayer.

Spray the wash evenly from side to side, covering the entire surface with a thin, smooth layer of kiln wash. As with brush application, thin layers are preferable to thick ones. It may be necessary to go over the surface several times to ensure sufficient coverage.

Because of the risk of inadvertently spraying kiln wash on kiln elements, it's a good idea to use a brush for applying kiln wash to the floor of a kiln. Also, a respirator or mask is recommended when using a sprayer.

When kiln wash begin to crack or chip or shows other signs of wear, it should be scraped from the kiln shelf using a paint scraper or similar tool. After scraping, use a damp paper towel or vacuum with a HEPA filter to remove the loose particles, then re-apply fresh kiln wash to the shelf. (Photo by Samantha Allen.)

When to reapply kiln wash

During normal fusing activities, a good brand of kiln wash will last for around half a dozen firings. Signs of wear include cracking, chipping, and visible uneven patches on the shelf. When kiln wash begins to stick to the glass, it's also a signal that it's time to reapply the wash.

To reapply, first remove the old kiln wash. Avoid the temptation to just brush new kiln wash over the old -- that will cause additional flaking and won't leave a smooth finish on the shelf. It's almost always preferable to completely remove the old kiln wash before applying the new.

A paint scraper, putty knife, or even a scrap of glass can be used to remove kiln wash. Medium grit sandpaper or a stiff wire brush can also work well. If you have one available, an electric hand sander will quickly remove kiln wash with a minimum of effort.

Because kiln wash particles may be hazardous if inhaled, it's not a good idea to breathe in the dust from the dried kiln wash. If your removal process is particularly vigorous or if you're sensitive to the dust, you should wear a respirator. In either case, as with many glass procedures, good ventilation is a must.

When the old kiln wash has been removed, finish cleaning the shelf by brushing or vacuuming loose dust and other particles off the shelf. Use a damp paper towel or a vacuum with a HEPA filter to do the job. Once the shelf is clean, reapply kiln wash using the same procedures as when it was originally applied.

Firing with opaque colors against the kiln shelf will tend to shorten the life of your kiln wash. So will firing to higher temperatures. It's generally a good idea to reapply kiln wash after any high temperature firing, such as for a pot melt or combing. Not only is sticking more likely at higher temperatures, kiln wash also degrades more quickly at higher temperatures.

Items such as slump molds, which are used in lower temperatures, last much longer between

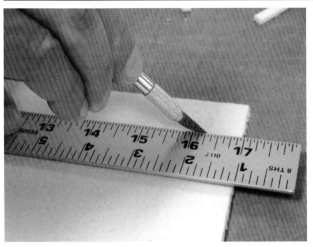

Fiber paper can easily be cut to shape using a craft knife or box cutter. (Photo by Jody Danner Walker.)

Scissors work well for cutting thinfire shelf paper. (Photo by the author.)

coatings. It's not unusual for a mold to last a year or more without having to be recoated with kiln wash. In many cases only a light sanding of a mold is necessary before adding new kiln wash. If the existing wash is crack free, new kiln wash can even be be applied directly over the old with minimal surface preparation.

Using fiber paper

Protecting the kiln shelf can be done with either kiln wash or with fiber paper. (Using both is not necessary.) If you decide to use fiber paper, first cut it to fit the shape of the shelf (a craft knife will work well). Then fire it to about 1300F/700C to burn out the binder that holds the fibers together. Good ventilation is helpful during this procedure, as it may smell (like burning sugar) and may give off a mild dark smoke. Although the smoke from the burning binder is not harmful, the odor can be unpleasant.

Once the fiber paper has been fired, it is ready to use. Most fiber papers have one side that is relatively smooth and a second side that has a light texture. You can fire with either side facing the bottom of your glass.

Fiber paper can also be re-used, but to do this it should be handled carefully so that it stays intact. Some fiber papers also have a tendency to stick to glass after firing (especially to opaque colors); this can be minimized by waiting for the fired item to totally cool before removing it from

the fiber paper. After cooling, peel any stuck paper away carefully, trying to minimize loose particles and wayward fibers. Any loose fibers are potentially hazardous if inhaled, so the best way to remove them is to place the glass item under water and lightly rub them off. Wear a mask or respirator if you must work for any more than a few moments with loose fibers in the open air.

Unless the fiber paper has become soiled, it can be saved and re-used. In addition to its use as a shelf protector, fiber paper can be used in several other ways, the most common of which is to control the flow of glass during a firing.

Some artists like to kiln wash over the fiber paper in order to create a more desirable texture on the underside of the glass being fired. There's no harm in doing this, but either kiln wash or fiber paper alone are sufficient to keep the glass from sticking to the shelf.

Lightly dusting the fiber paper with dry kiln wash powder before firing will help minimize sticking and prolong the life of the paper. Also, consider trying some of the rigid paper, such as Unifrax's 110 paper; these generally last much longer than conventional paper.

Using thinfire shelf paper

Thinfire shelf paper can also be used to keep the glass from sticking to the shelf. Although this paper is only good for a single firing, making it

Properly placed items in kiln. Note the use of kiln posts to raise the shelf off the floor of the kiln. (Photo by the author.)

more expensive than most other options, thinfire paper does have the advantage of expediency. It also leaves an attractive sheen to the underside of the fired item.

To use thinfire paper, simply cut it to shape and place it on the kiln shelf beneath your glass. The paper should be cut only slightly larger than your piece; if it is cut too large make sure to anchor the extra paper with small pieces of glass. Otherwise, the extra thinfire can curl over the edge of the glass and leave undesireable marks on the surface.

Be aware that when thinfire is fired it gives off a slight odor at around 900F/480C. If you peek at the paper at this temperature, it will appear brown and slightly wrinkled. But don't worry,

just continue firing and paper will turn back to white, leaving behind a layer of dust particles beneath the fired glass. Use a damp cloth or a vacuum with a HEPA filter to clean the thinfire residue.

Placing the kiln shelf in the kiln

While it doesn't matter whether you place your item to be fired on the kiln shelf prior to putting the shelf into the kiln or afterwards, you should make certain that you do not place the shelf directly on the kiln floor. It should be raised off the floor at least half an inch, so that air can circulate under the shelf. This will help the piece heat and cool more evenly.

Damming, discussed in detail in Chapter 14, is required to keep thicker pieces from spreading during the firing. (Photo by Jody Danner Walker.)

A full shelf of pieces ready to be fired. Leave about 1/2" between pieces and along the outer edges of the kiln shelf. (Photo by Jody Danner Walker.)

The best way to do this is to use kiln posts, short "legs" that are usually made of the same kind of ceramic material as the shelf. Three posts are sufficient, although four may be used. Select posts that are at least half an inch high and place them under the shelf in the kiln. These support posts do not need to be kilnwashed, but there's no harm in doing so, if you prefer.

One question that's often asked is whether it's permissible to fire multiple shelves in a kiln, with one shelf supported several inches above another. This is common with ceramic kilns, but for the most part is not recommended for firing glass. The reason is that the temperature difference between a top shelf and a bottom one can be large enough to cause the glass on one shelf to fire significantly differently than the glass on the other. One piece could be fired perfectly, while another could be underfired. If you're experienced and know your kiln very well, you may be able to work around these temperature differences, but it's not easily done. Better to stick to one shelf at a time.

The first time you use your kiln, and from time to time during the life of the kiln, you should use a small level to check the levelness of the kiln shelf. If the shelf isn't level, pieces fired in the kiln could be slightly thicker on one side. If necessary, adjust the height of the posts under the shelf (or adjust the kiln itself) until the shelf is

level. If it is uneven, your pieces could be slightly thicker on one side. This check is especially critical for thick pieces and castings. It should be done when you first set up the kiln, anytime the kiln is moved, or when firing thicker pieces.

Another important test for kilns is to check the evenness of heating throughout the kiln. One easy way to do this is to create several tiles from inexpensive clear glass. Cut small squares from the glass and stack them two layers high (1/4"/6 mm) at various places in the kiln. Fire a standard full fuse firing, then examine the tiles to make certain that they're fused evenly. If there are hot spots or cold spots in the kiln, the tiles that were placed in those areas will have a different appearance than the other tiles. It's not necessary to do this test the first time you fire your kiln, but it does give you valuable information that will help you get the most out of your kiln.

Once the kiln floor and shelf have been protected and the shelf is level and supported in place, you are ready to begin your kilnforming projects.

Chapter 7

Keeping a firing log

Keeping a notebook • Documenting the firing schedule • Making comments

In many ways the firing log is the most underappreciated glass tool. All too often, the eagerness to fire overcomes the need to keep records of the firing, resulting in loose scraps of paper with illegible writing, disorganized rambling, or generally useless comments.

This is a huge mistake. The firing log is one of the most important tools you have. The combination of your kiln, your firing schedule, the glass you select, and the designs you create are unique to you. No one else can precisely duplicate your firing conditions, so it's up to you to keep records that are detailed enough to allow you to repeat good firings and avoid repeating bad ones.

Keeping a notebook

Some people suggest that a printed firing log is best, but a simple notebook is more flexible. You want to document all important information. Some firings will require minimal comment, others might demand several paragraphs.

Most importantly, keep the notebook in your work area. Use it religiously and enter essential information about each firing.

- **Date of firing.** If you plan multiple firings each day, you may also want to enter the time of the the firing.

- **Type of firing.** Possibilities include slumping, fusing, kiln casting, and fire polishing. Include information about the item being fired (bowl, plate, etc.) and the mold being used.

- **Type of glass.** Enter brand, color and texture, and any other significant features of the glass, such as thickness, opacity, or iridescent or dichroic coatings.

- **Design specifics.** It's often useful to enter specifics about your design, such as number of layers of glass or unusual arrangements. This isn't as important with simple projects, but becomes more valuable as your projects increase in complexity.

- **Firing schedule details.** Include enough information to allow you to duplicate this firing completely.

- Some people also document their firings with sketches or digital photographs of the pieces being fired. This is a great way to have a visual record of your firing.

Documenting the firing schedule

For those who use a computer controller, this information is as simple as listing each step of the specific firing schedule entered into the kiln. But even if your kiln is not equipped with a controller, it's good form to enter the rate of temperature increase, ending temperature, and hold time for each step of the firing. This will allow you to analyze problems and to duplicate the firing in the future.

Making comments

As important as it is to keep a record of the firing schedule, it's even more important to make comments about the success or failure of the firing. What went well? What do you want to avoid the next time?

Your comments might include:

- **Any cracking.** If the glass cracked, indicate the kind of crack, the number of cracks, and whether it split into pieces.

- **Nature of edges.** Are they smooth and well formed or uneven and irregular?

- **Degree and type of bubbles.** How many, how large, probable cause?

- **Placement of item in kiln.** Was it centered or close to the edge, was it closer to the elements than normal?

- **Fiber paper or kiln wash.** Each fires differently, so indicate the one being used, especially if you've change your process.

- **Uneven slumping.** Did the item lurch to one side or the other?

- **Any devitrification or other discoloration.** Did the glass devitrify? Did it change color or behave unexpectedly?

- **Opened kiln.** Document the opening of the kiln to vent during initial heating, to peek at the firing, or to accelerate cooling. Don't forget to mention how long the kiln was kept open.

- **Apparent hot spots**. Does one part of the kiln appear to be hotter or colder than other parts?

- **Other unusual events.** Anything that happened during the firing that seems out of the ordinary.

Rather than being a hindrance, a firing log can be viewed as the glass artist's best friend. It's the place to document what happened and why. Document your experiences and your theories.

As you become more experienced, you may find that many of your firings are similar and require little (or even no) entries. But regardless of your experience level, your firing log can be used as an invaluable tool in helping you learn and document the intricacies of your kiln and the glass you use.

A very basic firing log. This is the minimum information that should be kept for each firing.

Date and Time:	Firing type:	Glass info:
Rate of firing (dph)	**To temperature**	**Minutes held**
Firing Results:		

Chapter 8

Fusing coasters and tiles

Designing the piece • Cutting out the glass • Cleaning the glass • Loading the kiln • Fusing the glass • Care and cleaning • Variations • Beyond the coaster

Glass coasters and tiles are simple, basic shapes that make perfect first projects. If you can master the intricacies of making perfectly shaped tiles, you'll be a long way toward understanding volume control and being able to tackle more complicated projects.

As with all fusing projects, it's critical that you either use "tested compatible" glass or test the glass you plan to use for compatibility. Prior to starting the project, you should also have properly kiln washed and prepared your kiln and kiln shelf for firing.

For the project you will need a pen and some blank paper, a glass cutter, a working kiln, some kiln wash, fiber paper, or thinfire paper, and about half a square foot of glass (460 square cm) for each coaster you wish to make. You can choose any glass colors and textures you like.

The major steps in this project are:

• Designing the piece
• Cutting out the glass
• Loading the kiln
• Fusing the glass to form the tile or coaster

Sample coaster design with two layers: a design layer in green and red and a second layer of clear to add the necessary thickness. (Designed by Samantha Allen, photo courtesy of the artist.)

After a full fuse, a layer of clear capped with miscellaneous frit will yield the mottled appearance shown here. For best results use 1/4" (6 mm) of clear. (Photo by the author.)

Designing the piece

The design for the tile coaster can be as simple or as elaborate as you would like. If you have experience with cutting glass, you can come up with a design that gives you the opportunity to show off your cutting skills. For those with less experience, start with a more geometric design that uses mostly straight lines. Or use a design that involves stringers and frit, which don't require extensive cutting skills.

If you don't want to try your own design, you can use a copyright free stained glass pattern or just modify one of the design ideas shown on these two pages.

If you want to create your own design, it's often helpful to first sketch it out using a sheet of paper. Start by drawing a square on the paper the size of the tile or coaster you wish to make. Three and 1/2" (about 9 cm) squares work very well, but you can use any size that seems right to you. You can even use a circle or other different shape if you prefer, but these are generally more difficult for beginners.

Sketch your design inside the shape you've chosen. Don't worry if your design isn't perfect. Frank Lloyd Wright didn't design a masterpiece the first time out, either. The key is that you start to think about the different glasses that are available and how they can work together.

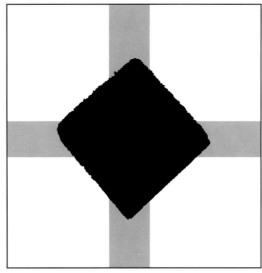

This simple design, which is demonstrated in this chapter, consists of a base layer of clear, a second layer with four squares and strips of glass, and a single square place on top of the two layers below. (Sketch by the author.)

The basic designs illustrated on these two pages are all made with a base layer of glass (usually a solid square of opaque glass) and a group of design elements placed on top of the base layer. This is the most common way of creating pieces that are two layers thick.

In some of the example designs, a few design elements are placed on top of the second layer. Generally, this is done with stringers, frit, or smaller pieces of glass. In most cases, you'll get better results if these small design elements are placed on top of the top layer, rather than in between the base layer and the top layer. Placing

An assortment of coaster designs, all two layers thick and using various colors and types of glass. The tile on the far left has a partial third layer, with black Uroboros noodles placed on top. (Photo by the author.)

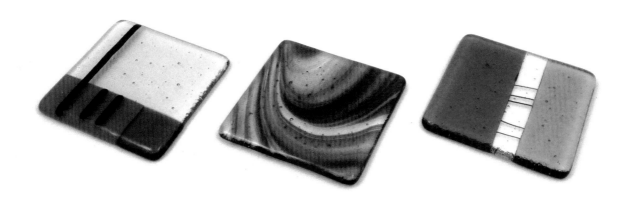

Glass required for our sample coaster project: four squares of yellow, one square of dark blue, several wide strips of white, and one large clear square the size of the final piece. (Photo by the author.)

frit and stringers between two layers can trap air and create ugly air bubbles in the finished piece.

Cutting out the glass

One of the best things about fusing is that it's possible to make beautiful and interesting pieces without having first-rate glass cutting skills. Of course it's a great benefit if you can cut well, but even if you can't you can use frit, powder, and other elements to create your designs. If you do that, then you can probably get by with just the ability to cut simple straight lines.

For coasters and tiles, start with a base layer of around 3 1/2″ (around 9cm) in size. Your second layer should be around the same size as the first. Try to avoid cutting the base layer larger than the layer on top; if you do that, then the edges of the finished piece may not round properly.

Although it's not essential, some people cut the base layer about 1/4″ (6 mm) smaller than the top layer. This allows the top layer to overhang the base layer up to 1/8″ (3 mm) all around. (For example, a base layer with 3 1/2″ would require a 3 3/4″ top layer.) If the coaster is properly fired, this overhang melts and curves around the bottom layer, creating nicely rounded edges.

If you need help with glass cutting fundamentals, check out the suggestions in Chapter 4.

Cleaning the glass

By now you should have designed your piece and cut out the glass. You should have also prepared the kiln for fusing by applying kiln wash or deciding to use fiber paper. You're almost ready to load and fire.

But wait. Before you can load the kiln, you need to make certain the glass is clean. Washing with clean water is often sufficient, but you may need to use dish washing liquid or another cleanser to thoroughly rinse away the oil from your cutter. Since some commercial glass cleaners have a tendency to leave a haze on the glass, many glass artists prefer to use isopropyl alcohol or acetone to clean their glass. Avoid denatured alcohol, as it can sometimes leave the glass hazy after firing. But whatever you use to clean the glass, make certain you remove any smudges or residual oils.

When you're finished cleaning the glass, take time to dry each piece with a lint-free cloth. From this point on you should wear latex gloves or handle the glass only by the edges. Avoid getting fingerprints on the glass -- they can show up as smudges in the finished work and can sometimes lead to devitrification.

Loading the kiln

Once the glass is cleaned thoroughly, it's ready to be assembled on a kiln shelf that has been

The coaster project, loaded on the kiln shelf and ready to fire. The yellow squares and white strips fit together to form the bottom layer of the piece. Next a layer of clear caps the base layer and it's topped with a single blue square. (Photo by the author.)

why doesn't blue stay "on top"

protected with kiln wash, fiber paper or thinfire shelf paper. It doesn't matter if the shelf is inside the kiln or outside. Do whichever is easier for you, but if you assemble the project outside the kiln you will need to be careful not to disturb it when placing it in the kiln.

Arrange the glass on the shelf. Glue shouldn't be needed to hold the piece together, but if your design requires glue, use as little as possible. Glue smells when it's fired, can leave behind ugly carbon deposits, and makes devitrification more likely. Avoid its use where ever possible.

If you absolutely must use glue, use a non-carbon based glue such as a gel glue or a glue that's especially formulated for fusing such as Klyr-fire. If you use a white (PVA) glue, it's generally a good practice to dilute the glue 50-50 with distilled water. Use as little glue as possible. Avoid super glues, which give off a poisonous fume when fired. And never use glue to counteract gravity and hold pieces in place in unnatural positions; the glue will burn off before the glass fuses. If you can get by without the glue, you should.

Once you've arranged your piece on the kiln shelf, transport the shelf to the kiln if it's not already there. Double check to make certain that everything is positioned properly, then take a moment to make the proper entries in your firing log. Keep the information that seems most important to you, but at a minimum the log

should include the date, a description of what is being fired, and information about the firing schedule used.

Fusing the glass

For this initial fusing firing, we will use a basic schedule that's appropriate for fully fusing two layered pieces of art glass up to about a square foot in size. The major steps follow below.

Please note that these temperatures are for average kilns and typical glass types -- your kiln and materials may require you to adjust the temperatures and times slightly up or down.

- **Begin firing the kiln**

Let the temperature increase evenly, at a rate of no more than 400F/222C per hour. For many fuse firings an even slower rate is used, around 300F/167C per hour. To avoid thermal shock, larger, thicker pieces require slower rates of temperature increase than smaller pieces.

- **Slow down and hold to reduce trapped air bubbles**

When the temperature reaches 1100F/600C, slow down the ascent to around 200F/111C per hour.

View of several pieces glowing in the heat of the kiln. This photo includes both the sample coaster described in this chapter and the square plate discussed in Chapter 10. (Photo by the author.)

A good rule of thumb is to slow down to half the rate you used in step one. Going slowly from 1100F/600C to 1240F/670C reduces the likelihood of trapped air bubbles between layers of glass.

In some situations, such as when trapped air bubbles are unlikely due to the design or the size of the pieces, it's possible to use a faster, more aggressive firing schedule. But in most cases the reduction in firing rate through this temperature range will be time well spent.

Once the kiln reaches 1240F/670C, hold the temperature for a while to allow air bubbles to escape. This soak period isn't necessary if there's no possibility of trapped air bubbles in your piece (or if you want trapped air bubbles), but in most cases you want to include it. Soak for around 30 minutes for small pieces and an hour or longer for thicker, larger ones.

- **Heat to full fuse and hold**

After the bubble soak, turn the kiln up and fire to your full fusing temperature as quickly as your kiln allows. Then hold for a time to allow the glass to fully fuse together and the top of the piece to become smooth.

For two or three layer items like the coaster, Bullseye recommends a ten minute hold at 1480F/804C. Spectrum recommends a ten minute hold at 1450F/788C. These are good starting points, but you'll need to find the temperature and hold time that works best for you, your kiln, your particular glass, and the way you work.

For glasses other than Bullseye and Spectrum, your full fuse temperature may be higher or lower than the temperatures recommended above.

How fast can you fire?

For two or three layer items up to 4" across, it's theoretically possible to fire from room temperature to 1100F/600C as fast as 900F/500C per hour. That's 15F/8.3C per minute. However, many fusers report much better results when they fire slower. A rate of temperature increase of around 400F/222 C per hour (6.7F/3.7C per minute) will usually give you better results than firing at a faster rate. And if your kiln has only side elements, you should consider going even slower.

What's the best full fuse temperature?

A full fuse is when the glass flattens out and the top surface is smooth and bump-free. Full fusing occurs as a result of several factors, including the temperature, the rate of temperature increase, the particular kiln, and the type of glass. Conventional schedules tend to hold (or soak) for 10 minutes at around 1450 to 1500F (788 to 815C), but you can achieve similar results by soaking for longer at lower temperatures or even by not holding at higher temperatures. Try different approaches to see which works best for you.

Try firing to around 1450F/788C and then adjust as needed.

Once the kiln reaches full fusing temperature, maintain that temperature until a full fuse is achieved. When fully fused, the edges should be completely rounded and the pieces on the top layer should flow together and the top of the piece should be smooth.

For most firings you shouldn't need to open the kiln during the firing, but it's sometimes necessary to get a closer look at the progress of the firing. If you must open the kiln, then do so carefully, using safety gloves and glasses that block infrared radiation. Open the kiln door and look in for only as long as necessary to quickly examine the piece. Then close the kiln quickly and quietly (don't slam the lid!) and allow the firing to continue.

• **Cool to the annealing range**

Once the glass has fully fused, it's time to begin the cooling process. The best way to accomplish this is to simply allow the kiln to cool naturally, without adding more heat and without opening the kiln.

The concept of flash venting, or crash cooling, while once popular with fusers, is no longer recommended. The advent of computerized controllers and glasses treated to minimize

devitrification have made it unnecessary in most situations. Also, if you open the kiln to speed up the cooling process, then it's possible to thermal shock the kiln brick or to knock dust particles from the roof of the kiln onto the glass below.

• **Anneal**

Annealing is the process of controlling the cooling of the glass, so that stress is removed and the glass won't crack once it cools to room temperature. In most kilns, small items such as coasters and tiles can be annealed by simply allowing the kiln to cool undisturbed, from fusing temperature all the way to room temperature. So long as the kiln is unopened and the time required for cooling to room temperature is four hours or more (as is the case in most kilns), then annealing can take place as the piece cools inside the closed kiln.

For kilns equipped with an electronic controller, annealing is best accomplished by controlling the rate of temperature descent, rather than simply allowing the kiln to cool naturally. To do this, the kiln is typically cooled naturally to the recommended annealing temperature for a particular glass, then the kiln is held at that temperature to allow annealing to take place.

A good rule of thumb for basic fuse firings is to hold the glass at the annealing temperature for about 15 minutes per fused layer. This is 30 min-

---

What's the right annealing temperature?

The glass manufacturers generally recommend a specific annealing temperature for their glass. Since the actual "textbook" annealing temperature varies based on color and type of glass, the recommended temperature is generally an educated guess that combines the different kinds of glass in the manufacturer's product line. This guess is an approximation, not a definitive temperature.

To make things even more complicated, the manufacturers's recommended temperature changes from time to time. This can be confusing, but it needn't make it harder to anneal. Simply use the latest recommendation and your pieces will anneal without difficulty. And remember that for most

pieces the exact temperature isn't as critical as making sure you anneal soak for long enough for stress to be removed.

Bullseye currently recommends an annealing temperature of 900F/482C, but for many years their recommendation was for a soak at 960F/515C. Spectrum recommends a soak at 950F/510C, while Uroboros recommends 960F/515C. Other manufacturer's recommendations can differ, so it's a good idea to check if you're uncertain.

The float glass manufacturers don't generally recommend an annealing temperature, but typically a range from 1000F/540C to 1030F/554C is used.

utes for a typical two layer fused piece, but you should add an additional 15 minutes for pieces that are tack fused, have metal inclusions, or are unusual in any other way. Better to be safe than to rush the annealing process.

After the anneal soak, the annealing process should continue by gradually cooling the piece until the temperature drops below the annealing range. For items such as coasters and tiles, the rate of cooling should be around 200F/111C per hour. For most glasses, cooling to a temperature of around 750F/400C works well.

• **Cool to room temperature.**

Once the temperature falls out of the annealing range, annealing is complete. You may let the glass slowly cool to room temperature. Larger, thicker pieces require controlling the rate of temperature decrease during this range, but for simple pieces that are 3/8″ (9 mm) or less the kiln can be shut off and allowed to cool naturally.

To be absolutely safe, the kiln should not be opened until it reaches room temperature. However, since most kilns cool very slowly over the last few hundred degrees, most people speed up the final cooling by opening the door or lid slightly toward the end of the cooling process.

A good rule of thumb for basic two layer pieces is to open the kiln about one inch (25 cm) at around 300F/150C. Open another inch at around 200F/90C. In most situations with small pieces, it's safe to open the kiln completely once the temperature drops to around 150F/65C, but be careful to allow a few moments more for the piece to be cool enough to touch. And avoid washing or handling the piece extensively until it has cooled to room temperature.

For larger, thicker pieces, it's best to let the kiln cool completely, unopened and undisturbed. Impatience has caused more than one thick piece to crack from sudden exposure to cool air. And if you plan extensive coldworking with the piece, it's a good idea to wait a day or more before beginning the job.

Sample fusing log for fused tile project; all temperatures are in degrees Fahrenheit.

Date / Time	Firing type	Glass type	Other
February 2nd	*Full fuse*	*Bullseye*	*Basic Coaster*
Starting Temperature	**Ending Temperature**	**Temperature change in degrees per hour**	**Minutes to hold**
Room	1100	400	10
1100	1240	200	30
1240	1480	Full	10
1480	900	Full	45
900	750	150	0
750	Room		
Comments:			

- **Inspect the finished piece**

Inspect it for uneven edges, rough spots, or other problem areas. Note anything unusual or significant in your log.

The most common problems experienced with simple fusing firings are needling, uneven edges, unwanted bubbles, and devitrification.

Small pin pricks of glass along the edges are called "needles." **Needling** is caused when the piece sticks slightly to the kiln shelf or paper beneath and can be prevented by firing slightly lower. Reducing the fusing temperature by as little as five or ten degress can make a big difference. Needles can be removed with a fine (400 or 600 grit) diamond hand pad or by gentle grinding with a fine grinding head.

Uneven edges are caused by overheating, under heating, or by poor cutting. They can also be caused by bulging from pieces placed on a third layer of the piece. In all cases the solution is to smooth out the edges with diamond hand pad or a glass grinder and then fire polish if necessary. (To fire polish to achieve a shine, re-fire the piece to around 1375F/746C. See the chapter on finishing for more on this process.)

Even with a bubble squeeze, small bubbles are almost inevitable between the layers of fused glass, but larger, misshapen, **unwanted bubbles** are usually prevented by the bubble squeeze. If you have them despite a long soak at 1240F/670C, then it's likely that something in your design (such as sandwiching frit between two layers) has caused the problem.

Devitrification is most often caused by either poor cleaning or by overheating. Some glasses, such as opaques, are more prone to devitrify than others. If other efforts to prevent devitrification fail, then consider using a devitrification spray.

You can read more details about these and other common fusing problems and their solutions by visiting Chapter 10, the Troubleshooting Guide.

The finished sample tile, fully fused, with rounded edges and a smooth top surface. (Photo by the author.)

Care and cleaning

So long as you use compatible glass, the key to long lasting glass projects is good annealing. When you hear of a glass bowl or plate that "just cracked" or an item that broke when barely touched, it's almost certainly a case of not being properly annealed. While it's not recommended, a well-annealed, relatively thick glass piece is about as durable as ceramic ware, and can withstand fairly rough handling and even occasional drops. The thinner the glass piece, of course, the more gently it needs to be handled.

Cleaning a finished coaster or similar item is simply a matter of wiping occasionally with a damp cloth. Mild cleaning solutions can also be used if desired, but water is generally sufficient. A well annealing piece should be dishwasher safe.

Sometimes the bottom of the coaster will have a rough surface that can scratch the top of the table it sits on. To prevent this, cover the bottom with felt or use small rubber bumper cushions in each corner. These cushions, which are often used to protect framed artwork from damaging the wall, are available from many framing supply outlets. One common type, made by 3M and several other manufacturers, are called bump-ons.

Variations

The coaster and tile designs covered so far have all been simple designs with either two layers of glass or two layers with a few small elements on top. A variety of other, more complicated techniques are illustrated on these pages. Many of these techniques are discussed in greater detail in later chapters of this book.

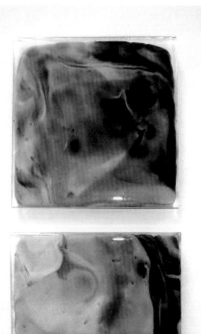

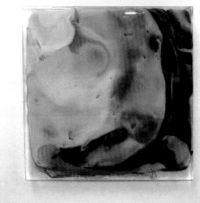

Reactive glasses. A simple design such as this one gains additional impact when the two glasses react with each other to create the thin dark line between the blue and the vanilla glasses. (Photo by the author.)

High temperature. When larger pieces, such as those created by pot melts, combing, or other high temperature firings, are cut into coaster size pieces, each tile will be unique. (Photo and design courtesy of Brock Craig.)

Strip construction. One way to achieve two layer thickness without placing one layer of glass on top of another is to cut strips of glass and then arrange them on edge to form the tile or coaster. For best results, the strips should be about 5/16 to 3/8" (7 to 9mm) wide. After cutting, arrange the strips edge to edge and then fuse fully to obtain the finished pieces shown above. (Photo by the author.)

Air bubble inclusion with powder and stringer. This coaster starts with a piece of Bullseye textured reed glass, placed reed side up on the kiln shelf. Powder is lightly sifted onto the reeds and stringers added to create the design. A second square of reed glass is placed reed side down criss-crossed on top of the first square. After fusing, a pattern of small bubbles is trapped with the powders and stringer between the layers of reed. (Design by Samantha Allen, photo courtesy of the artist.)

Powder migration using frit. *The tile above was created by first sifting red and black glass powder onto a base layer of glass to form the shape of the hand. After sifting the powder, the top layer of the glass was covered with a layer of coarse frit. The frit application should be about the thickness of one layer of glass, but no heavier or else unwanted air bubbles will be trapped. After applying the top layer of frit, fire to a full fuse; the powder will magically migrate to the edges of the frit.*

Powder migration using glass squares. *First sift blue powder onto a base glass, then place small squares of scrap glass directly on top of the powder to form a top layer. After firing, the blue powder will migrate to the edges of the small squares, creating the dark lines in the tile above. Any color of powder can be used, but due to their more intense colors opaque powders tend to work better than transparent ones. (Both powder migration photos by the author.)*

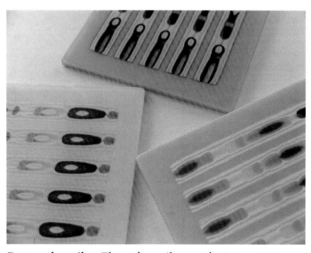

Sifting over textured glass. *Begin by placing textured glass on top of a base layer, then sift black powder over the top surface of the glass. After firing to a full fuse, the top of the glass will become smooth, but the impression of the texture will be left behind. This pieces uses Uroboros's radium glass to achieve the snakeskin look. (Photo by the author.)*

Pattern bar tiles. *These three tiles use the totem pattern bar process, discussed in Chapter 14, to achieve their unique look. Pattern bar slices make excellent coasters and tiles. (Photo and design courtesy of Brock Craig.)*

Beyond the basics

As your design, cutting, and fusing skills develop, you'll be able to tackle more complicated projects. The artwork on these two pages, for example, builds upon on basic fusing principles.

As always, feel free to draw inspiration from the artist's pieces used throughout this book, but please respect the artists ideas, designs, and copyrights.

Left: Kari Minnick, "Bite Me." Glass frit fused onto glass sheet. (Photo courtesy of the artist.)

Below top: Ruth Gowell, "Collection of Optical Objects." Fused with bubble inclusions. (Photo courtesy of the artist.)

Bottom: Jody Danner Walker, "An Autumn Wash." Fused and kiln-carved with glass powder (Photo courtesy of the artist.)

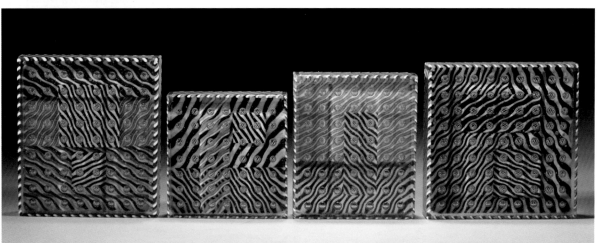

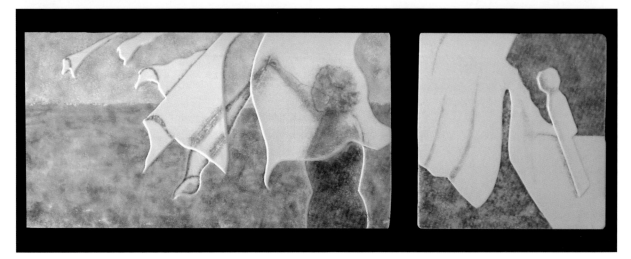

Top right: Marcia Newren, "The Dust Belt." Sheet glass, frit, handpulled stringer - fused, sandblasted and torchworked glass. Photo transfer process used on some small sections. (Photo by Margot Geist, courtesy of the artist.)

Bottom left: Richard Parrish, "What on Earth." Fused, kilncarved. (Photo courtesy of the artist.)

Bottom right: Dorothy Hafner, "Bongos." Fused glass panel, stainless steel pedestal. (Photo by George Erml, courtesy of the artist.)

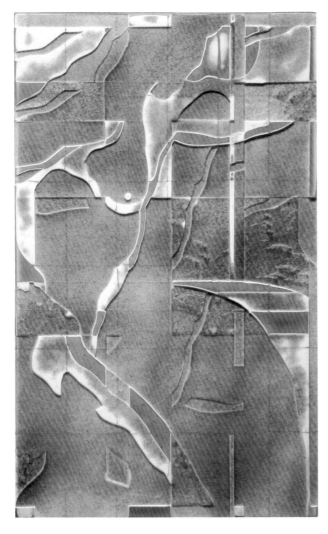

Chapter 9

Molds for slumping

Ways of slumping • Mold materials • Vitreous clay • Stainless steel • Fiber blanket • Fiber board and Ceramaguard • Plaster/silica • Refractory cement • Found molds • Applying kiln wash to molds • Using fiber paper with molds • Molds to avoid or use with caution

Molds, sometimes spelled "moulds," are essential if you want your glass to take on a third dimension. They are most frequently used for glass slumping and shaping in the kiln. This chapter focuses on molds for slumping and draping; molds for kiln casting are covered in Chapter 17.

Ways of slumping

Molds for slumping can be used in several different ways, but the most common are slumping into the mold and draping over a mold. It's also possible to have molds that combine both approaches.

- **Slumping into the mold.** The most widely used way to slump, this approach allows heat and gravity to act on the glass so that it droops down into the mold. Shapes frequently formed in this manner include bowls and platters.

  Most molds of this type are made from vitreous clay, but stainless steel molds may also be used so long as the sides aren't too steep. Molds used in this way need to have small holes in the bottom in order to allow the air to escape when the glass slumps.

- **Draping over the mold.** This approach, in which the glass is allowed to fall over the out-

side of a convex or upturned mold, generally uses molds made of stainless steel. Bowls and vases made using this technique are characterized by their wavy sides, like folds of cloth.

- **Combination molds.** Molds that combine both slumping and draping must be designed carefully to prevent the glass from being trapped on the mold. Usually this is accomplished by engineering a gentle drape, rather than a severe one, which allows the piece to simultaneously drape and slump without cracking or deforming in unexpected ways.

- **Drop rings.** A drop ring is a unique kind of mold that is slumped *through*, rather than into or over. This is possible because the drop ring has a large hole in the center.

  Smaller drop rings made of clay are commercially available, but larger ones must be custom made by cutting them from a refractory material like fiber board or Ceramaguard ceiling tile.

Commercial molds for commonly slumped forms such as bowls and plates are widely available, but molds for more specialized shapes need to be custom made. Fortunately, the materials to make your own molds are fairly easy to obtain and shape.

Janet Kelman, "Brilliant Green and Teal Seafan" was sandblasted from a blown form, then slumped to shape in the kiln. (Photo by Leslie Patron, courtesy of the artist.)

Mold materials

Some materials do not make good molds. Aluminum won't work; it will either melt or deform badly in the heat of the kiln. Steel can sometimes be used, but it is likely to oxidize and "spall," leaving small metal flakes inside the kiln and on the finished piece. Steel is also prone to warp, as may copper and many other metals. Cast iron tends to hold its shape, but it is very heavy and prone to rust.

Commercially made molds for slumping tend to be made of either stainless steel or vitrious clay. These materials can also be custom fabricated, but in most cases custom molds are made of fiber blanket, fiber board, Ceramaguard, plaster/silica, or refractory cement.

Vitreous clay molds

Vitreous clay simply refers to clay that has been previously fired, so that it tends not to absorb water. Clay can make excellent, long lasting molds. Clay is also inexpensive, making it the most widely available mold material.

If you buy a commercially manufactured vitreous clay mold, it should be good for a hundred or more firings. You'll just need to make certain you cover it well with kiln wash before using it the first time. Although some people advocate applying up to ten coats, just four or five coats with a haike or similar brush should suffice. Just brush on one coat in each compass direction. Reapply kiln wash when the previous application starts wearing thin. For most slumping situations, the kiln wash should last for dozens of firings before reapplication is required.

Many clay molds are specifically made for use in slumping, but it's also possible to use some regular pottery shapes for slumping. Typically, this is done by using "bisque ware," which is simply clay pottery that has been fired, but not glazed. While bisque ware (commonly called "bisque") is sometimes marketed specifically for use for slumping, it's more often found at ceramic supply houses or "paint-your-own-pottery" stores. If the purchased mold has not been pre-drilled, use a small drill bit (1/8"/3 mm or less) to drill holes in the lowest part of the mold, so that trapped air can escape during the firing.

In most situations, you'll obtain the best results from slumping *inside* a clay mold. Since clay shrinks less than glass when it cools, the glass easier slips from the mold after firing. Slumping over the outside of a clay mold (or drooping over the edges of the mold) can sometimes cause the glass to crack as the mold cools.

An assortment of molds for slumping, including vitreous clay molds, stainless steel molds, square drop ring, and a curved mold made from wet felt. (Photo by the author.)

If you must slump over clay (such as over an upturned terra cotta pot), then it's best to add a protective layer of fiber paper between the mold and the glass. This will allow for the different rates of expansion and contraction and prevent the glass from getting permanently stuck on the mold.

Stainless steel molds

Stainless steel molds are lightweight, difficult to deform, and able to last for a thousand firings or more. Simple bowl forms are relatively inexpensive to buy; you can even use cheap stainless steel bowls. As with most bisque ware, you'll need to drill three or four small (1/8"/3 mm or less) holes in the bottom for air to escape.

Like clay molds, stainless steel molds need to be covered with kiln wash to prevent glass sticking. This is difficult to do when the mold is at room temperature, but it can easily be accomplished by heating the mold to around 350F/180C and then brushing or spraying on the kiln wash while the mold is hot. The water in the wash will evaporate, leaving a protective coating behind.

In addition to kiln wash, it's also possible to coat stainless steel molds with boron nitride, a specially formulated product which helps prevent glass from sticking to steel. Boron nitride is available in both spray and liquid formulations; it is fairly expensive, but is much easier to apply than kiln wash.

For some molds, such as the stainless steel floral former, it may be possible to protect the glass from sticking to the mold by using a layer of thinfire shelf paper between the mold and the glass. The thinfire will turn to powder during the firing, but it will still keep the glass from sticking.

It's important to realize that, as it cools, steel contracts more than glass. (That's the opposite of clay, which contracts less than glass as it cools.) As a result, stainless steel molds are the mold of choice when slumping floral former or similar shapes where the glass folds over the outside of the mold.

Still, you can get away with slumping inside gentle stainless steel bowl forms; just make certain they're well covered in kiln wash (you might even sprinkle a little kiln wash powder inside) and be aware that slumping inside stainless steel forms with steep sides may not work.

Fiber blanket molds

Fiber blanket resists the heat of the kiln well. It can be used as a mold material on its own or it can be shaped and then hardened with the addition of a rigidizing solution.

"Parchment" by Dick Ditore. Fused, then slumped over fiber blanket. The left piece is ceramic with glass frit, the right is glass with glass frit. (Photo courtesy of the artist.)

Unadorned fiber blanket is best used for shapes that only require gentle bends, such as the piece depicted above. To use this material, simply arrange fiber blanket on the kiln shelf (a thickness of 1/2"/12 mm works well), place the glass on top (no kiln wash is needed), and fire using a slump schedule with a long hold at approximately 1150F/620C. The glass will conform to the shape of the blanket and can be easily removed after the firing.

A second way to use fiber blanket is to use it to make a more permanent mold. This requires the addition of a rigidizing solution, which gives the mold strength and allows it to stay in the desired shape in the heat of the kiln. Rigidizing solutions, which are usually made of colloidal silica, are commercially available uner the name of "fiber mold hardener." Fiber blanket can be soaked in the solution, then used to create a mold.

This process is fairly straightforward. Start by sculpting your desired shape from clay or any other material. Cover the sculpted shape with plastic wrap (cling film); this will keep the blanket from sticking to the custom form.

Once the form is ready, saturate fiber blanket with rigidizing solution. A blanket thickness of 1/2" (12 cm) works well. Squeeze the excess solution from the blanket and shape it around the sculpted form. Allow several days for the saturated blanket to air dry, or dry it more

quickly by heating in a kiln at 250F/121C for about half an hour. When the fiber blanket mold is dry, remove it from the sculpted form and fire it by itself in the kiln to 1150F/621C. This firing will harden the blanket and complete the curing process.

Once the blanket cools, touch up any soft spots with a small amount of rigidizer. The mold can be sanded lightly if desired, but wear a mask during this process. Kiln wash the mold thoroughly before use.

Although these kinds of molds are fragile, they can last for years if they're handled properly. Kiln wash should be reapplied frequently.

It's also possible to purchase fiber blanket that has already been saturated with the rigidizing solution. This is marketed under the names "wet felt" and "moldable fiber blanket."

Fiber board and Ceramaguard molds

More rigid refractory materials, such as fiber board and Ceramaguard, may also be used to create molds. Most often, these are either used as drop rings or carved into to create designs on fused and slumped pieces.

For use as a mold, a fiber board thickness of around 1/2" to 1" (12 to 25 mm) will work well.

73

The board can be cut with an exacto blade or similar sharp tool. Since many fiber boards are carcinogenic or cause respiratory issues when particles are inhaled, always wear an appropriate mask or respirator when cutting or shaping the board. Although some brands of fiber board have been pre-fired by the manufacturer, many brands need to be pre-fired to around 1400F/760C before use as a mold.

Ceramaguard, a commercial ceiling tile manufactured by Armstrong, is a less expensive alternative to fiber board for many applications. It is also non-carcinogenic, making it safer to cut and carve than fiber board. It produces a slight amount of nuisance dust when worked, requires kiln wash, and needs to be pre-fired to remove the paint layer on the top side.

Avoid other brands of ceiling tile. Ceramaguard is unique in that it can withstand slumping temperatures without deforming or losing strength. It can be cut with a craft knife or with any woodworking tool, making it ideal for use as a drop ring material.

Although Ceramaguard works well for slumping, care should be taken if firing it to fusing or higher temperatures; it can warp and lose its shape, especially when unsupported. Also, note that almost all other ceiling tiles will not perform well at temperatures above 1000F/540C.

Plaster/silica molds

People who work with clay and similar materials often use plaster to make their molds. Pottery plaster, which is made of gypsum, has the advantages of being fairly easy to find, easy to work with, and relatively inexpensive. By itself, however, it won't work for making molds for glass work that needs to be fired in a kiln.

That's because plaster alone can't withstand the heat of the kiln. In order to keep it from deteriorating when it's fired, it's essential to add one or more refractory materials to the mixture.

The most common refractory material used with plaster is silica, which is sometimes known as flint. Silica, available with very fine particle size (around 300 mesh, often called "silica flour"), helps the plaster maintain its strength at fusing and slumping temperatures.

Doug Randall, "Jazz Dancer." Fused, then drop formed, cut, and coldworked. (Photo courtesy of the artist.)

Plaster/silica mixtures can also be used without kiln wash. Molds made from these products are generally single use molds, making them best suited for making molds for pate de verre and kiln casting. If used for making custom slumping molds, use them in applications where the mold only needs to be used a few times.

Despite their usefulness, making plaster/silica molds is not as simple as making many other types of molds. Proper mixing requires practice and specific safety procedures must be followed. These are discussed in detail in Chapter 19.

Refractory cement molds

There are three major types of cement molds: castable cements, insulating cements, and gypsum cements. All are dry mixtures to which you add water and allow to harden to form the mold.

Cements are usually used to make a form for slumping over or for pate de verre (filling a mold with glass frit and then firing to fusing temperatures). They tend to stick to the model being used, so the model usually needs to be coated with a parting agent such as Pam cooking spray or liquid soap. Insulating cements tend to be less dense than the other types of cements.

Both castable cements and insulating cements require that kiln wash be applied to the finished mold to make sure that the glass doesn't stick. By contrast, gypsum cements do not need kiln washing. They are also able to pick up more detail than the other kinds of cements.

There are two major types of gypsum cements: hydrocal and hydroperm. They both work very well for casting into as well as for slumping over or for pate de verre. Hydrocal tends not to be as strong as hydroperm.

Found molds

You'd be surprised how many found items can serve as molds. We've already mentioned inexpensive stainless steel bowls and old pottery, but molds can be made from river stones, from steel hubcaps, from empty tuna cans, or from just about any material that can withstand the heat of the kiln.

Just be sure to use kiln wash on the found item and heat it slowly in an initial firing until certain how it will behave in the kiln. Some items, such as rocks, may have water trapped inside and could explode or fracture if heated too quickly.

But just because a found item can't stand the heat, it might still be worth using as a form around which to cast a more usable mold using clay or another refractory material.

Applying kiln wash to molds

Not all molds require kiln wash or a similar barrier to keep the glass from sticking, but many do, especially molds made from vitreous clay or stainless steel.

Applying kiln wash to clay molds is similar to kiln washing a shelf. Spraying usually leaves a smoother finish than brushing, but either method can be used. Just make certain the mold is dried thoroughly before using. If you're in a hurry you can dry in a kiln heated to about 500F/260C.

If the mold has holes in the bottom, examine the holes after kiln washing to make sure they haven't been blocked by the dried wash particles.

Beginning the process of applying kiln wash to a slump mold. Four or five coats is generally sufficient. (Photo by Jace Allen.)

If they are blocked, use a straightened paper clip or thin wire to clear the holes so that air can escape when slumping.

Some molds, notably those made of stainless steel, need to be heated in order to get the kiln wash to stick. In addition to heating, kiln wash sticks better to a stainless steel mold that has been sandblasted to slightly roughen the texture. If you don't have access to a sandblaster, rub the the stainless steel with steel wool, sandpaper, or emory cloth to give it a bit of tooth.

Once prepared, place the mold in the kiln and heat to around 350F/180C. A higher temperature can be used, but it's not really needed, and the lower temperature is a bit safer. Since stainless steel won't crack from being fired quickly, the kiln can be fired as rapidly as desired.

While the kiln is heating, prepare your kiln wash materials. Determine if you want to brush or spray the kiln wash. A brush takes less time to set up, but using a sprayer or airbrush will result in a smoother finish than using a brush.

Once the temperature in the kiln reaches 350F/180C, turn off the kiln. Put on your gloves, reach inside, and carefully remove the stainless steel mold. Place it on a nonflammable surface, next to the kiln wash.

Spraying on kiln wash is a simple matter of applying a thin, even coating on the outside of the mold. The kiln wash will sizzle as it hits the mold. That's the sound of the water in the mixture evaporating and leaving the protective powder behind.

When applying kiln wash with a brush, make certain the brush will resist the heat of the stainless steel. Foam brushes will not work, but a good quality brush can withstand the heat.

Quickly use the brush to apply the kiln wash. Cover all areas that might come into contact with the glass. As with a spray application, the kiln wash will sizzle as it goes on. After a few moments, the mold will cool to the point where the kiln wash no longer sticks. Return it to the kiln and repeat the process. It may take several applications before the mold is and ready to use.

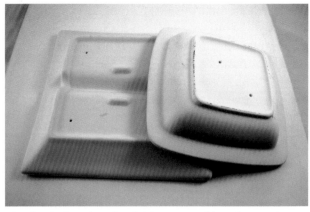

The finished underside of these two molds indicates they were made as pottery, not as molds for slumping. This doesn't mean that they won't work in the kiln, but it is a warning flag. Not all pieces of pottery make good slumping molds, even if they're being sold for that purpose. (Photo by the author.)

When you finish, the mold should be smooth to the touch, with no visible gaps or bumps. The kiln wash application should last for several firings, but if it flakes away, starts to look thin, or discolors slightly, you should reapply the kiln wash. For best results, lightly sand the mold with very fine steel wool before reapplying.

Finally, if you choose to kiln wash stainless steel without sandblasting, sanding, or otherwise roughing up the texture, it's a good idea to fire to 1200F/650C before kiln washing. The heat will remove oils or other contaminants that may remain on the steel from the manufacturing process.

Using fiber paper with molds

Sometimes, especially when you're using a mold for a purpose that's contrary to its design, it's helpful to use fiber paper to form the barrier between the mold and the glass.

In situations where the mold is likely to contract more than the glass, such as slumping over clay or into stainless steel with deep sides, the layer of fiber paper helps compensate for the different expansion characteristics and makes it possible to slump without cracking the glass.

Molds with steep rims, such as this one, are difficullt to use because the sides will draw in as the glass slumps. (Photo by the author.)

An example of a piece that was slumped on the mold to the left. The dogboned edges are curved, rather than straight. (Photo courtesy of Samantha Allen.)

Molds to avoid or use with caution

Not all molds are created equal. Some work much better for slumping than others. Some are designed for other purposes and may not work well in the kiln. And some molds are designed in ways that make slumping more difficult.

When purchasing any mold, it's a good to idea to examine it carefully to determine if it will be easy to use for slumping, or if it will be difficult to use. A few moments of reflection prior to the purchase can save hours of frustration later on.

For instance, many unglazed pottery pieces (also known as "bisque ware," or simply "bisque")

Because of the higher temperature required, molds with rippled edges, such as the two illustrated below, are more difficult to slump than molds without textured rims. (Photo by the author.)

make great slumping molds, but not all do. Just drilling a hole in the bottom of a piece of pottery doesn't make it a perfect mold for slumping.

Examine the mold to determine if it was made for slumping. Turn the piece over and examine the underside. Molds made for use as pottery have a finished bottom, allowing the mold to sit firmly on a flat surface. Molds made for slumping often have an unfinished underside. In addition, molds made for slumping often have sides that raise the bottom of mold slightly off the kiln shelf. This, along with one or more large ventilation holes in the mold sides, allows for good air circulation beneath the mold as it heats and cools.

Although this mold was made for slumping, the steep sides make it much more difficult to use successfully. (Photo by the author.)

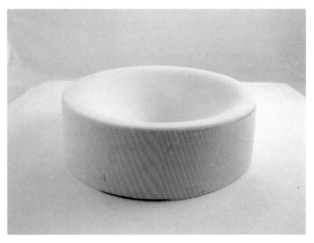

Don't eliminate a mold from consideration if it turns out to be a piece of pottery with holes drilled in the bottom. And don't automatically assume that a mold made specifically for slumping is a perfect mold. Instead, examine the way the mold is designed to get an idea of how it will perform in the kiln.

Watch out for are rims that are very narrow or steep. This makes slumping more difficult and can lead to dogboning, where the center of the sides draws in as the glass slumps. Particularly deep molds, as well as molds with steep sides, should be used with caution. These can slumped successfully, but rarely do beginners have success.

Use molds with texture with caution. Molds with wavy edges, for instance, can be slumped but are more difficult to use than molds with smoother rims. Use caution when firing any mold that has anything other than a smooth surface.

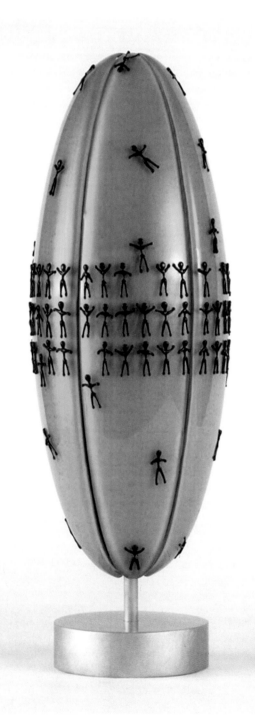

Amy Buchwald, "Falling Away." Torchworked, fused, and slumped glass on an aluminum frame. (Photo by Charles Buchwald, courtesy of the artist.)

Chapter 10

The basic slumping process

Fuse first, then slump • Selecting the mold • Designing the piece • Cutting out the glass • Preparing and loading the kiln • Fusing the glass to form a flat "blank" • Slumping the glass • After the slump • Beyond the basics

This project, which covers the steps involved in making a simple fused and slumped piece, assumes that you have either successfully tested your glass for compatibility or have obtained "tested compatible" glass.

The materials required include some blank paper, a glass cutter, a working kiln, some kiln wash or fiber paper, and enough glass to complete the project. Choose any colors and textures you like.

You will also need to either make or purchase a mold for slumping. We'll be using a shallow, square mold, but the steps can also be followed to slump any fairly shallow mold.

The major steps in this project are:

- Designing the piece
- Cutting out the glass
- Preparing and loading the kiln
- Fusing the glass to form a flat "blank"
- Slumping the glass

Fuse first, then slump

Before we begin the project, let's take a few moments to review the concepts of fusing and slumping and to make certain we know how the two processes work together.

Fusing is the process of heating two or more pieces of glass, so that they melt and join together. The fusing process results in a relatively flat piece of glass, like a coaster, a tile, or a two-dimensional work of art. This flat piece of glass is sometimes called a "blank."

Slumping, by contrast, is the shaping of a piece of glass using a mold. Slumping results in a three dimensional object such as a bowl, a plate, or a piece of sculpture. Some people use terms such as "sagging" and "draping" to differentiate among different types of forming with a mold, but most people use the umbrella term "slumping" to refer to any glass forming technique that uses heat, gravity and a mold to shape glass.

It's possible to do a one-step project where you just take a piece of glass and slump it to a particular shape. This is often done when making simple, inexpensive forms and draped shapes. More often though, a glass project involves two steps. First, the glass is fused together to form a blank. Second, the fused blank is slumped into (or over) a mold to form the final shape.

Because fusing typically takes place at higher temperatures than does slumping, you have to do slumping and fusing in the correct order. If you slump first, then fuse, the higher temperature required to fuse will cause the glass to lose the shape taken on during slumping. And if you try to both fuse and slump in one firing, you'll most likely be disappointed because the glass pieces will distort and move around significantly before they fuse together. As a result, in most cases you must fuse first, then properly cool the piece and use a second firing to slump it to the shape you want.

Selecting the mold

Before designing or fusing your piece, it's a good idea to determine the shape of the mold you want to use. The mold will not only determine the size of the blank to be made, it will determine its precise shape and even suggest particular designs. Don't make the mistake of fusing your blank without giving some thought as to the mold you're going to use.

This first project uses a very simple mold with a slight, all over curve, rather than a deep, more complicated shape. For your first slumps, choose molds with shallow, gentle curves, instead of more difficult deeper molds with steeper sides.

The mold we'll be using is called a "square slumper." Since squares are easier to cut than circles, the square shape of this mold also makes it a good choice for first slump firings. Always start with simple projects and attempt more difficult ones after you're learned the basics.

A simple vitreous clay mold with a gentle curve. The square shape of this mold explains why it is called a "square slumper." These molds can also be used to slump circles or more abstract shapes. (Photo by the author.)

Designing the piece

The design for the piece can be as simple or as complicated as you would like. If you have experience with cutting glass, then you can come up with a design that gives you the opportunity to show off your cutting skills. If you're new at glass cutting, you can make a very simple design that uses mostly straight lines. If you don't want to try your own design, you can use a stained glass pattern or just modify the design idea that is suggested at the bottom of the page.

Start by getting a sheet of paper. Measure the size of your mold and draw the outline of the piece on the paper. You want the outline to be approximately the same size as the rim of the mold. In most cases it's ok if the outline is a bit larger (as happens when you trace around the outside of a mold that's been turned upside down). It's also ok if your shape outline is a bit smaller than your mold. But don't overhang the edge any more than about 1/4" (6 mm) and don't be so much smaller than the mold that you're unable to take advantage of its curves.

Your design must fit into the shape you have drawn. You can just draw a simple design, or even use pencils or paints to sketch something more elaborate. Some people dispense with the formal design phase altogether. Instead, they just arrange pieces of glass on top of a base sheet of glass until they find an arrangement they like.

One possible design. This simple geometric pattern is easy to cut and assemble. (Photo by the author.)

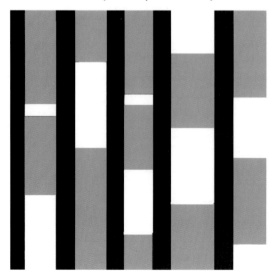

The glass pieces required for the project. The black and yellow strips will be cut into smaller pieces and assembled on the blue layer to form the pattern. (Photo by the author.)

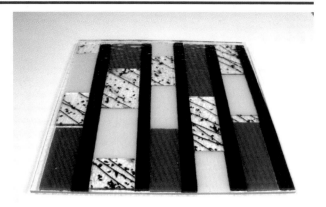

The assembled glass pieces, ready for fusing in the kiln. A full square of clear glass has been placed on top of the assembled pieces. (Photo by the author.)

But even with this approach it's helpful to have an idea of how your design will look in glass.

Once you have a sketch you're happy with, determine the colors you will use and pick out the glass you'll need. Now you're ready to move on to the next step, cutting out the glass.

Cutting out the glass

The simplest fused glass projects require two layers of glass. One, called a design layer, is created from as many different pieces of glass as are necessary to make up the design. As with fused tiles and coasters, stringers, frit, and small glass pieces can also be used as design elements if desired.

The second layer is often a single color that is used either as a base beneath the design layer or a cap on top of the piece. Any color is appropriate for use as a bottom layer, but clear glass is generally used as a cap on top.

For our piece, we'll start with an assortment of strips that will be cut to fit together to make up our design. In this case our square has 8″ (20 cm) sides and the strips are either 1/2″ (12mm) or 1/8″ (3mm) wide, in a variety of complementary colors.

Our design layer will be on the bottom, with a clear square of glass placed on top. We could have built the piece the other way around, with a base layer beneath and a design on top. Or we

could choose a more complicated configuration; the key, as with our coaster and tile designs, is to create a piece that will be approximately two layers thick when complete.

Remember, if the large piece of clear is on top, the weight of the glass on top will push the individual pieces of glass closer together, making for crisper lines. And if the individual pieces are on top of a base layer, the lines between the pieces will be a little less sharp, and the piece may have a bit more texture.

After cutting the glass for the two layers of the piece, the next step is to clean the glass thoroughly and then dry it with a paper towel or lint-free cloth.

Preparing and loading the kiln

If you're not familiar with the process of preparing your kiln for firing, please read through Chapter 5 for suggestions. If you have fired in your kiln before, take a moment to examine the kiln shelf to make certain the kiln wash is still intact and smooth. If necessary, remove the old kiln wash and re-apply new. If you've decided to fire on fiber paper rather than kiln wash, make sure your paper has been pre-fired and is still in good shape. If using thinfire shelf paper, cut a fresh piece and place it on the kiln shelf.

Before placing the glass into the kiln, it must be cleaned. From this point on, handle the glass only by the edges to prevent getting fingerprints on the smooth surface.

If you are using glass that is prone to devitrify, apply devitrication spray. Devit spray is not usually necessary for glasses formulated for fusing, such as Bullseye and Spectrum tested compatible glasses. The spray may either be brushed or sprayed onto the top surface of the glass. Take care not to spray the kiln shelf or underside of the glass. A thin layer of spray is best; be sure the spray is dry before firing.

Once the glass is ready, it should be assembled on the prepared kiln shelf. Take care to arrange it toward the center of the kiln, at least half an inch from the outer edges of the shelf.

For our sample piece, we'll start by placing the elements of the design layer into the kiln. Since these elements are fairly small, they'll each be cleaned and dried individually as they're laid into place on the shelf. When the design layer is complete, the clear layer will be centered on top. In our design the top layer is slightly larger than the bottom one. This will help the edges round

properly. In most cases the top layer should be the same size or just slightly larger than the layer beneath; if it is smaller, the edges may have difficulty rounding fully. Be sure not to overhang the bottom layer by more than 1/8 inch (3 mm).

Once you are satisfied that the pieces of glass are in position, it is time for the firing. If the shelf is not already in the kiln, carefully set it into place, on top of the kiln posts on the floor of the kiln. If the glass shifts during the loading process, take time to rearrange the pieces, making certain that you avoid leaving fingerprints and smudges behind. The last step is to record the information about the firing in your log.

Fusing the glass to form a flat "blank"

For this initial fusing firing, we will use a very simple, straightforward schedule that's appropriate for two layered pieces of art glass. The steps are basically the same as the ones in the fusing step of the coaster project, but additional com-

Sample firing log for fusing portion of bowl project; temperatures are in degrees Fahrenheit.

Date / Time	Firing type	Glass type	Other
March 13th	Full fuse	Bullseye	Bowl project
Starting Temperature	Ending Temperature	Temperature change in degrees per hour	Minutes to hold
Room	1100	400	10
1100	1240	200	30
1240	1480	Full	10
1480	900	Full	45
900	750	150	0
750	Room		
Comments:			

ments have been made to help illuminate some of the reasons for the specific items.

• **Begin firing the kiln**

Let the temperature increase evenly, at a rate not to exceed 400F/222C per hour. That rate works well for most basic fusing projects. It's sometimes possible to go faster, but doing so risks thermal shock. As the size and thickness of your project increases, you'll need to fire slower. When encountering firing problems, the solution is often to slow down the rate of temperature increase. You'll be surprised how many problems sort themselves out just by firing a bit slower.

• **Soak for ten minutes at 1100F/593C**

The purpose of this soak is to encourage even heating of the glass. A short soak (ten minutes works well for two layer pieces) allows the temperature of the glass to equalize in all areas. It also gives the glass time to reach the temperature shown on the controller or pyrometer and makes for a more accurate, even firing.

• **Don't forget the bubble squeeze step**

Fire slowly from 1100F/293C to around 1240F/670C, then hold at 1240F to allow air bubbles time to escape. A good rule of thumb is to go from 1100F to 1240F at half the rate of step one. For this firing, our rate in the first step was 400F/222C per hour, so we'll decrease to 200F/111C per hour in the bubble squeeze step.

Once the kiln reaches, 1240F/670C, hold the temperature for half an hour. Hold longer for thicker pieces or for pieces that are prone to trapping air. If trapped air bubbles are not a concern in your piece, you can skip the bubble squeeze step and fire faster through this stage. But it won't hurt to include the squeeze anyway.

• **Continue heating to full fuse**

After the bubble soak is complete, you can fire as quickly as you would like to full fusing tem-

perature. The exact temperature depends on your glass and the specific kiln you're using, but in most situations a range from 1450F/788C to 1500F/816C is appropriate. 1480F/804C is a good choice for most glasses.

• **Soak at full fuse temperature**

A ten minute soak will work well in almost all situations. For a full fuse, the idea is to hold the temperature until the edges are fully rounded and the pieces on the top layer flow together. If it takes longer than about 15 minutes to achieve the appearance you want, then try soaking at a slightly higher temperature the next time you fire.

Remember, the "right way to fuse" can vary from person to person and from kiln to kiln, so use these temperatures as a starting place, not a definitive guideline.

• **Allow the kiln to cool to the annealing temperature**

There's no need to open the kiln during this phase. Instead, simply allow the kiln to cool naturally without firing. This will take anywhere from about an hour to several hours, depending on the size and shape of your kiln.

• **Anneal**

Once the temperature inside the kiln reaches 960F/516C, begin the anneal soak. For a typical two layer piece, a thirty minute hold is sufficient. Fifteen minutes per layer is a good rule of thumb that works well for pieces up to around four layers (roughly half an inch or 12mm) in thickness.

After the anneal soak, cool the glass to 750F/400C, then turn off the kiln. A good cooling rate is about 150F/83C per hour.

There are many different ways to anneal, but the key with all of them is to remove stress from the glass so that it doesn't crack once it reaches room temperature. If in doubt, increase the annealing soak and slow down the rate of cooling. If you're uncertain about the exact annealing temperature, the manufacturer's latest recommendations can usually be found on their website.

• **Cool to room temperature.**

Annealing is complete when the temperature falls below the annealing range. A temperature of 750F/400C is safe for almost all types of glass.

From this point, simply allow the glass to slowly cool to room temperature. For two to three layer projects the size of this one, you will avoid thermal shock if your kiln cools no more rapidly than around 500F/260C per hour. If it cools faster than that (very unlikely), you will need to slow down the rate of temperature decrease.

• **Inspect the finished blank.**

When the kiln reaches room temperature, remove the fused piece from the kiln. Inspect it for uneven edges, rough spots, or other problem areas. Note anything unusual or significant in your log.

Now your fused piece is ready to be slumped. If the piece is significantly distorted or out of round, you may want to grind the edges and fire polish to smooth the piece and do a better job of rounding the edges.

Fire polishing is a separate firing, not unlike the fuse firing, except that you only fire to around 1350F/732 C and soak a few moments until the edges round and the heat of the kiln melts the

The fused blank, centered on the mold and ready for slumping. (Photo by the author.)

glass enough to form a nicely polished surface. It's not always necessary, but it's often useful when the piece emerges from fusing in less than perfect shape.

You can also re-fuse if desired; just fire a bit slower. The more times a particular glass is fired, the more you need to slow down the rates of ascent and descent.

Slumping the glass

Once fusing is complete, you should have fused a "blank" that is sized to fit the mold. The mold should have been previously prepared for use by applying kiln wash. Make sure the kiln wash is totally dry before use. Chapter 8 has more on applying kiln wash to the mold.

Once the mold is ready and the glass is clean and dry, get ready to set everything into place. Verify one last time that the air holes on the bottom of the mold are clear. Center the fused glass piece on top of the mold. It should rest lightly on or just inside the edges of the mold. Extend no more than 1/4" (6 mm) past the outside edge of the mold; any further risks cracking either the glass or the mold during the firing.

Don't forget to note the date, type of glass, firing schedule, and other information in your log. Also note that this is a slump firing.

• **Begin the first step of the slump firing**

Let the temperature increase evenly, at a rate not to exceed 300F/167C per hour. When the temperature reaches 1100F/600C, hold for around ten minutes to even out the heat in the glass.

It's important to note that the thicker the piece of glass you are firing, the slower your rate of temperature increase must be. A previously fused two layer piece needs to be fired slower than two layers of glass that have not been fused. Also, the more times a particular piece of glass has been fired, the slower you should fire. These points won't matter much for simpler projects, but as your projects become larger and more elaborate, adjusting the firing schedule becomes increasingly important.

• **Heat until the piece slumps.**

After the brief soak at 1100F, heat the kiln slowly to the appropriate slumping temperature for the mold being used. The exact temperature varies depending on the mold. Shallow molds generally work at lower temperatures, while deeper or more complicated molds require higher temperatures. For this reason, it's important to adjust your slumping temperature and soaking time depending on the specific mold being used.

For our simple square slumper mold, we'll fire from 1100F/600C to 1150F/620C at 100F/56C per hour, then hold for thirty minutes. This should be long enough for the piece to slump fully into the mold. It's even possible that it will slump more quickly, but with shallow molds such as this one it won't hurt if the glass sits at slumping temperature for a few extra minutes.

It's sometimes necessary to open the kiln when slumping to glance at the piece being fired. If you do this, take proper safety precautions, such as wearing protective gloves and eyewear. Open the kiln quickly, look in for only as long as necessary, then gently close the kiln again, taking care not to dislodge loose particles from the ceiling of the kiln and onto your piece.

At normal slumping temperatures, the glass will not pick up significant texture from the mold. It may smooth out slightly, but only slightly. If your mold has significant texture, it's probably a mold made for casting, not slumping, and shouldn't be used at slumping temperatures.

In general, a longer soak at a lower temperature is preferable to a short soak at a higher temperature. Slumping at a lower temperature leads to a more even slump and also prevents picking up kiln wash or unwanted detail from the mold. It's almost never necessary to slump at a higher temperaure than 1300F/704C.

• **Cool to to annealing temperature.**

In most situations the schedule for cooling to anneal and for annealing is the same for slumping as it is for fusing. Simply allow the kiln to cool naturally to the annealing temperature for your

Sample firing log for slumping portion of the project; temperatures are in degrees Fahrenheit.

Date / Time	Firing type	Glass type	Other
March 15th	Slump	Bullseye	Square slumper
Starting Temperature	**Ending Temperature**	**Temperature change in degrees per hour**	**Minutes to hold**
Room	1100	300	10
1100	1150	100	30
1150	900	Full	45
900	750	150	0
750	Room		
Comments:			

The finished piece. The square slumper mold gives a gentle, all over curve to your piece. (Photo by the author.)

glass, then hold the temperature for the required length of time.

Occasionally, especially for more complicated slumps such as drop rings and slumps using very deep molds, it may be necessary to open the kiln to allow the piece to stop additional movement of the glass and help the piece cool more quickly. But in most cases this is not necessary or recommended. Letting the kiln cool naturally is both safer and easier.

• **Anneal and cool to room temperature.**

For these steps you should follow the same procedures that were recommended during the fusing firing discussed in the previous section.

After the slump

When the kiln reaches room temperature, remove the mold and the slumped piece it contains from the kiln. The finished piece should easily slip out of the mold. Inspect it for uneven edges, rough spots, or other problem areas. Note anything unusual or significant in your log.

Slumping can be much more complex than fusing. There are many different ways to slump and many different philosophies about the "right" way to slump. Molds vary considerably and some glass requires higher or lower temperatures to slump. The key is to experiment with different methods and temperatures until you find the

one that works best for you, your kiln, and your particular kilnforming projects.

Sometimes a piece emerges from the kiln absolutely perfect and with nothing required but to wash it off and find a place to display it. More often, though, it won't be quite perfect and will require some additional finishing work before it's ready to display.

Complete disasters can be fired again or even broken into pieces and used as elements in a new work. You can also re-slump if necessary, or even re-fuse flat and start again. Just be aware that you may need to heat and anneal these "second efforts" a bit longer than normal. Pieces that have been fired many times are also more prone to devitrification, so consider using a devit spray if you must fire numerous times.

You can also improve the success of your fused and slumped pieces by "coldworking." This operation, which is discussed in greater detail in Chapter 18, involves using various tools to shape and polish the edges and surface of the glass.

Coldworking can be very tedious and often involves expensive equipment, but the final polishing process can remove baked-on kiln wash, smooth out rough edges, and bring a finished sparkle to the piece.

Good planning, accurate glass cutting, and attention to detail during the fusing and slumping processes can minimize or eliminate the need for coldworking.

Above: Lisa Allen, "Cognition." Fused and slumped. Full piece above left, detail above right. (Photo courtesy of the artist.)

Middle: Dick Ditore, "Stone Bowl." Fused and slumped. (Photo courtesy of the artist.)

Bottom: Doug Randall, "Woven Window." Fused, drop formed, cut and coldworked, hand polished. (Photo courtesy of the artist.)

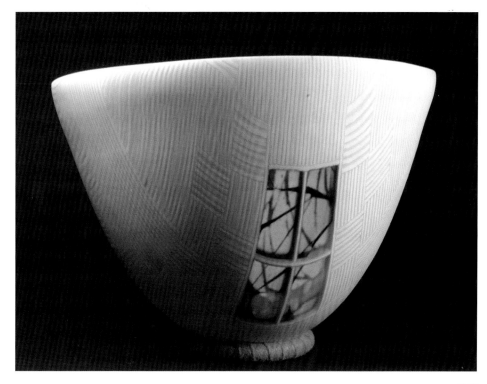

Steve Immerman, "Corolla." Assembled from strips, fused, slumped, coldworked.
Detail at top, full bowl at bottom. (Photo courtesy of the artist.)

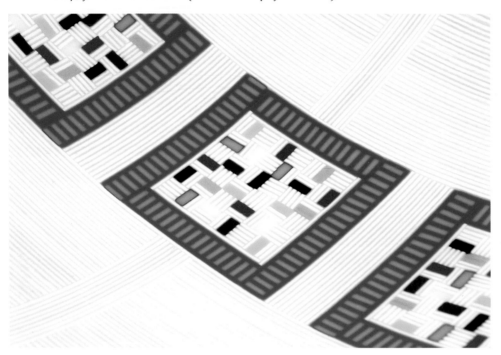

Martin Kremer, "In Depth." Fused glass bowl. Detail at top, full bowl at bottom. (Photo courtesy of the artist.)

Beyond the basics

While it's great to create functional items like bowls and platters, you don't have to confine your projects to such basic shapes. With a little practice and some imagination, you can explore the possibilities of slumping to create both functional and non-functional art pieces.

It's possible to use slumped components as elements in a larger, more complicated piece, to slump and then assemble pieces using adhesives or other methods, or even to arrange slumped forms with other items to create a piece that is greater than the sum of its parts.

Chapter 17 has more information about slumping and suggestions for slumped items that aren't made in the conventional way.

Left: Karl Herron, "Dolmen Cairn #0309."", "The Ancestors." Fused and slumped (Photo by Brian Rutledge, courtesy of the artist.)

Below: Nina Falk, "Nested Waves." Fused to create texture, then slumped. (Photo by Greg Staley, courtesy of the artist.)

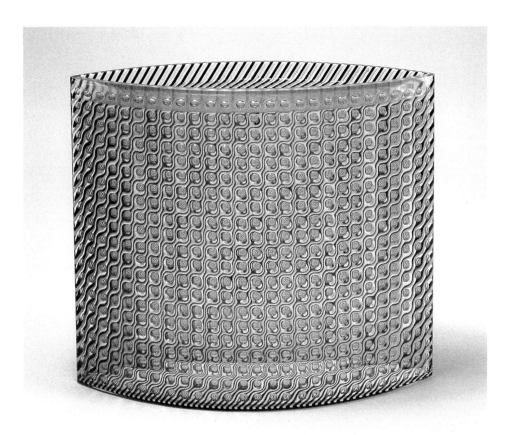

Right: Ruth Gowell,"Optical Vase." Fused, slumped, assembled. (Photo by Pete Duvall, courtesy of the artist.)

Below: Emily Brock, "Intimate Encounter." Assembled from fused, slumped, and lampworked components. (Photo by Terry Brock, courtesy of the artist.)

Chapter 11

Troubleshooting

Cracked glass • Unwanted air bubbles • Dull patches and devitrification • Baked on kiln wash • Uneven fused edges • Uneven slumping • Sticking to the slump mold • Fused panel slightly bowed

Unfortunately, not all glass projects emerge from the kiln in pristine condition. Sometimes the item is cracked, sometimes there are unwanted bubbles, sometimes the edges aren't rounded properly, the surface looks hazy, or a piece slumps crooked or misshapen. Here's a discussion of possible problems and their solutions.

Cracked glass

There are few things more frustrating to the glass artist than opening the kiln to find that the piece you've fired has cracked. The only bright spot is in figuring out why the piece cracked so it doesn't happen again.

First, let's assume you didn't drop the piece. Let's also assume you didn't remove it while it was still warm and then "accidentally" put it on something cold or splash it with water.

Now that we've set those obvious reasons aside, let's try to figure out the less obvious reasons for glass to crack. You can learn a lot by examining the nature of the cracks. Do they go all the way across the glass? How are they shaped? Is the piece broken entirely or still intact? What's the

When thermal shock occurs, it's possible for the force of the break to shatter the glass into several pieces. This break occurred during the initial heating phase and the edges were rounded during later stages of the firing. (Photo by the author.)

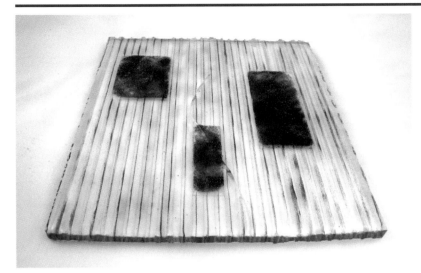

Poor annealing often shows up as an S-shaped crack in the center of the piece of glass. The crack can split the piece into two or it can stop mid way through. Often it will continue to grow with time. Annealing cracks can emerge immediately after firing or they can show up many months later. Full piece above, detail to the right. (Photos by the author.)

shape of the broken pieces? By analyzing the kind of cracks you're experiencing, you can determine what caused them, then change your kiln processes to prevent their re-occurrence.

• **Cracks with rounded edges that break the glass into several pieces**

These cracks, which can occur with such force that they split the piece into two, three, or even more pieces, are caused by thermal shock. The edges of the pieces are rounded because the crack occurs early in the firing cycle (usually around 300 to 500F/150 to 260C) and the edges round during later phases of the firing. The cure for thermal shock is to fire more slowly during the initial phase of your firing (below 1100F/600C.

In most cases this kind of thermal shock splits the piece into two or three pieces. Since the edges round during the firing, it's not usually possible to fit them precisely back together and refire.

• **Curved crack across the middle of the piece**

Improper annealing causes this kind of crack. It most often shows up as a gentle curve (often S-shaped, but sometimes as straight lines) that run across the middle of the piece. Sometimes the crack will curve sharply as it nears the edge

of the glass. The piece can be split in two by the crack, but often the crack only goes part of the way across the piece and it remains intact.

The cure for this problem is proper annealing. Lengthen the soak time at the annealing temperature and cool more slowly in the bottom half of the annealing range. Pieces that have already been cracked can be re-fused and then properly annealed to repair the crack, but in almost all cases the line of the repaired crack will be visible.

• **Slit marks, usually on top side of a piece**

These cracks, which look like deep knife slits on the top of a piece, are also caused by thermal shock. They are most likely to occur during slumping and are caused by being too close to a kiln's top elements, often while slumping on a bowl mold. The temperature difference between the very hot top of the piece and the cooler bottom side leads to thermal shock and causes the slits to form.

• **Cracks where two different glasses come together.**

Glass incompatibility causes these cracks. The cracks can be very small or they can cause the

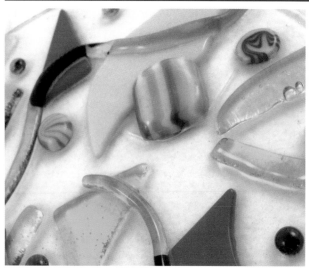

Closeup of an incompatibility crack, barely visible just around the bottom edge of the striped piece, which is incompatible with the base glass. (Photo by the author.)

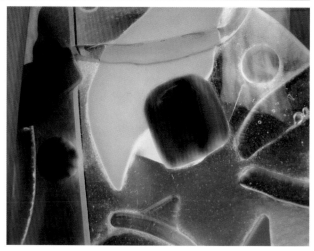

The same piece, viewed through polarized film. Note the characteristic stress halos where the crack has formed around the bottom of the incompatible piece. (Photo by the author.)

pieces to break apart, but they will usually show up as curves around the intersection between two pieces of glass. To prevent this problem, use "tested compatible" glass or conduct your own compatibility tests. See page 14 for a discussion of the procedure for testing compatibility.

Aside from cutting out all of the incompatible glass and then adding fresh glass and refiring, there is no way to salvage a piece that has cracked due to incompatibility.

- **Extreme cracking, shattering the piece into small pieces**

Extreme cracking, most likely caused by incompatibility. These cracks will continue to increase over time until the piece falls apart. (Photo by the author.)

This kind of cracking, illustrated in the photo to the lower left of this page, is most often caused by extreme incompatibility. When the piece is badly cracked, but still intact, the incompatibility cracks are likely to spread over time, until the piece falls apart.

When the incompatibility is especially severe, the piece will fall apart while still in the kiln or when picked up from the shelf. Severe incompatibility is most often caused when using glasses not made for fusing or inadvertently fusing large quantities of incompatible glass. A single isolated piece of incompatible glass will generally not cause a reaction this severe.

- **Small, interconnected cracks (like a spider web)**

These cracks generally extend from a single spot on the underside of the glass. They aren't usually severe enough to cause the item to split into pieces. Sometimes shelf primer will also be stuck to the underside of the glass. Most likely, this kind of crack is caused by glass sticking to the kiln shelf. A close examination of the shelf may also reveal small glass pieces that are embedded in the shelf.

The obvious solution is to scrape the shelf clean and apply fresh kiln wash. Using thinfire shelf paper or fiber paper will also prevent this kind of crack.

- **Cracks that occur long after firing.**

Sometimes a glass piece will just be sitting on a table when you hear a sharp ping. It might be quite loud, and perhaps there's a second (or even a third) ping. When you check it out, you discover that the glass piece you thought was beautifully finished has cracked. This cracking can even be severe enough to shatter the piece, leaving the artwork in pieces on the table.

The reason for this disaster is related to stress left in the piece from improper annealing or incompatibility. Incremental stress from "normal" wear and tear, such as from the sun hitting a piece in the window or the warmth of a hand holding the piece, adds to the stress already in the glass to cause the crack. If this occurs, go back to your log -- you do keep a log of your firings, don't you? -- and examine the firing schedule to see if you notice anything out of the ordinary.

If you used the same schedule you've always had success with, then perhaps this piece of glass was a bit thicker or more irregular than normal. Perhaps it was a different glass than you usually use. Perhaps your "normal" annealing schedule needs to be adjusted to anneal just a bit longer and slower.

Unwanted air bubbles

Some people like air bubbles in their finished glass pieces. They claim that they give the work character and are even attractive in their own right. It's even possible to work with bubbles by manipulating them between layers of glass.

But most people think of bubbles as a nuisance. They'd like their finished pieces to be bubble-free and as smooth and untroubled as a piece of plastic. This isn't always possible, but there are some techniques that will help minimize bubbles in the glasswork.

The first step is to identify the kind of bubbles you have. There are many different kinds, from large ones that pop like a balloon and leave a hole behind to very small bubbles trapped between the layers of glass. Each of the types of bubbles has different causes and solutions.

- **Bubbles in unfused, unheated glass**

Sometimes a "new," unfired sheet of glass will have small bubbles captured inside. These bubbles, called "seeds," are manufacturing defects. They cannot be eliminated. If you find them undesireable, take the time to examine your glass sheets closely prior to purchasing.

- **Small bubbles between layers of glass**

These are the most common types of bubbles, caused by air that has been trapped between the layers of the glass. It's very difficult to totally eliminate these relatively small bubbles (many people find them attractive), but proper design and firing techniques can minimize them and eliminate unsightly, large trapped air bubbles.

In addition to lengthening the bubble squeeze cycle, proper design and layout of your pieces can help with this problem. Avoid glass "sandwiches" that trap frit or small pieces between layers of glass. If you must have small pieces of glass between layers, use smaller pieces, rather than large ones, and give some thought to designing ways for trapped air to escape.

The trapped air bubbles in this piece are caused by sandwiching small pieces of glass between the top and bottom layer. (Photo by the author.)

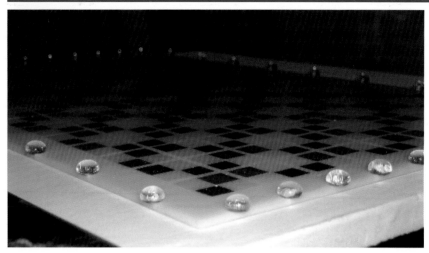

Closeup of small beads lining the outer edge of a piece. After capping, the piece should be fired so that the top piece of glass slowly pushes the air bubbles out. Once fused, the rim of the glass can be coldworked to achieve a gently scalloped edge. (Photo by Brock Craig.)

If you want to absolutely eliminate air bubbles between layers of glass, consider supporting the edges of the glass with tiny, nugget-sized, pieces or "beads" of glass. Use clear glass or glass that is the same color as the base glass. Place the pieces in several different places along the outside edge. This will give the air additional room to escape. It will also change the character of the edges slightly and may require coldworking the edges to achieve the desired finish. When using this technique, make certain to use a long bubble squeeze to allow the top piece of glass to slowly slump down over the bottom piece and push the air bubbles out.

- **Large bubbles, sometimes breaking through to form a hole**

These bubbles are two inches (5 cm) across or greater. They start in the space between your piece and the kiln shelf and generally increase in size when the piece is fired above 1300F/693C. If heated long enough, they can expand until they pop, leaving behind a hole in the glass. Normally, this problem occurs when fusing on kiln wash; the most likely cause is an uneven kiln shelf.

There are several ways to prevent these large bubbles. One is to lengthen the bubble soak and fire more slowly from 1100F/600C to your final fusing temperature. A rate of around 150 to 200F/83 to 111C from 1300F/700C to fusing temperature is often slow enough to allow the trapped air and gas to escape. Other options are to switch to another kiln shelf, flip the one

you're using, or fire on fiber paper rather than kiln wash. Note that firing on thinfire shelf paper will reduce the likelihood of large bubbles forming, but it will not eliminate it entirely.

Dull patches and devitrification

Dull patches on a fused piece, where the glass appears rough or has lost its shine in spots, is most often related to devitrification, a scummy white crystallization that can ruin the best of pieces. Normally, this occurs when glass lingers too long in the temperature range just before it becomes molten. For most glasses, this is above 1300F/693C.

If the dull parts are only along the edges of the glass, then this is most likely due to devitrification caused by the edges of the glass remaining hot for longer than the middle. To alleviate this problem, consider "baffling" the side elements of your kiln by placing a barrier (kiln furniture or kiln brick) between the elements and the piece. This will keep the hottest air from directly hitting the sides of the piece and should reduce the risk of edge devitrification.

Note that some glasses are more prone to devitrification than others. Glass that hasn't been cleaned thoroughly is more likely to devitrify. Opaque glasses are more problematical than transparent ones. Thinfire shelf paper can cause a loss of shine on the bottom of a piece or if touches the top of a piece during a firing. And float glass can exhibit "tin bloom," a discoloration that looks very similar to devitrification.

Large bubble in a fused piece. This kind of bubble is between the kiln shelf and the piece. (Photo by the author.)

An extreme example of large bubbles beneath the piece. Some of the bubbles are large enough to break through the top surface. (Photo courtesy of Steve Immerman.)

The treatment for all of these problems begins with cleanliness. Failure to thoroughly clean cutting and other oils from the glass can lead to devitrification; even the oil from a single fingerprint can smudge the surface of the glass and leave a dull patch behind. Once the glass is thoroughly cleaned, make certain you handle it only by the edges or while wearing gloves.

Other options for preventing devitrification include applying a devitirification spray ("devit" spray) prior to fusing. This process involves spraying or brushing a thin, even layer of spray on the top surface of the item. Be sure to allow the spray to dry thoroughly before firing. See Chapter 3 for more on devit sprays.

Since devitrification occurs when the glass no longer flows at full fuse temperature, careful monitoring of a firing can also help prevent devit in some cases. Minimze the time spent at fusing temperatures and in extreme cases consider flash venting to quickly "crash cool" from the fusing temperature to just above the annealing zone.

Once it occurs, there are several approaches to removing devitrification and related dull spots. If the equipment is available, a light sandblasting of the surface of the glass, followed by a fire polish firing, will remove the discoloration and restore the shine.

Another treatment option which works well for flat pieces is to sift a layer of clear glass powder on top of the piece. Take care that the layer is very thin (no more than one or two grains of powder in thickness); if the layer is thicker, it's possible to trap air bubbles between the individual grains and leave a cloudy appearance after re-firing. Once the glass powder has been sifted, fire the piece to around 1450F/788C and hold for about five minutes. This is long enough to smooth out the particles of powder and should also leave a bright, shiny surface behind.

Baked on kiln wash

Sometimes kiln wash becomes baked on to the bottom surface of the glass. This is sometimes unavoidable, as when firing to very high temperatures for combing and pot melts, but in most situations it can be minimized or eliminated entirely.

Avoid firing on a damp kiln shelf, firing to a higher temperature than necessary, or firing on used kiln wash that should have been scraped and reapplied. Use kiln washes that have been formulated for glass, rather than ones made for pottery. Wherever possible avoid placing opaque glass against the shelf. Opals are much more likely to stick to kiln wash than transparents, and white is the worst of all.

Another option is to give your kiln wash some help by sifting another barrier beneath the piece. Sprinkle loose kiln wash powder, dry plaster, mica, or whiting directly on the kiln shelf. Then

97

place your piece on top of the sifted material and fire as normal. The extra layer will help keep kiln wash from sticking.

You might also consider firing with iridized glass, irid side down against the shelf. Not only will this leave the glass with an attractive, shimmery finish, it will also help keep kiln wash from sticking to the glass.

When firing, it also helps to fire a bit slower and to a slightly lower fusing temperature than normal. Reducing hold time will help; a very long soak can aggravate the problem. And you can sidestep kiln wash problems entirely by fusing on fiber or shelf paper.

If kiln wash does stick and needs to be removed, try scrubbing gently with a scrubbie or similar mild abrasive sponge. A wire brush or very fine steel wool can also work for stubborn situations. Kiln wash particles can also be loosened by a brief soak in vinegar. Stronger solutions, such as CLR, Limeaway, or muriatic acid, are much more caustic and should be avoided if at all posssible.

If you have access to the equipment, then sandblasting is fast and effective. However, it does have the potential to change the appearance of the piece. This may not be a problem for the backside of a platter or similar object, but sandblasting can dramatically alter the appearance of a more three-dimensional piece.

As with many problems, prevention is preferable to removal. Frequent reapplication of kiln wash will help, paying special attention to removing the old kiln wash thoroughly prior to applying the new. Making certain that the kiln shelf is dry also helps, as does avoiding reducing your top temperature or hold time if at all possible. And selecting a good brand of kiln wash can be a factor; some brands do not work as well as others.

Uneven fused edges

One of the most common complaints voiced by beginners concerns uneven or unattractive edges in fused glass. Since the perceived quality of a finished piece is often directly related to edge quality, this is a significant issue that should be addressed. Often the difference between a second-rate work of art and one that is worthy of display lies with the quality of the edge work.

If the edges of a fused piece are not as smooth and well rounded as desired, then the piece may not have gotten hot enough. Just heat the piece again, this time firing a bit higher (or soaking for a bit longer). If possible, watch the piece as it soaks until it rounds completely.

Be aware that certain designs will be more prone to misshapen edges. If the top layer is significantly smaller than the bottom one, then the edges will be unable to round fully. If large pieces of glass are placed near the edges, the the glass will often push out in those spots, causing an uneven edge. To avoid this situation, place large design elements at least one half inch (13mm) from the outside edge of the piece.

If the fused piece has needle-like projections along the edge, then you've overfired. Use a fine (400 grit) diamond hand pad or extra fine grinding head to grind the projections away. Re-fire to fire polish (1350 to 1400F/730 to 760C) if the sanding process also removes the shine, but with small needles this is generally not necessary.

More elaborate coldworking techniques, such as using a wet belt sander, lap wheel, or similar tool, can also improve the edges following fusing. These techniques are discussed more fully in the chapter on coldworking.

Normally, edges should be worked to the desired shape and form prior to slumping. The slumping process will reshape the glass, but it won't turn ugly edges into pretty ones. Sometimes, however, despite our best efforts, the slumped pieces still have rough or distorted edges. The best way to improve this is to use coldworking equipment to grind and polish the edges.

Uneven slumping

The crooked slump, where one edge of the piece slumps further down into the mold than another, has several possible causes. Most often, it's caused by firing too high or too quickly. A lengthy soak at a lower temperature is almost always better than a short one at a higher temperature.

This problem can also be caused by starting the slump with a piece that is uneven in the mold. Use a small level to check that the piece is even in the mold before the firing begins. Check the levelness of the piece in the mold, not the kiln shelf of kiln.

Creating a slight bevel to the underside of a piece can also help the piece to move evenly down the sides of the mold. This suggestion is especially appropriate for stainless steel molds. For many of these molds, which tend to have small rims and steeper sides than many ceramic molds, it's also a good idea to start your slump with the piece inside the mold, rather than resting on the top rim. For very deep slumps, slump in several firings, each deeper than the previous, rather than all at one time.

At times it may be necessary to reach into the kiln during a slump to manipulate the mold or rearrange the piece on the mold. This is an extreme maneuver that should only be taken when wearing the proper safety equiment, especially gloves and eye protection.

A piece will also slump unevenly if the air holes in the mold are blocked, so always check that the holes are clear before starting your slump.

Sticking to the slump mold

Occasionally a piece will emerge from a slump firing with the glass stuck to the mold. This can happen if the mold was not properly covered with kiln wash. It can also happen if the glass blank was significantly larger than the mold and the glass becomes trapped around the outside edges of the mold.

Although it may be necessary to break the glass or the mold in order to get the two apart, this can often be avoided by careful re-firing. Start by turning the piece upside down, so that the mold is on top and the glass is on a prepared

kiln shelf. Re-fire the piece slowly from room temperature to the slumping range. When the temperature reaches around 1150F/620C, allow it to soak for 30 minutes or more. Watch the kiln carefully; in many instances the glass will separate from the mold and drop onto the kiln shelf. Sometimes it helps to put on gloves and safety glasses and reach inside the kiln and move the mold to help the glass come loose. Once the two are separated, anneal and cool as you would for a normal piece.

Fused panel slightly bowed

A flat piece will sometimes emerge from the kiln slightly bowed. The bowing is more pronounced with long panels, when one layer of glass is thicker than the other (such as a 6mm sheet over a 3mm), when the glass is close to the elements, or in situations where there is a tendency for uneven cooling.

Left unchecked, stress can build up in the bowed panel and eventually cause it to crack. Even if cracking doesn't occur, an uneven panel can be unattractive or difficult to install or hang.

To address this issue, first verify that the shelf is level and that the kiln is heating evenly. If neither of these seems to be the issue, then try changing the cooling and annealing portion of the firing schedule as follows.

Instead of cooling rapidly from the final fuse temperature to the annealing temperature, stop just above the annealing range and hold the temperature for thirty minutes to an hour. (For Bullseye and Spectrum glasses, hold at 1050F/565C.) After this hold, anneal and cool the glass as normal. The extra time spent just above the annealing range gives the glass time to better relax and even out the temperature.

A more extreme version of this process, generally used for thicker or more complicated panels, is to cool the glass to below the annealing range (around 750F/400C for Bullseye and Spectrum), reheat to above the annealing range and hold for thirty minutes to an hour, then anneal and cool as normal.

Chapter 12

Surface techniques for fusing

Adding texture • **Tack fusing** • **Texturing with tiles, molds, and related materials** • **Kiln carving** • **Powder, frit, and stringer** • **Glass paints and enamels** • **Decals** • **Mica** • **Reactive glass**

Although it's possible to fuse using nothing more than cut up sheets of glass, fusing becomes much more interesting when also adding additional techniques. The ones discussed in this chapter all focus on changing the surface appearance of the glass by:

• **Adding texture** by tack fusing, firing on textured tiles, or kiln carving;

• **Using powder, frit, and stringer** to expand design possibilities;

• **Screenprinting and painting** on the top surface of the glass;

• **Using decals and resist papers**;

• **Using mica**;

• **Exploring reactive glass**;

Adding texture

So far we've emphasized the creation of pieces that are smooth and shiny on the top surface. For many beginners, this is the preferred finish.

But more experienced fusers often opt to create pieces that are textured, rather than smooth, on the top surface. This can be done either by tack fusing, which creates a textured top surface, or by fusing on a textured shelf or other surface, which creates a textured bottom surface.

Once a piece has been textured, the texture will remain during additional firings, so long as they are done at a temperature below full fuse. This means that slumping a textured piece, which is normally done below 1300F/704C, won't cause the texture to go away.

Tack fusing

The simplest way to texture the top surface of the glass is to create a design that has high spots and low spots. Then fire to a temperature that is high enough to fuse, but low enough so that the highs and lows don't even out across the glass. This is called "tack" or "contour fusing."

In most cases a standard fusing schedule will work, adjusted so that the top temperature is lower than a full fuse temperature. An appropriate top temperature of between 1375F/746C and 1450F/788C will leave the top surface textured.

The reason a range is given is that there are many different levels of tack fusing. A top temperature of 1375F/746C, for instance, is enough to permanently fuse the glass pieces together, but it will leave the edges of all the pieces fairly straight

Tack fusing, as in the detail from this piece, gives a very different final appearance than fully fusing. Anneal a bit longer than normal to accommodate the added texture. (Photo by the author, courtesy of Jody Danner Walker.)

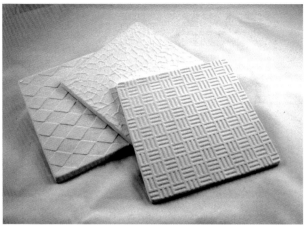

Textured tiles, such as the ones shown here, are best used by first fusing a piece on the kiln washed tile so that the glass takes on the texture of the tile, then slumping. The texture remains during the slump. (Photo by the author.)

and unrounded. As the top temperature increases, the edges will round more and more, and the piece will begin to flatten out. By the time the temperature reaches 1450F/788C, it will be getting close to a regular full fuse, if not completely fully fused. The specific glass, kiln, and design configuration can cause the exact temperature required to vary, so it's essential to keep good records to find the specific look you prefer.

Texturing with tiles, molds, and related materials

Texture can also be created on glass by firing the piece to a full fuse on top of a textured tile, kiln shelf or other surface. This will transfer the texture from the tile to the bottom of the piece.

Textured tiles and shelves must be covered with kiln wash prior to use. Don't use shelf paper or fiber paper on the tile; they're too thick to allow the texture to be transferred to the glass. Once the tile is prepared and the wash is dry, simply place the glass on top of the tile and fuse. At least two layers (1/4" / 6 mm) of glass is required. using a full fuse firing schedule will guarantee that the texture fully transfers to the glass , so be sure to fire to a temperaure in the 1450F/788C to 1500F/816C range.

After firing, the texture will be transferred to the glass. Because it's on the bottom surface of the glass, it will not be shiny. If you want to give it a

shine, flip the piece over so that the textured side is up and then re-fire using a fire polish schedule (generally, to around 1375F/746C). Be careful not to fire too high or the texture will be lost.

Although a textured tile or kiln shelf is one of the easiest ways to achieve a texture on the underside of a piece, it's not the only way. Texturing can also be accomplished with a powder such as whiting or dry kiln wash, on a textured refractory cloth, or on carved fiber board or paper.

Whiting, or calcium carbonate, is a white powder that can be sprinkled on the kiln shelf to give texture. Kiln wash can also be used in this fashion. It's also possible to mix whiting with water to form a creamy paste that can be applied to the kiln shelf using a large syringe, turkey baster, or piping bag (like the kind that's used to decorate cakes). Once the whiting dries, place glass on top and fire to around 1450F/788C. The glass will take on the texture created on the kiln shelf and the whiting can be easily removed.

Another way to create a texture on the underside of the piece is with fiberglass cloth, This cloth, also marketed under the brand "Lava Cloth," is a fiberglass product that doesn't stick to glass. To use, place the cloth on the kiln shelf, cover with about two layers of glass, and then fire to full fuse. The texture will transfer to the glass.

The texture from fiberglass cloth can be very rough to the touch, so the textured glass may

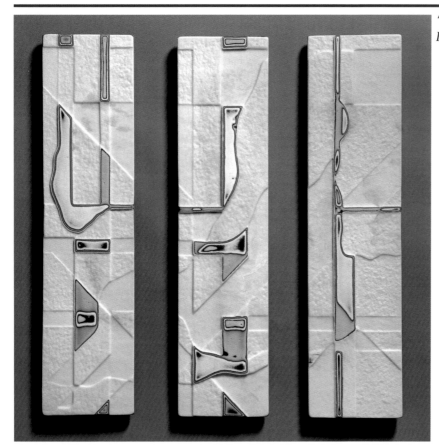

"Linear Settlements" by Richard Parrish. Kiln carved and coldworked. (Photo courtesy of the author.)

need to be smoothed a bit with a diamond hand pad or similar tool. The cloth will last approximately a dozen firings. Sprinkling a small amount of dry kiln wash powder on top of the cloth before the fuse firing softens the texture and helps the cloth last longer. Note that fiberglass cloth shrinks roughly 10% the first time it is fired.

Although textured slump molds are available, it's generally not a good idea to attempt both texturing and slumping in the same firing. That's because the temperature required to transfer the texture to the glass is much higher than the temperature needed to slump. As a result, firing the glass high enough to take on the texture will probably cause the slump to be uneven or distorted. So if you want texture on your piece, fuse over a textured surface first, then slump. In most cases, heavily textured slump molds are better used as pottery than molds for slumping glass.

Once textured, a piece can be flipped over texture side up and then fired a second time, so that the desired texture appears on top of the piece. This approach, called "flip and fire," is discussed in greater detail starting on page 104.

Kiln carving

Using fiber board or fiber paper to texture the underside of a piece is called "kiln carving." This involves firing the glass on top of a piece of fiber paper that has been cut to shape. As with firing on a textured tile or cloth, a full fuse is required to make the glass take on the desired texture.

Most of the time, kiln carving is done with fiber paper, but it can also be done by carving into thicker fiber board. Thinfire shelf paper is also thick enough to use in kiln carving, but of course the texture created with thinfire is very subtle. To kiln carve, start with one or more pieces of fiber paper. The paper can all be of one thickness or it can be of various thicknesses. Using a pair of scissors or a sharp knife such as an Exacto blade, carve a pattern into the fiber paper. It's important that the carving go all of the way through the paper to form a pattern. The pattern can be as elaborate and intricate as desired.

If desired, detailed holes and lettering can even be carved in the paper. This technique is sensitive enough to pick up very fine detail, especially

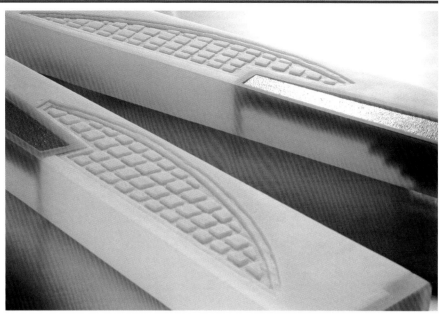

Alyssa Oxley, "Twin Pools." Dammed and kilnformed, then coldworked and sandblasted. Fiber paper used to kiln carve relief areas. (Photo by Doug Abdulnour, courtesy of the artist.)

when thinner papers are used. When carving, use the blade at about a 45 degree angle, rather than straight up and down. This will cut through the paper more easily, without tearing. A fresh blade is preferable to one that has been used. And it's best to cut on a soft surface (such as a scrap of cardboard), rather than on a hard ceramic tile.

Once the pattern is carved, prepare to place the carved paper into the kiln. If the paper has developed small fiber balls from pilling, smooth the paper out using a gloved hand; latex, nitrile, and vinyl gloves are all appropriate. Pre-firing the paper is not always necessary, but if you find that finished pieces have a hazy appearance pre-firing to 1300F/704C can help minimize the hazing. No kiln wash is necessary.

Once the paper is ready for firing, place it on a kiln shelf in your kiln. Glass should be laid directly on top of the paper. A single 1/8" (3 mm) layer of glass is usually not thick enough, so two or three layers is preferable. If you're firing so that the glass drops into a carved area (as opposed to over a carving) then three layers are essential.

To avoid trapped air bubbles between two layers of glass, either pre-fire the single layers to fuse them together or use glass that is 6 mm (1/4") thick. Clear or light transparent glass will work best for pieces that will be viewed from the top surface, but opaque glass can also be used, especially for pieces that are flipped over and re-fired.

Fire to a full fuse, in the range of 1460F/793C to 1500F/816C. Carvings with more detail should be fired to a temperature on the higher end of this range. For very thick firings with many layers of fiber paper, it may be necessary to fire even higher, to 1525F/830C or more.

Because of the fiber paper, it's a good idea to anneal for a bit longer than normal. A good rule of thumb is to anneal for a thickness that is double the actual thickness of the glass.

After firing, the glass will conform closely to the fiber paper and take on the texture of the paper. A unique pattern will emerge as the glass slumps through the carved holes in the fiber paper.

In most cases, the fiber paper can be removed from the glass without too much difficulty. Waiting until the glass and paper are totally cool will make this easier. Opaque glasses will have a greater tendency to stick to the fiber paper than transparent glasses. Also, glasses with iridized or dichroic coatings will tend not to stick to fiber paper, making them good choices for many projects.

Sometimes the fired fiber paper can be peeled away from the glass in once piece and then re-used. More often, the paper is too fragile to survive more than one firing. A stiff paper, such as Unifrax's 110 paper, can often be used more than once. If desired, ordinary paper can be made more durable by spraying with a colloidal silica

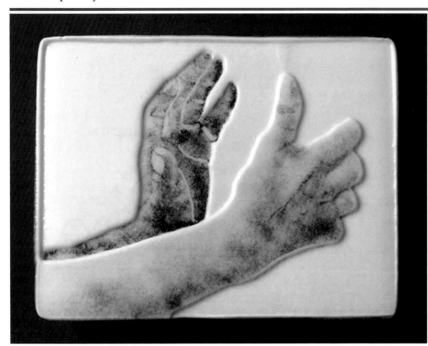

"Pushing Hands" by Jody Danner Walker. Kiln carved with powder additions. (Photo courtesy of the artist.)

solution (sometimes called "fiber mold hardener"). After the solution dries, the paper should be pre-fired to around 1300F/700C and then coated with kiln wash before using.

As with all fiber products, handle fiber paper with care and in a well-ventilated area. The paper will give off some fumes and will smell like burning sugar during its first firing, as the organic binder burns away. Avoid breathing loose fibers. A respirator or mask is recommended, as are gloves if direct contact with the skin can not be avoided. Using a non-carcinogenic paper such as Isofrax is preferable to using a standard paper.

- **Flip and fire**

One significant side effect of texturing glass using textured shelves or kiln carving techniques is that the underside of the finished piece does not necessarily have a shiny appearance. To achieve a shiny surface, first clean the piece thoroughly with water. Then flip it so that it is carved side up and re-fire to a fire polishing temperature (around 1350F/730C). Take care not to fire too high or soak for too long or the detail from the kiln carving will be lost. Spraying an overglaze on the piece prior to firing may allow you to achieve a shine by firing to a lower temperature. Follow the manufacturer's recommended firing schedule if using this approach.

Another option with this "flip and fire" technique is to embrace the matte appearance and use it as part of your finished piece. This works best when the piece is flipped and then altered by sandblasting, using glass powder, or with related techniques. Done properly, a final firing can yield a matte finish that has richness and a depth that is sometimes lacking in the standard shiny surface finish.

Powder, frit, and stringer

Glass powder, frit, and stringer can be sprinkled or arranged on top of sheet glass and fired to create a wealth of different patterns and effects. Some of these effects are illustrated in Chapter 8, which covers basic coaster and tile projects. Some of the more common approaches include:

- **Powder sifting**

Most powder effects start by sifting glass powder onto the top surface of the glass. Sifters are widely available from both glass and enamel suppliers; even a household tea strainer can make a good sifter. Most powders will sift well through a sifter with a mesh size of around 80.

Opaque powders tend to yield darker and more intense colors than transparents ones, but both kinds of powder generally require a thicker application than you think to achieve a solid, dark appearance. Powders will darken in color when fired, but it may still require sifting three or four layers of powder onto the glass to get the desired color intensity.

Remember that pieces that don't emerge from the kiln as dark or as brightly colored as you would like can be enhanced by adding more powder, then re-firing. Also, using fine frit instead of, or in addition to, powder will create a more dense appearance.

• Using stencils

One of the most interesting uses of powder is to sift it through a stencil to achieve a more detailed design. A single color can be used, but using multiple colors will yield more intricate and interesting final pieces.

Stencils can be made from any stiff paper, such as card stock. Stencils made of plastic or thin metal can also be purchased. Stencils made from a thicker material, such as the ones from Josa Stencils, are easier to lift from the glass after sifting. They can also be filled with more powder if the design requires.

Firing schedule recommendation

The firing schedule for most of these powder and frit effects is adapted from the basic fusing schedule discussed in Chapter 8, with the schedule varied slightly depending on the precise look desired. A top temperature of 1300F/704C is enough to stick glass powder or fine frit to the glass, but it won't round edges or cause the particles to shine. Firing to 1375F/730C or higher will yield a shine. Larger pieces of frit or stringers will need to be fired close to a full fuse temperature if you want them to be fused totally flat, rather than remaining textured on top of the base glass. Remember to use two layers (1/4" / 6 mm) of glass when firing to 1400F/760C or higher to avoid the glass distorting or shrinking from the heat.

• Powder manipulation

Powder can be sifted onto glass, then manipulated using a brush or other tool, to form detailed patterns such as the veins in a hand, shown in the piece on the top of the page to the left. Given sufficient talent and patience, even very intricate portraits and designs can be achieved.

It's easier to rearrange powders if the glass is properly prepared prior to applying the powder. This can be done by sandblasting or by firing the piece face down on fiber paper. Another approach is to lightly sift clear glass powder on a sheet of glass, then fire the glass to 1300F/704C. This is hot enough to stick the powder to the surface of the glass, but it still leaves enough texture to make it easy to maneuver sifted powder additions.

• Sgrafitto

One of the most common kinds of powder manipulation is sgrafitto, which comes from the Italian word for "scratched." In this technique a design is created by scratching away portions of a painted or otherwise prepared surface. The easiest way to create a sgrafitto effect with glass is to sift powder on top of a layer of glass, then use

This image was created by sifting various colors of frit through a stencil. Firing to only a tack fuse will retain the texture of the frit. (Photo courtesy of Jody Danner Walker.)

a comb or a pointed item to remove part of the powder. As with all of these techniques, after the powder is prepared, the glass should be fired to make the design stick permanently in place.

• Sifting over textured glass

Glass powder can be used in combination with textured glass to duplicate the patterns in the glass. To use this technique, simply sift powder over a textured glass (texture side up). Sift it on fairly heavily; about three or four layers of sifted powder is usually enough. With a glass such as reed or fibroid glass, you should barely be able to see the individual lines of the glass.

After sifting, the glass should be fired to a full fuse. That's enough to smooth out the texture and leave the top of the glass shiny. The sifted powder will be left behind, magically arranged in the same pattern as the original glass.

• Frit painting

Frit painting, sometimes called "painting with light" or "fritography" is a technique that arranges frit, stringers, and other small glass pieces on sheet glass, then fuses to obtain realistic or more impressionistic "paintings." Frit can be used dry or mixed with a binder. This technique requires a careful hand and attention to fine detail. Often, multiple firings are required to achieve the desired effect.

• Bending stringer

Stringer can easily be bent in the heat of a candle. Simply hold the stringer in the flame for a few seconds. Wait for it to soften, then bend quickly and remove it from the flame. The stringer will be hot for several minutes, so take care. If soot from the candle appears on the stringer, wait for the stringer to cool, then clean it with water and a soft cloth. Soot will generally burn off in the kiln, but it's a good idea to remove it anyway just in case.

Stringer can also be bent on any slump mold. Just lay it in place and fire to your slumping temperature. Because stringers are so thin, they can be fired and cooled as rapidly as your kiln permits.

• Creating small balls or beads

Many designs and effects can be achieved by fusing small balls or beads of glass onto the top surface of the piece. The easiest way to make these small balls is to fuse them separately in the kiln, prior to using them in the finished piece.

To make frit balls, sprinkle coarse frit onto a kiln shelf that has been kiln washed or covered with thinfire shelf paper. (Fiber paper will not work well for this technique.) Use a brush or the tip of a pen or pencil to spread the pieces of frit so that no two are touching. Then fire to 1500F/816C

"Attention Distraction" by Michael Dupille. Frit painting. (Photo courtesy of the artist.)

Top: "Between Hope and Fear" by Kari Minnick. Fused glass and powder. (Photo courtesy of the artist.)

Below: "Awaiting the Day" by Jody Danner Walker. Fused glass and powder. The small book in front of the piece was fused. (Photo courtesy of the artist.)

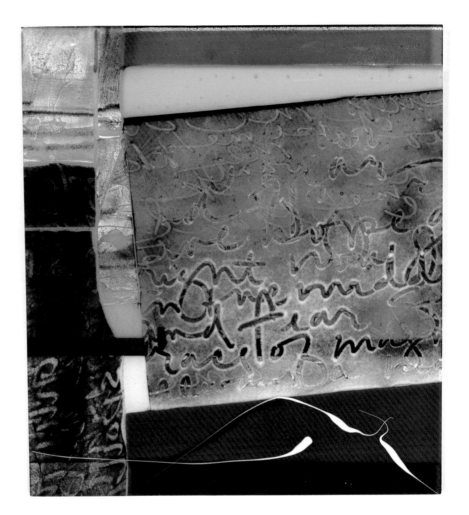

and hold for about ten minutes. Because of the very small nature of the pieces of frit, you can fire as quickly as you would like. You can also turn the kiln off once the soak at 1500F is complete. Allow the kiln to cool naturally to room temperature before removing the finished balls.

An alternative way to make balls is to use small scraps of glass. Scraps of any size can be used, but scraps smaller than about 1/2" (12 mm) in size will round up best. Cutting a strip of glass about 3/8" (9 mm) wide and then nipping it into small squares is a quick way to prepare a large batch of glass for firing. Once the kiln is loaded with glass scraps, just fire to a full fuse as previously described. Larger or multiple layer balls may need a slightly higher temperature or longer soak to fully round into balls.

Once you have an assortment of these small balls, they can be tack or fully fused onto glass to make interested design elements and patterns.

Glass paints and enamels

The subject of glass painting is extensive enough to fill a book of its own. There are literally dozens of ways to paint on glass, ranging from using traditional oil paints to using specialized glass paints that require firing with a kiln. For our purposes, we'll focus on products specifically made for use with glass.

- **Air-dried and oven-cured glass paints**

Air-dried and oven cured glass paints, marketed by companies such as Delta and Pebeo, have the advantage that they're easy to use and that no kiln is required. However, there are a number of disadvantages to these kinds of paints.

In most cases, the colors start out very vivid, but tend to lose their intensity with time. Because they're not permanently fused to the glass, they're also prone to chipping. Although these kinds of paints are suitable for decorative purposes on surfaces that won't be handled much, they may not be the products of choice for the long haul.

- **Traditional stained glass paints**

Because these are fired onto glass in a kiln, traditional stained glass paints are far more permanent than air-dried or oven-cured paints. This kind of painting, which is actually closer to drawing than painting, was originally done to add details such as faces and folds of clothing that couldn't be added with traditional lead lines. It was also used to cover up portions of stained glass works, so that light was kept from shining through.

In most cases, the glass paints used for stained glass painting are predominately browns and gray-blacks. The colors tend to be water or gum arabic based, and can be applied with a brush in a method similar to the way watercolors are applied. In most cases, these paints are fired onto the glass using a kiln. The heat of the kiln causes them to bond permanently with the glass.

Types of traditional stained glass paints include vinegar trace paint, matte paint, and silver stain. Most of these have very special application processes and are fired to around 1100 to 1250F (600 to 675C). If you are interested in learning more about the traditional stained glass painting process, obtain a copy of Albinus Elskus's *The Art of Painting on Glass*, widely considered the classic in the field.

- **Glass enamels**

Glass enamels offer a much broader range of colors than traditional stained glass paints. Not only are they available in both transparent and opaque colors, they can also be intermixed, yielding a virtually unlimited color palette.

Most glass enamels are made from tiny glass particles which have been mixed with additional coloring agents and a flux which allows the enamels to flow at a relatively low temperature. Because the particules are small, good ventilation is essential when working with enamels. A respirator or a mask may also be needed. Inhaling fine glass particles can cause silicosis, a serious and potentially fatal lung condition.

"Harbor Impressions" by Jody Danner Walker. Glass enamels on sheet glass. (Photo courtesy of the artist.)

Care must also be taken to ensure that the particular enamel being used is compatible with the base glass being painted on. Otherwise, incompatible enamel can cause cracking or poor adhesion to the glass.

Enamels are generally available in a powder form which can be sifted or mixed with a binder to create a liquid that can be painted, sprayed, or air brushed. Enamels are often applied and then fired in several thin layers, rather than in a single thick application. This maintains the integrity of the colors and also helps to achieve effects that would not be possible in a single firing. It is not uncommon for enamels to require four or five or more firings before the work is complete.

• **Using enamels**

Enamels may be sifted just like powders; many of the powder techniques already discussed will work equally well with enamels. The colors will be more intense, so a smaller quantity of enamel can normally be used. Enamels made by Thompson work very well for sifting and are less expensive than many other enamels, such as those in Ferro's Sunshine series, which work better for

painting, screen printing, and similar applications that use the enamel in liquid form.

To apply enamels with a brush or air brush, they must first be mixed with a binder to obtain the desired consistency. Binders (or "mediums") can be either oil or water based, but water based mediums have the advantage of generally being safer and easier to clean up. The key criterion is that the medium fires clear without leaving a residue. Commonly used binders include squeegee oil, gum arabic, and water miscible mediums such as Thompson's A-14 or Klyr-fire. Even glues or sugared soft drinks can sometimes be used.

The proper consistency varies depending on the specific enamel and on how it is to be used. It's a good idea to mix the paints on a smooth surface (a sheet of window glass is ideal), adding the binder drop by drop until the desired consistency is reached. Leftover mixed enamels can be stored in a capped container and reconstituted, if necessary, by adding a few extra drops of binder.

Once enamels have been mixed, they can be applied using an air brush, a good quality paint brush, or even a palette knife or similar tool. It's possible to achieve a wide variety of results by varying the method of application. Enamels can be mixed very thin and splattered or drizzled onto the glass à la Jackson Pollock. They can be applied in a wash like watercolor or painstakingly like acrylic paint. They can be applied, allowed to dry, then scratched partially off to yield interesting patterns. Often, the best results come from very thin applications and multiple firings; thicker applications tend to result in a dark, muddy appearance. The enamels are also more likely to crack, if used thickly.

Firing in the kiln should take place after the enamels are dry. Enamels will mature at various temperatures, with opaques generally requiring higher temperatures (around 1450 F/788 C) and transparents needing only to be fired to around 1200 F/649 C. Follow the recommendations from the manufacturer for the particular enamels you're using.

For enamels that fire at a lower temperature, it is possible to both slump and fire on enamels in the same firing. Many lower-firing enamels contain lead, so care should be taken not to use them on food-bearing surfaces.

The "reverse painting" technique is often used with enamels. This approach, which is contrary to "normal" painting techniques which start with the background and add details as a final step, starts on the backside of the sheet of glass. Working from the top layers to the bottom, successive layers of paint are added and fired until the picture is complete. Then the piece is flipped and fired with the bottom side on top, resulting in a work with an exceptionally clear and glossy surface.

Remember that when firing enamels you must follow the normal fused glass procedures to heat, anneal, and cool the glass to prevent cracking and thermal shock. Fired properly, the enamels will bond to the glass, resulting in a permanent, lustrous finish.

• **Screen printing**

In the traditional screen printing (sometimes known as silk-screening) process, ink is forced through holes in a mesh screen and onto paper or cloth. Wax or other substances are used to fill some of the holes and make patterns by controlling where the ink goes. By combining this procedure with multiple print runs (a different run for each color), it is possible to create elaborate and multi-colored works of art. You can even make multiple copies of the same item by using the same screens again and again.

Today this process has been adapted to print on items as diverse as posters, T-shirts, and coffee cups. It can be automated, and has even been combined with photographic techniques to yield extremely precise, detailed images.

By using glass enamels instead of standard screen printing paints, which aren't made for firing on glass, it's possible to use the screen printing process to print on glass. Once a frame has been constructed and the screen has been stretched tightly across the frame, you are ready to transfer the image to be screened to the screen.

Traditionally, screen preparation was done by brush, using a liquid "screen filler" to block out parts of the screen, or by stencil, using commercially available stencil film and a sharp knife to cut out the desired design. The "photo" screen printing process, used to transfer a photographic image onto the screen, has been developed more recently. It's more complicated than the traditional processes, but can result in much more detailed images.

Ulano and Speedball, traditional manufacturers of supplies for screen printing, offer "photo emulsion" products that can be used to transfer photos to the screen. More recent innovations, such as PhotoEZ screen printing paper, greatly simplify this process by eliminating the need for laborious and delicate screen washing.

Regardless of the process used to prepare the screen, the next step is the same. Use glass enamels instead of regular screen printing paints. Either sift dry enamels directly through the screen and onto the glass or else mix the enamels with a binder and then screen them onto the glass and and allowed them to dry. Just make sure to fire to the appropriate maturation temperature for the enamels being used.

Lesley Nolan, "Memories of the Dance." Screen printed glass -- fired, cut and pieced. Slumped on hand bent stainless steel mold. (Photo courtesy of the artist.)

Decals

Decals made for ceramics will often work when fired onto glass, but glass decals do exist. They are useful for imparting unique patterns or repetitive designs to the surface of the glass prior to fusing.

Most decals have a thin enamel coating which is affixed to a backing material that must be removed prior to firing in the kiln. Although the process for using decals can vary from manufacturer to manufacturer, the general process involves cleaning the glass, cutting the decal to shape, sliding the decal onto the glass, removing the backing material, and then firing to the required maturation temperature.

The smoother the glass used, the better the decals will adhere. Pre-firing glasses with a slight texture will usually yield better results. A simple firing to around 1400F/760C works well.

Decal transfer paper, often called water-slide paper, is available from several manufacturers, including Beldecal and Lazertran. Some of these products can be printed with a laser or inkjet printer, but many of the common inks will burn off during a firing. It's also possible to use screen printing techniques to print on decal transfer paper.

Mica

Mica is a mineral that is used commercially in such products as fingernail polish and interference paints to create a glittery appearance. It is commonly sold in powder form, but is sometimes available as small chips or flakes. It is available in 20 to 30 different shades, mostly in shades of silver, gold, and bronze, but occasionally dyed to appear green, red, or other colors. Some mica powders, such as those sold by Sepp Leaf, are formulated to withstand temperatures up to 1650F/900C. Other powders, such as those

111

sold under the PearlEx brand name, are not formulated for the kiln and will start to fade as the temperature exceeds 1300F/700C.

The simplest way to use mica is to sift the powder onto a base layer of glass, then cap with a second clear layer and fuse. The powder can also be sifted directly on top of the glass, rather than used as an inclusion. If desired, a stencil or resist can be used to precisely place the mica. It's also possible to coat the top surface of glass with a glue or an overspray, then sift on mica. The coating acts as a binder to help keep the mica in place.

Mica can also be mixed directly with a binder such as Klyr-fire to create a liquid solution that can be painted or airbrushed. Airbrushing mica probably creates the most even appearance, while painting is more difficult and often requires a dabbing motion, rather than normal brush strokes. One technique is to airbrush mica on the top surface of glass, fire to about 1400F/760C, and then use a resist and a sandblaster to remove unwanted mica and create the desired pattern. A final firing will usually be required to give a shiny or matte finish.

The smoother the underlying glass, the better mica will stick. Pre-firing glass to reduce or minimize texture will often result in better results.

Note that mica tends to stick to sifters and other tools, so careful cleanup is essential. Mica is generally not considered hazardous, but some persons are more sensitive than others. Avoid prolonged contact with the skin and be sure to wash thoroughly after use. Breathing in the fine powder particles should also be avoided.

Reactive glass

A reactive glass is one that changes color when it comes into contact with a particular glass or metal. The color of the reaction appears brownish, but it can also have a reddish or grayish cast.

In order to understand reactive glass, it's helpful to have a basic understanding of some of the chemicals used to color glass sheet. Copper, for instance, is often used to create "cool" blue and green glasses. Sulphur and selenium are used to make "warm" reds, yellows, and tans. Lead is used to make some whites and many pinks and purples.

Because glass chemistry is complicated, it's not always easy to tell which glasses contain which chemicals. Not all glasses are reactive. Some blues are made with cobalt, which doesn't react, instead of copper. And some greens are made with sulphur, instead of copper. Moreover, the amount of a particular chemical can vary from sheet to sheet of glass.

The resource area of the Warm Glass website has a list of reactive glasses, but it should be used only as a starting point. It's essential to conduct tests to determine both if a reaction between two glasses exists and if the resulting color change is desirable.

Firing to at least 1300F/704C is usually necessary for the reaction to occur. Higher temperatures will generally yield a stronger reaction. In most cases a standard full fusing schedule gives good results.

Reactions generally occur in the following situations:

• **Glasses containing copper will react with glasses containing either selenium or sulfur**

This reaction shows up as a dark brown line where the two glasses touch. The intensity of the reaction, as well as the precise shade of brown, varies depending on firing temperature, degree of contact, and specific glasses used.

• **Copper will react with glasses containing either selenium or sulfur**

Not only will copper containing glasses react, copper foil, copper leaf, and copper wire will also create this reaction. Reactions with copper often have a reddish cast. These reactions tend to be more intense when the copper is on top of the glass, rather than sandwiched between layers.

A typical reaction between a blue glass containing copper and a second french vanilla glass containing sulfur. The reaction creates the dark line where the two glasses touch. (Photo by the author.)

The reaction between silver and glasses containing sulfur or selenium is particularly strong. The dark circles in this piece were punched from silver foil and fired on top of a reactive layer of glass. (Photo by the author.)

- **Glasses containing lead may react with glasses containing either selenium or sulfur**

This reaction, which tends to leave a more grayish tint, is less prevalent than some of the other reactions, but it can be used to marvellous effect when it does occur. For an example, see the Karl Herron piece on page 115.

- **Silver will react with glasses containing either selenium or sulfur**

The reaction between silver and selium/sulfur glasses is usually very strong. They can be made even stronger by using the silver on top of the reactive glass, rather than as an inclusion. If the silver used is thin (as in foil or leaf), then the metal will melt into the glass and leave a smooth finished surface.

In addition to silver wire, leaf, and foil, it's possible to create this reaction using a silver nitrate solution. Just mix a few crystals of silver nitrate with water and spray on the glass before firing. Silver nitrate can discolor the skin, so wear gloves and handle the solution with care.

The section on metal inclusions in Chapter 13 has more information about using silver in glass.

Image of a pot melt made with turquoise blue and french vanilla glass. The blue has reacted with the vanilla to create the dark brown color. (Photo by the author.)

Given enough time and heat, the reaction between two glasses will spread, as in the square on the top of this piece. (Photo by the author.)

Far left: "Golden Spring, Opus 463" by Roger Thomas. Fused panel with powders and frits.

Near left: "Wine Forthcoming, Opus 437" by Roger Thomas. Fused panel with powders, frit, and stringer.

Below: "Last Leaves, Opus 474" by Roger Thomas. Fused panel with powders and frit.

(All photos courtesy of the artist.)

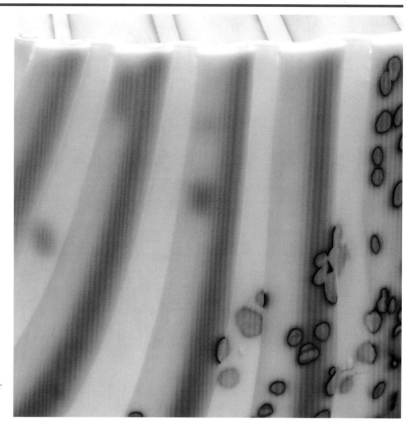

"Artefact 058b" by Karl Harron. Fused, then slumped. This deep bowl (approximately 8 inches/20cm) required three careful slumps, each a bit steeper and deeper than the previous.

Detail to the right, full piece below. (Both photos courtesy of the artist.)

Chapter 13

Inclusions in fused glass

Firing schedules for inclusions • Metal inclusions • COE and melting point for common metals • Organics and other materials • Air bubble inclusions

An "inclusion" is a material that is trapped within the layers of glass when it fuses. Inclusions can give a piece texture, character, and color that glass alone can't achieve.

Aside from air bubbles (both intentional and unintentional), the most frequently used inclusion is probably copper, but many other substances may be used, ranging from other metals to mica to fiber paper to organic materials such as leaves and shells.

Firing schedule for inclusions

The schedule given below is for typical two layer firings in which the inclusion is sandwiched between two layers of glass. It's essential that there be space between the inclusion and the edges of the glass. Otherwise, the top layer of glass will not seal to the bottom.

Except as noted, most inclusions can be fired with a full fuse schedule, such as discussed in detail in Chapter 7. The main steps of this schedule are:

- **400F/222C to 1100F/593C hold 10 minutes**

Slow down more than this for thicker or previously fired items, or for kilns that lack top elements.

- **200F/111C to 1240F/671C hold 30 minutes**

This bubble squeeze may need to be lengthened for some designs. For some effects it may be desireable to go faster or slower through this temperature range.

- **Full speed to full fuse temperature**

For most glasses, this is in the range from 1450F/788C to 1480F/804C. Some techniques, glasses, and kilns will require firing slightly higher or lower than this range.

- **Full speed to anneal**

Use the appropriate annealing temperature for your chosen glass. For most inclusions, it's good practice to lengthen the anneal soak slightly, to perhaps an hour for a basic two layer piece. This helps compensate for variations in temperature caused by the inclusion and will make it more likely that the piece will anneal properly.

After the anneal soak, cool slowly through the remainder of the annealing range and then allow the kiln to cool down to room temperature. If in doubt, be a bit more conservative than when firing glass without inclusions.

Metal inclusions

The most important factor when using metal inclusions is that the metal is thin enough not to crack the glass after firing. As the chart below illustrates, metals have very different expansion characteristics than glass. Using metal that is too thick or taking shortcuts in annealing will almost certainly cause the glass to crack as it cools.

Most metals are available in sheet form, often in rolls of various widths and thicknesses. Sheets for common metals such as copper, aluminum, and brass rangle in thickness from as thin as two mil (millionths of an inch, 24.5 microns equals one mil) to 5 mil (.005 inch/127 micron) and more. These sheets, sometimes called "tooling foil," are slightly thicker than a common aluminum soft drink can. Sometimes they're labeled by gauge; one very common gauge is 36 gauge, which is 5 mil/127 micron.

Because of the expense, more precious metals, such as gold and silver, are more often purchased and used in either foil or leaf form. Although the terms foil and leaf are sometimes used interchangeably, foil is generally thicker than leaf. Gold and silver leaf, for instance, is usually 0.2 to 0.4 microns thick, while foils are much thicker. Household aluminum foil, for instance, is approximately 16 microns (0.016 mm/.00064 inches) thick.

As should be apparent, metals are available in a wide variety of sizes, shapes, and forms. In addition, quality and purity can vary significantly from product to product. Moreover, different firing schedules yield different results, and the results from kiln to kiln can also differ. For these reasons, it's absolutely essential to keep good notes when firing inclusions.

• **Aluminum**

Aluminum, known as aluminium in Britain, is a very common, relatively inexpensive metal. Its melting temperature of 1218F/659C is well below most fusing applications, making aluminum

COE and Melting Point for Common Metals

Metal	Coefficient of Expansion (10 (-7) per degree C)	Melting temperature (Fahrenheit/Celsius)
Aluminum	248	1218 / 659
Brass, navy	212	1650 / 899
Copper	176	1981 /1081
Gold	140	1945 /1061
Iron	295	2300 / 1260
Silver	191	1764 / 962
Steel, high carbon	121	2500 / 1374
Steel, stainless	171	1600 / 1430
Zinc	297	788 / 420

COE is the change in length for each degree Celsius change in temperature.
This chart is for pure metals or typical alloys. Other alloys can differ significantly.
Source: U.S Military Training Circular No. 9-237, "Welding Theory and Applications."

Aluminum sheet, cut from a soft drink can and fused between two layers of clear glass. (Photo courtesy of the author.)

Closeup of the piece to the left, showing large air bubbles generated by the fired aluminum and trapped between layers of glass. (Photo courtesy of the author.)

unsuitable for use as a slumping mold. But don't let that fool you. Aluminum is still a very versatile and fascinating metal to use as an inclusion in glass.

One of the best things about using aluminum as an inclusion is that it's very inexpensive. Cut up soft drink cans work well, and are virtually free. Household aluminum foil can also be used, and the cost is only pennies a firing.

In addition to being inexpensive, aluminum is easy to use. It does not react with the ingredients in some glass colors, as silver and other metals sometimes do. And once you've tested your particular variant, its behavior is consistent and predictable.

The easiest way to try out aluminum as an inclusion is to cut a small piece from a soft drink can. Although tin snips work best, this can even be done with common household scissors. Just be careful not to cut yourself on the sharp edges of the can.

Sandwiched between two layers of clear glass and fired to a full fusing temperature, a thin sheet of aluminum takes on a fascinating appearance. The silvery appearance becomes a mass of dark brown bubbles, with lighter highlights scattered throughout the piece. After the piece cools, the bubbles remain captured between the layers of glass and the color remains brown, rather than returning to its original bright silver.

An aluminum foil dragonfly, demonstrating that thinner layers of a metal take on very different characteristics than thicker ones. While aluminum sheet remains opaque when fired, aluminum foil becomes transparent. (Photo courtesy of the author.)

When fired to a temperature just above full fuse, sheet brass will bubble ferociously, as on the piece on the far right. Firing to a lower temperature, as on the left, will result in smaller bubbles. The difference is not unlike what happens when water begins to boil, with higher temperatures leading to larger bubbles. (Photo by the author.)

Like most metals, different thickness of aluminum behave differently when fired in the kiln. A single layer of household aluminum foil, for instance, leaves behind a scattering of small brown bubbles and silvery patches of metal. The effect, as in the diaphanous dragonfly, shown above, can be mesmerizing in the right design.

Inclusions made with more layers of foil, different sheet thicknesses, and other forms of aluminum (such as wire and screen) result in even more variations of color and density. For instance, fully fusing small balls of aluminum will create a single gas bubble around each ball, with a scattering of dark patches as well. And if the aluminum ball gets large enough, the bubble of gas can burst through the glass.

As with many materials, experimentation is the order of the day. Don't be afraid to try fully fusing different thickness and types of aluminum. Just be careful not to use metal that's so thick it will crack the glass.

Although inclusions with aluminum tend to be fully fused most of the time, interesting effects sometimes emerge when firing to a lower temperature. For example, firing an aluminum inclusion to around 1250 to 1300F (675 to 700C) will fuse the edges of the glass together but still leave the aluminum intact. The paint on soft drink cans, for instance, will lose its color and darken, but the text will still remain legible.

Since aluminum tends to be non-reactive with other substances, it is usually one of the safest metals for experimentation in the kiln. However, there are two situations to watch out for when working with aluminum:

First, take care that stray pieces of aluminum don't fall onto the kiln shelf or the floor of the kiln. It's possible for the pieces to eat through the kiln wash and into the kiln shelf. It's not hazardous, but it can be a mess to clean.

Second, avoid experimenting with aluminum powder, which can irritate the eyes, skin, and respiratory tract. Aluminum powder is also flammable and can burn violently at temperatures above 1400F/760C. Other forms of aluminum work well in the kiln, but it's a good idea to avoid aluminum powder.

• **Brass**

Brass is an alloy of copper and zinc. The precise makeup of the alloy can vary from sample to sample, so it's always a good idea to test your particular brass sample. Not all brass alloys behave the same in the kiln.

Sheet brass can be cut with scissors or lightweight tin snips. Its melting temperature of 1650F/899C (as high as 1675F/913C for some alloys) means that it will behave quite differently than a metal like aluminum, which melts below fusing temperature.

If you've ever watched a pot of water on the stove as it heats and prepares to boil, you will have

A range of copper effects, demonstrating that the thinner the copper sheet, the more likely it is to turn blue. The sheet on the left is 5 mil thick (36 guage), the one in the middle is only 2 mil, and the one on the right is thin copper leaf. All have been sandwiched between layers of clear glass and fired to full fuse. (Photo by the author.)

seen that prior to boiling the bottom of the pot will be lined with small bubbles. As the water gets hotter, the bubbles get larger and larger, until they finally erupt in a full boil. Heating brass is very similar -- the size of the bubbles created will vary depending on the firing temperature. At temperatures in the range of 1450F/788C, there will be only small bubbles. By around 1525F/830C, the bubbles become larger. Yet at both temperatures the bubbles remain encased inside the glass, and they won't be as ferocious as the bubbles trapped from fused aluminum.

The rate of temperature increase can also impact the appearance of the brass inside the glass. Firing more quickly from 1240F/671C can cause the outer edges of the brass to take on a different look than the middle.

Brass screen and mesh can also be fired in the kiln. The bubbles generated will tend to collect in the holes of the screen or alongside the metal, rather than throughout.

Also, note that brass will behave differently when it touches copper during a firing. This phenomenon will be discussed further in the next section, on copper inclusions.

• **Copper**

Copper is one of the most common inclusions in glass. Not only is it widely available in sheets,

foils, and wires of various thicknesses, it's also available in powder form and as a component in many common pigments, such as copper oxide.

Copper has a higher melting temperature than either aluminum or brass. As a result, only very thin pieces bubble the way that aluminum or brass do when heated. Instead of bubbling, copper sheet changes color when heated. The color change can range from light blue to bluish-green to vivid reddish-orange to black, with dozens of shades in-between. The precise color depends on the the temperature, the thickness of the copper and the amount of oxygen that touches the copper during the firing.

Thinner copper sheet will tend toward blue, while thicker sheet will be purplish in appearance. Copper that has wrinkles, or a pronounced texture, retains the texture during the firing. Texture can also change the nature of the color change, allowing more oxygen to reach the copper and leaving a more purplish appearance.

Very thin copper (usually called copper leaf, although it is not often as thin as gold or silver leaf), will leave a mass of brilliant blue bubbles when fired as an inclusion.

Left uncapped and exposed to the air, copper will stick to glass but will turn black and appear corroded. Sometimes it will have a tendency to flake or spall. To prevent this, use copper sheet and wire as an inclusion, rather than as a layer on

120

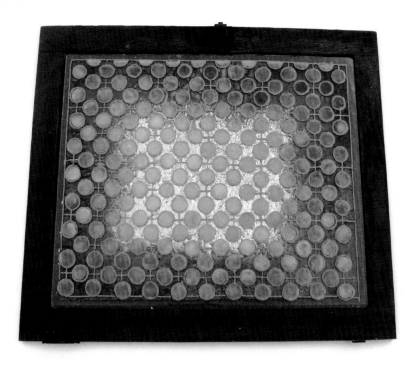

This panel by Emily George combines glass enamels with copper. Careful firing causes the edges of the copper inclusion to darken while the center remains shiny. (Photo courtesy of the artist.)

top of glass. Or use a commercial copper cleaner such as Penny Bright to clean the exposed copper and restore it to its original color.

There are several ways to stop copper sheet from changing color during a firing. One method, illustrated at the top of this page, is to fire quickly from 1100F/593C to full fuse, preventing the copper from changing color. A second is to coat the copper thoroughly to keep oxygen from reaching the metal during the firing. A devitrification spray can do the job, as can a clear enamel or paint such as Ferro's Mixing Flux or Unique's Clear. Even common white glue can sometimes retard the color change.

To successfully use these coatings, the copper must first be cleaned. This can be done by hand or by a brief soak in vinegar. Scrubbing with an emory brush or similar fine brush to give the copper some tooth will also help. Airbrushing results in more even coverage than painting with a brush. After the coating dries, the piece is ready to be fused. Remember, the basic principle is to keep air from reaching the glass, so the denser and more even the application, the better.

The behavior of copper sheet can also be changed by torching it lightly with a hand torch just prior to firing. More than any other metal, copper is very sensitive to degrees of cleanliness and oxygen exposure; even the oils from your fingerprints can impact the color change.

In addition to being available in sheet form, copper is also available in mesh, screen, powder, and oxide forms. Mesh and screen will behave much the same way as copper sheet, with the additional ability of screen to capture a pattern of air bubbles.

Copper powder can be sprinkled lightly on glass or used as an inclusion, but the color will tend toward dark blue or black, with occasional light blue areas. The precise color varies depending on the thickness of the application and the degree of oxidation.

Copper oxides are available in two main varieties: black and red. Like copper powder, they can be used either as an inclusion in glass or sprinkled on top. If mixed with water to create a solution and then sprayed between layers of glass, the oxides will behave much like copper leaf, leaving a mass of blue bubbles behind. Varying the strength of the solution can change the color of the bubbles, which can range from green to almost black.

Variegated red, a variety of leaf used in the picture framing and sign painting industries, is mostly copper, so will yield the same blue

121

Enamel, copper, and brass panel by Emily George. When copper and brass touch during a firing, both behave differently than if they had been fired without touching. (Photo courtesy of the artist.)

bubble result as normal copper leaf. Two similar products, variegated black and variegated green, can also be used as inclusions. When fused, they leave behind blue bubbles that are laced with dark lines from the other substances in the leaf.

One of the most exciting facets of working with copper is that it will react with other materials. For instance, when copper touches brass during a firing, the combination changes the way both the brass and the copper behave. Brass will bubble only slightly, if at all, and its color will lighten slightly. Copper will tend to remain copper-colored, rather turn blue or purple. This reaction will occur if only a small amount of copper touches the brass.

In addition, copper will react with many glasses that contain sulfur or selenium. When used as an inclusion, the reaction will show up as a thin, darker color along the edges of the copper. As with most reactions, the intensity of the reaction can vary from sheet to sheet and color to color, depending on the amount of chemical present in the glass. When fired on top of glass, rather than as an inclusion, the reaction will be stronger and much more widespread. For more on metallic reactions with glass, as well as reactions from glass to glass, see Chapter 12.

As with brass and aluminum, the precise results can vary greatly from piece to piece. Even pieces of the same material can yield very different results when fired in different kilns. Keep very good notes if you want to duplicate your results. And don't be afraid to experiment, experiment, experiment.

• **Silver**

Silver is most often used in thin foil, leaf, or wire forms. As a precious metal, it can be expensive if used in thicker varieties. In most fusing applications fine silver is preferable to lower grades, such as sterling.

When fired as an inclusion, silver will sometimes retain its silver color. However, when capped it does have a tendency to turn yellow when it reacts to impurities in the clear glass cap. Using a "Crystal Clear" glass from Bullseye or Spectrum may prevent or minimize this reaction, as will capping with an iridized glass face down against the silver inclusion. Note that fine silver is less likely to yellow than silver of a lower purity, but any grade of silver can turn yellow after firing.

When silver is fired on top of glass, rather than used as an inclusion, it will tend to tarnish in the heat of the kiln. Uncapped silver on top of a piece also tarnishes over time.
In addition to potentially reacting with clear glass on top, silver will react with glasses which

The reaction between silver and sulfur or selenium is more muted when silver is used as an inclusion, (on the left) and much stronger when the silver is fired on top of the piece (to the right). (Photo by the author.)

contain sulfur or selenium. The reaction is relatively weak when the silver is used as an inclusion; when the silver is placed on top of the glass, the reaction is much stronger.

In addition to the potential for yellowing, silver wire will often become brittle if fused between layers of glass (for example, to make a loop for jewelry). Better to use less expensive nichrome wire, which is not as likely to tarnish or discolor in the kiln and is much less likely to become brittle after firing.

It's also possible to use silver powder as an inclusion or sprinkled on the top surface of glass before firing. Mixing silver with glass enamels can also produce interesting effects.

When firing with silver in your kiln, it's extremely important to clean the silver from your kiln shelf after firing. Residual silver on the shelf may react with glass used in subsequent firings. The residual silver is not always visible, so it's best to assume that the shelf will need to be cleaned thoroughly before being used again.

• **Gold**

Gold leaf is generally too thin to use as an inclusion or as a layer on top of glass. If it is used, it will tend to disappear or become barely visible in the finished piece. For this reason, it's best to either multiple layers of leaf (at least three) or thicker gold foil.

Working with thin metal foil and leaf

Very thin metal foils and leaves can be difficult to cut without tearing. For best results, place the metal between a folded sheet of notebook or typing paper and cut through the paper and the metal simultaneously.

After cutting, use tweezers to move the metal into place. If you have difficulty with the metal moving after being placed on the glass, use a small amount of mineral spirits to help hold it in place. Just brush the mineral spirits on the glass, then drop the metal on top. It will stay in place, and the mineral spirits will burn off cleanly in the firing.

Small pieces will adhere better if the glass is smoother. For single and double-rolled glasses a previous firing to the 1400F/760C range will smooth out the texture in the glass. Once previously fired in this manner, the thin foils can be fired to a lower temperature for fusing if desired.

Remember also that incompatibility can be a problem when using metals. Avoid thick layers (even of foils), especially when almost all of the surface of the glass is covered with metals. This can lead to incompatibility cracks and make annealing much more difficult.

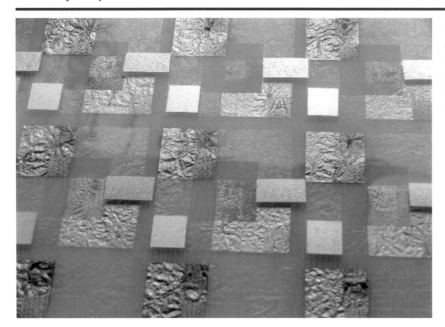

An array of gold, silver, and copper foils, both as inclusions and on the top surface of the glass. Note that copper over gold shows as green. (Detail of a piece by Brock Craig, photo courtesy of the artist.)

Although gold tends not to react with other materials, it will change color if fired under copper. This stems from the gold being viewed through the blue bubbles left behind by the copper.

Gold powder, like silver powder, can be sprinkled on or inside glass and then fired.

• **Zinc**

Zinc melts at 788F/420C, but doesn't boil until the temperature reaches around 1650F/900C. This is important because zinc fumes, which are given off when zinc boils, are potential hazardous. For this reason, it's a good idea not to use zinc at temperatures of 1650F/900C or greater.

When fired to normal fusing temperatures as an inclusion, zinc bubbles ferociously, not unlike aluminum. The bubbles tend to be larger than the bubbles from aluminum, but are similar in color, though a bit darker around the edges.

Zinc is also found in galvanized metal, such as buckets that have been coated to resist rust. Because of the potential hazard, take care when firing these to high temperatures in the kiln.

Since 1983, the U.S. penny has been made of 97.5% zinc, with a thin copper coating. Sandwiching a penny between glass and firing to a full fuse is an easy way to get a first hand look at a zinc inclusion.

• **Other metals**

Other metals can also be used as inclusions. A few, such as steels and related alloys, will spall significantly in the kiln, making them poor candidates for fusing. (Spalling is when heat causes a metal to shed small flakes during the firing. With steel, these flakes take on the appearance of rust and can be difficult to clean off the shelf after firing.

Some other metals, such as palladium or platinum, can be successfully fused as inclusions, using techniques similar to those previously discussed in this chapter.

• **Coins**

Since most coins are made from metals that can survive the heat of the kiln, they tend to be excellent candidates for inclusion experiments. Coins made from metals with a fairly low melting point will usually survive the firing without cracking, but coins made of metals with a higher melting temperature will most likely be too thick to survive fusing in a kiln.

Organics and Other Materials

Although metals are among the most common kinds of inclusions, many other materials have

124

Left: Mica and leaf inclusion, created by coating a leaf with mica powder, sandwiching between two layers of glass, and firing to a full fuse.
Right: Leaf print with mica inclusion.
(Photos courtesy of Jody Danner Walker.)

the potential for use as inclusions. Chief among these are mica, various papers, and organic materials, such leaves and shells.

The key to success with these materials is careful experimentation to find the particular combination of material, firing schedule, and process that gives you the look you like. In most cases it's essential to allow any moisture in the inclusion time to escape; firing too quickly can trap a large air bubble inside the glass. Use a long bubble squeeze, going slowly from 1100F/593C to 1240F/671C and adding a lengthy soak at 1240F. This allows moisture to escape, rather than being trapped between layers of glass.

• **Mica**

Although mica is more commonly used on the top surface of a piece, as discussed in Chapter 12, it can also be used as an inclusion. One advantage of this approach is that mica is less likely to burn off when used between layers of glass. This is especially important if using the mica formulations has not been made specifically for fusing.

Mica can be used as an inclusion either dry, by sifting onto a bottom layer of glass or wet, by mixing with a binder such as Klyr-fire or glue before application. In either case, once the mica

is applied to the base layer of glass, it can be capped with a clear layer and then fused.

Since mica has a different appearance on top of glass rather than as an inclusion, the same color of mica will often appear to be a different color, depending on how it is used.

Mica can also be used with fiber paper to create a inclusion that combines ease of application with mica shimmer.

• **Fiber paper and thinfire shelf paper**

Although fiber paper is generally used as a mold material or to protect the kiln shelf, it can also be used as an inclusion, as can thinfire shelf paper. Simply cut the paper to shape, sandwich between two layers of glass, and fuse.

This process works better with thinner fiber papers than with thicker ones; if the paper is too thick or if there are too many layers it may hold too much heat during cooling and prevent proper annealing.

One interesting variation is to dip thin fiber paper or thinfire paper into a solution of mica or enamel, so that the paper takes on the color of the solution. Allow the paper to dry, then sandwich it between layers of glass and fuse. Fired correctly, the result will be a brightly colored fiber inclusion.

• **Leaves**

Leaves won't survive the heat of the kiln, but if prepared properly they can still be used as inclusions. For best results, use dried leaves, rather than fresh ones. If you must use green leaves that contain a significant amount of moisture, give the moisture additional time to escape during the firing.

When fired, leaves will leave a residue of ash behind; the color and intensity of the the ash depends on type of leaf, specific firing schedule, and even the individual leaf. Keep in mind that leaves vary in mineral and moisture content depending on weather and time of year, so there is likely to be considerable variation in the results achieved, even from leaf to leaf of the same type.

It also helps to create a pathway for air and moisture to escape. To do this, allow the stem of the leaf to extend slightly beyond the layers of glass, so that air escapes during the firing.

Note also that because of the moisture they contain, many leaves will shrink when fired. The residue that remains will generally be ashen in color, but if you want a more colorful appearance, coat a dried leaf in glass paint or enamels and then fuse. Or simply use the leaf to "print" on the glass and dispense with firing the leaf altogether. It's also possible to soak the leaf in a solution of mica and a binder and then fire.

An alternative method is to fire the piece twice, once to create the ghost image of a leaf and a second time to permanently trap it between two layers of glass. In this approach, start by placing the leaf against a kiln washed shelf. Cap the leaf with a single layer of glass and fire to around 1350F/730C. The leaf will burn off during the firing, leaving an ashen image behind.

After this initial firing, carefully pick up the glass layer. With luck and care, the ashes from the fired leaf will stick to the glass rather than to the kiln shelf. Place the fired layer of glass on top

of a second layer, so that the image of the leaf is trapped in the middle. Re-fire to fuse the two layers of glass together. You'll trap the image and have only minimal trapped air.

• **Sea shells**

Another organic material that can be fired in the kiln is sea shells. Unfortunately, sea shell inclusions are rarely successful. Most often, the shells disintegrate and crumble, leaving behind a whitish powder. Alternatively, the shells can create large gas bubbles or trapped air in the glass. Successful fusing sometimes occurs, but this is less common.

It's difficult to predict how a particular shell will behave when used as an inclusion. Even two shells of the same type may behave differently when fired. This is because shells contain impurities and chemicals that can't be detected with the naked eye. As a result, there's no easy way to tell how a shell will react to the heat of the kiln just by looking at the shell. And since trial and error most likely results in the shell turning to powder, shells are more often successfully used as forms to create molds and cast items, rather than as inclusions.

• **Paper currency**

The paper used in bills won't survive the kiln, but the inks used will often remain or turn to ash during the firing. When bills are fired they will tend to generate gas that results in a large air bubble; to minimize this it's important to fire slowly, especially from 1100F/593C to 1240F/671C. As with many organic materials, a long bubble squeeze will also help minimize trapped air bubbles.

Air bubble inclusions

Rather than being a defect to be avoided, air bubbles can be encouraged and exploited for their unusual shape and appearance. This is accomplished by creating a pattern of deliberately trapped air bubbles between layers of glass.

"Hot Air" by Marcia Newren. Fused with bubble inclusions, then slumped, and assembled. (Photo by Margo Geist, courtesy of the artist.)

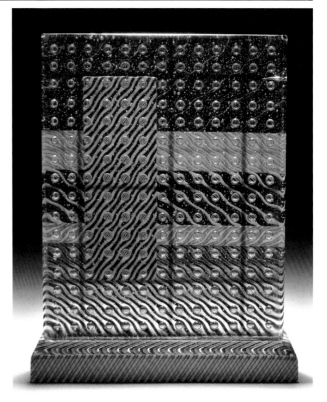

"Optical Study #4" by Ruth Gowell. A more detailed photo of this piece is on the next page. (Photo by Pete Duvall, courtesy of the artist.)

The basic concept behind encouraging air bubbles to form is the creation of air pockets between the layers of glass. This can be done by sandblasting, drilling, or arranging cut pieces to promote the forming of bubbles. The tendency of bubbles to form at the intersection of ridges of glass can also be used creatively.

• Bubbles from textured glass

Textured glass can also be used to promote the formation of bubbles. Two pieces of ribbed glass, for example, can be criss-crossed and placed face to face in the kiln and fired to seal the edges and trap air bubbles at the intersection of the ridges. Chapter 8 contains an example of this technique using Bullseye's Reed glass.

• Bubbles from stringers

This approach to air bubble inclusions uses glass stringers to create ridges on sheet glass. In its simplest form, a fusible glue is used to glue stringers in place both on the top and bottom layers of glass. Once the glue dries, the layers are fused face to face (with the stringers on the inside) to trap air bubbles between the layers. Variations in stringer thickness and the space between stringers will yield different effects, as will using iridized or dichroic glass.

• Bubble powder

Bubbles can also be created by using chemicals or solutions that generate gas that is then trapped within the layers of the fused glass. Commercial "bubble powders" are available in a variety of colors. These tend to be more reliable than household options such as baking soda (sodium bicarbonate) or borax. With all of these products the approach is basically the same. First, sprinkle the powder between layers of glass. Then, heat, fuse, and anneal as you would normally. Experimentation is needed to determine the amount of powder that works best. Using clear glass allows the bubbles to show up best. Varying the strength of the solution can also change the results.

Detail from Ruth Gowell's "Optical Study #4." A photo of the full piece, which incorporates both air bubbles and reactive glass in a thick slab, is pictured on page 127. (Photo by Pete Duvall, courtesy of the artist.)

Chapter 14

Beyond two layers

Pattern bars • Slabs, sinks, and related thick items • Coldworking

Typically, fused glass pieces are two layers, or roughly 1/4″ (6 mm) thick. That's because of the natural tendency for fused glass to level out at about that thickness. Fusing glass to achieve a greater thickness than 1/4″ is more complicated than simply stacking up layers of glass; instead, the piece usually needs to be restrained, or dammed, so that it doesn't spread and lose some of its thickness.

Making thicker pieces is also more technically challenging than making pieces of a standard thickness. In addition to the need for damming, thicker pieces have a greater tendency to trap air bubbles. They also require longer heating and cooling cycles, and may require extensive cold-

working to achieve acceptable edge quality. This chapter will cover several ways to create thicker pieces, starting with the basics of simple pattern bars and finishing with some tips for successful coldworking of thicker pieces.

Pattern bars

A pattern bar is a thick bundle of glass that has been fused together to form a solid mass. The size of pattern bars can vary, but most are long brick-like bars about one to inches (25 to 50 cm) high and one to two inches wide. After fusing, these bars can be cut into slices with a glass saw, tile saw, or trim saw and then re-fused to make new items.

A basic pattern bar bowl by Brock Craig. Fused pattern bars, sliced 3/8″ thick, then assembled side by side on the shelf and re-fused. Slumped and coldworked. (Photo by the author, bowl courtesy of Brock Craig.)

Pattern bar design

A simple pattern bar, constructed by stacking one inch (25 cm) wide strips of glass eight layers high, damming, and then fusing. (Photo by the author.)

Two more pattern bars designs. The left bar was built with spaces, so the glass would flow into gaps during the fuse. (Photo by the author.)

A small selection of various pattern bar slices. Rods, stringers, and frit can be used to create detail. The bars to the upper left and the lower right incorporate reactive glasses. (Photo by the author.)

Round pattern bars can be made by fully fusing scraps of glass in a ceramic tube, such as the one shown here. Line the tube with fiber paper to keep the glass from sticking and fire it standing up, rather than laying on its side. (Photo by the author.)

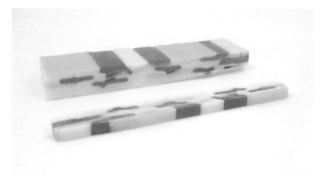

Totem bars and random progressive pattern bars, developed by glass artist Brock Craig, are made by creating a bar that will be sliced lengthwise, rather than from the end. These bars rely on glass flowing into intentional gaps to create their unique appearance. Lay up to the left, fused bar and single slice to the right. (Photos by the author.)

Greg Rawls, "Carnivale." Sliced pattern bars, reassembled, fused, then slumped into bowl mold. Full piece on right, detail of pattern bar slices on left. (Photo courtesy of the artist.)

• **Design the pattern bar**

The key to developing interesting pattern bars is the ability to think in cross section. That's because pattern bars are usually cut into slices that are each about 3/8" (9 mm) thick.

A simple pattern bar design consists of eight layers of glass, stacked to form a bar that is an inch (25 cm) wide and an inch high. The bar can be as long as desired. By varying the size, color, and space between strips, a broad array of bar shapes is possible. See the illustrations on Page 130 for some design possibilities.

• **Prepare the glass and assemble the bar**

Once the design is determined, the next step is to cut the glass required to form the bar and assemble the bar. In addition to sheet glass, stringer, frit, and scrap glass can also be used.

It may be easier to assemble the bar inside the kiln, rather than attempting to transport it from a work table to the kiln, especially if the bar has many small pieces. If this isn't practical, then consider assembling the bar on a separate kiln shelf outside the kiln, then transporting the entire shelf, bar and all, to the kiln. Constructing a glass box to contain frit and other small items is also a possibility. Because it generally fires off

cleanly in the kiln, hot glue can be used to hold the box together for easy filling.

Remember that if your layup has gaps between the pieces, either from spaces left between strips or from using frit, the bar will settle into the gaps and emerge from the kiln thinner in size than when it was created.

• **Construct the dam**

Once the bar has been assembled, it's time to construct the dam. Dams must be made from a refractory material that also has enough strength to hold back the weight of the glass at fusing temperature. For this reason, most dams are made of kiln brick, rigidized fiber board, or mullite or cordierite (which are also used to make kiln shelves). Dam material can be purchased ready made or can be fabricated from kiln shelves using a wet tile saw or similar tool. Dams approximately two to three inches (5 to 8 cm) tall will work in most situations.

In addition to the dam material, fiber paper is generally used to prevent the glass from sticking to the dam material. Paper of 1/8" (3 mm) or 1/16" (1.5 mm) thickness is ideal. Thinfire shelf paper will not provide a good barrier when used upright, so it should not be used for this purpose. Simply kiln washing the dams isn't sufficient; only using fiber paper strips will allow

To save space in the kiln, pattern bars can be dammed side to side. The strips of fiber paper extending past the ends of the bars will be cut off before finishing the dam. (Photo by the author.)

the flexibility of easily damming for the height of your bars.

Once you've obtained your dam material, start the damming process by cutting fiber paper to fit the bars being dammed. Cut the paper approximately 1/8" (3 to 4 mm) shorter than the height of your piece. For example, if your pattern bar is one inch tall (25 mm), then the fiber paper strip should be cut 7/8" (21 mm) wide. It's also a good idea to cut the strips slightly longer than needed; it's much easier to snip them off later than it is to have to cut a new strip if you accidently cut one too short.

Don't be alarmed if the glass looks much higher than the fiber strips. As the glass fuses, the glass will sink down and the top edge should round nicely as it fires. Cutting the strips too wide will usually cause needling around the edges of the glass, so stick to the 1/8" principle and minimize the potential for needling.

Begin the damming process by constructing two sides of the area to be dammed. Lay the brick or mullite strips on edge to form a right angle, then line them with the fiber paper strips. Gently slide the pattern bar into the angle between the two sides. Take a moment to make certain all is still intact, then place fiber paper strips on the side of the bar. Continue the process with each bar, until everything is in the kiln.

Finish by damming the final two sides of the dam. Include both fiber paper strips and the heavy dam material. For items such as a long row

of pattern bars, one long fiber paper strip for the ends of the bars is easier to cut than small strips for each bar.

- **Fire to full fuse, then anneal**

Once the bars have been dammed, they're ready to be fired. A standard full fuse firing is sufficient, with only a few minor alterations. First, fire to a slightly higher top temperature than normal, and soak for a few minutes longer than normal. In most cases, firing to 1500F/816C and soaking for fifteen minutes works well. The extra time and temperature allows the bars to fill in any spaces in the bars and to fuse fully.

The second adjustment to the standard full fuse schedule is to anneal for longer than normal. There are three reasons for this. First, pattern bars are thicker than normal, so more time must be spent in the annealing range. Second, pattern bars often involve many different colors of glass in close contact with each other; a longer annealing schedule helps the various colors anneal properly. And third, a longer annealing schedule will help pattern bars survive extensive coldworking on a tile saw.

Here's a typical firing schedule for one inch (25 mm) pattern bars:

1. 400F/222C degrees per hour (dph) to 1100F/593C hold 10 minutes

2. 200F/111C dph to 1250F/677C hold 10 min

132

Top view of a group of pattern bars that are ready for firing. Fiber paper strips surround each bar and strips of cut up kiln shelves are used to dam the perimeter around the bars. (Photo by the author.)

3. Full speed to 1500F/816C hold 10 min

Adjust temperature and hold time if needed.

4. Full speed to 900F/482C hold 4 hours

Adjust annealing temperature if your glass requires. The hold time is thirty minutes per 1/8″ (3 mm) layer of glass thickness.

Note that this hold time is longer than the one used for fusing basic two layer (1/4″/6 mm) pieces. The longer soak period helps minimize problems stemming from multiple colors and extensive coldworking often associated with pattern bars.

5. 100F/56C dph to 750F/399C
   no hold needed

6. Turn kiln off and allow to cool to room temperature.

Always allow the bars to cool completely before starting coldworking. Even when the outside of the bars feels cool, the inside of the bars can still hold considerable heat.

• **Cut up and reassemble to create your piece**

After cooling completely, pattern bars can be cut with a glass saw such as the Omni or the Taurus, but a wet tile saw equipped with a blade for cutting glass is quicker and more efficient. Bars can

be cut to any thickness desired, but a thickness of around 5/16″ to 3/8″ (8 to 9 mm) works well for re-fusing as a standard two layer piece.

With most pattern bars, cutting the cross section will give a different effect that cutting lengthwise or at an angle. If necessary due to a coarse blade or to uneven cutting or misshappen pattern bars, slices can be coldworked and shaped as desired on a stained glass grinder or more elaborate coldworking tool.

The resulting pattern bar slices can be fire polished and used as jewelry or decorative elements on other fused items. Or they can be arranged side by side on a kiln shelf and fired together to make a large pattern bar piece, as shown in the photo above. The ways to use pattern bar slices

Cutting pattern bars on a tile saw requires a steady hand and a blade specifically made for cutting glass. The larger the blade, the thicker the bars that can be worked. (Photo by Jody Danner Walker.)

Top: "Winter Song" by Karuna C. Santoro. Fused and slumped bowl formed from pattern bar strips. (Photo courtesy of the artist.)

Below: "Beyond Reason" by Lisa Allen. Fused and slumped. Full piece to left, detail to right. (Photo courtesy of the artist.)

Greg Rawls, "Solo on the African Plain." Sliced pattern bars, reassembled and fused, then coldworked. (Photo courtesy of the artist.)

are limited only by your imagination and the size of your kiln.

Slabs, sinks, and related thick items

Making pattern bars is an excellent way to learn the dynamics of working with thicker items and developing proper damming techniques. But sooner or later you'll want to try your hand at a thicker piece, such as a panel or a sink.

The basics of the process are the same, but there are several new considerations. First, many thicker pieces are best constructed by firing each layer individually, then stacking them all to create the thick piece. Second, thicker pieces require longer bubble soak and annealing cycles than pattern bars of the same thickness. And finally, thicker pieces often require time spent coldworking to achieve the desired edge quality and finish.

• Single versus multiple firings

If desired, thicker items can be constructed with a single firing. This process is not unlike the

process for creating pattern bars. Simply stack pieces of glass to the desired thickness, dam carefully, and then fire, taking care to include an appropriate bubble soak and annealing schedule for the thickness of the piece. Also, note that the need for cleanliness increases as pieces become thicker, so take extra time to thoroughly clean each layer of glass before firing.

Many thick pieces will benefit from a slightly different approach. Instead of firing all at once, consider firing layers of the piece separately, then stacking them and firing a second time to create the final slab.

The multiple firing approach has several advantages. First, an initial firing will smooth out the pieces and help reduce trapped air bubbles between layers in the final firing. Second, an initial firing will fuse design elements such as powder and frit in place, allowing for less distortion in the final piece. And third, an initial firing allows the opportunity to examine each layer to determine if adjustments need to be made before stacking to create the final piece. If necessary, layers can be fired more than once before being deemed ready for combining with other layers for the final firing.

135

Dorothy Hafner, "Spectral Dimensions." Multi-layer fused and kiln formed glass. (Photo by Austin Moore, courtesy of the artist.)

When using the multiple firing approach, a single 1/8″ (3 mm) layer can be fired to a low tack fuse to mature enamels or smooth out powder. 1375F/746C is often a good firing temperature for single layer smoothing. Another option is to stack two or three 1/8″ layers and fire to a full fuse. This works best when flattening design elements such as frit, stringer, or small pieces of glass. For some designs, both single layers and paired layers may need to be fired individually, sometimes multiple times, before they're ready for the final stacked firing.

• **Minimizing air bubbles**

Since many thick slab designs involve layers stacked on top of layers of glass, air bubbles are almost inevitable. Although a certain amount of bubbles can be attractive, adding a unique dimension to the finished piece, it's usually preferable to fire to minimize trapped air bubbles. Large, isolated, bubbles are especially distracting. In most situations the final piece should have

only a few unremarkable bubbles or a random pattern of small air bubbles to catch the light and help highlight the thickness of the piece.

The most common technique to minimize trapped air bubbles is to lengthen the bubble squeeze during the firing. For thick items, a two or three hour soak at around 1240F/671C will give trapped air additional time to escape from between the layers.

Bubbles can also be minimized by capping the top layer of a thick piece with a layer of glass that's at least 6 mm (1/4″) thick. The weight of this thicker layer will press down upon the layers beneath, helping squeeze out air bubbles during the firing. A single standard 1/8″ (3 mm) layer of glass is much more likely to trap air underneath than the thicker, heavier layer.

One option that can eliminate trapped air bubbles entirely is to use strips of glass laid on edge to create the thickness, rather than stacked layers of glass. This approach allows air to rise up and

"Exposure 27" by Steve Immerman. Fused and coldworked. Detail to right, full piece below. (Photo courtesy of the artist.)

Fusing with vertical strips, as in the black and white strips of this piece, can eliminate trapped air bubbles entirely. (Photo by the author.)

escape from between the vertical strips, eliminating bubbles entirely.

• **Annealing**

With any thick piece it's essential to use the appropriate annealing schedule for the thickness being fired. A rule of thumb such as thirty minutes per 1/8″ (3 mm) layer is a good starting point, but the rule of thumb isn't really applicable for pieces more than a couple of inches thick. It's always a good idea to double check with the glass manufacturer's latest recommendations. All of the major art glass manufacturers, including Bullseye, Spectrum, and Uroboros, have published schedules for annealing thick glass.

Also, note that many annealing recommendations assume a piece that is regular in shape, fully fused and without sharp outside curves or projections. If your piece has a complicated shape or if there's any potential for cooling unevenly in the kiln, then adopt a more conservative annealing schedule. For unusual shapes anneal for twice the thickness of the shape's thickest part.

• **Final cooling**

With small pieces such as pattern bars, most kilns will cool slowly enough to simply turn the kiln off after annealing and allow the kiln to cool naturally. This approach, however, isn't

recommended for thicker slabs, which need to be cooled more slowly, both through the bottom part of the annealing range and from below the range down to room temperature. As with any firing, the rate of temperature decrease depends on the total thickness of the glass, but large thick slabs generally require a multi-stage annealing process, followed by a controlled cool down to room temperature. Consult the manufacturer's published annealing and cooling schedules for thick items if uncertain about the proper cooling rate for your piece.

• **Typical firing schedule for one and a half inch (38 mm) thick glass slab**

This schedule is based on recommendations from Bullseye Glass, but will work for other manufacturers by adjusting the top temperature and annealing temperature as appropriate. The schedule also assumes single layers of glass, rather than thicker glass than has been previously fired.

1. 400F/222C degrees per hour (dph) to 1100F/593C hold 10 minutes

2. 200F/111C dph to 1250F/677C hold 2 hours

3. Full speed to 1500F/816C hold 10 min

Adjust temperature and hold time if needed.

4. Full speed to 900F/482C hold 6 hours

Adjust the annealing temperature if your glass requires. The hold time recommended is thirty minutes per 1/8″ (3 mm) layer of glass thickness. Note that this rule of thumb is more conservative than the hold time recommended for standard two layer pieces.

5. 12F/6.7C dph to 800F/427C

No hold is needed at the end of this stage.

6. 22F/12C dph to 700F/371C

No hold is needed at the end of this stage. Some kilns can be turned off at this point, but if your kiln cools faster than 72F/40C per hour, the firing should be continued to room temperature.

7. 72F/40C dph to room temperature

It's good practice to allow the piece to cool completely for another day or more before beginning coldworking.

Coldworking

Many thick pieces require some coldworking before they're complete. In some situations only a small amount of coldworking is needed, but in some cases hours of work may be required. The extent of the coldworking needed depends on the quality of the dam construction and the finish desired by the artist.

A well constructed dam will leave the edges of the glass gently rolled, with a minimum of needling or other rough spots. Haphazardly constructed dams are likely to require more coldworking time.

A broad range of coldworking equipment is available, from wet belt sander to lap wheel to sandblaster and more. Those tools can be very useful and can greatly reduce time spent coldworking. They can also be used to achieve finishes and textures that are more difficult, if not impossible, to achieve by hand.

But even without expensive equipment, it's possible to achieve a satisfactory finish with your

Els VandenEnde, "Cairn #14: Psittacine." Fused layers of glass, carved and textured. (Photo by Delores Taylor, courtesy of the artist.)

piece. Don't underestimate what can be accomplished with a simple grinder and a set of relatively inexpensive diamond hand pads.

With the addition of elbow grease, diamond hand pads can do wonders. For example, if your piece has been well dammed, diamond hand pads can quickly smooth out the rough spots. The edges of an 8 by 10 inch (20 by 25 cm) slab can be brought from rough edges to a smooth matte finish in about an hour's steady work with hand pads. Moreover, there's a satisfaction from working with your hands that working with tools can't match.

Check out Chapter 18 for more on coldworking.

Chapter 15

High temperature firing

High fire • Pot melts and wire melts • Combing • The vitrigraph kiln

When a glass kiln is fired to 1600F/871C or higher, it enters the range for high temperature firing. At temperatures in this range, glass behaves quite differently than it does at normal fusing and slumping temperatures.

In the range from 1600F/871C to 1700F/927C, glass begins to flow. The flow isn't like water pouring out of a cup; it's more like molasses or thick syrup. If the kiln shelf is uneven or if the glass is three or more layers thick, it can flow off the shelf and onto the floor of the kiln. In the high temperature range air bubbles in the glass rise and come to the surface. As bubbles from lower layers rise, they often disturb the layers above, creating interesting, unique color patterns and swirls.

When the temperature exceeds 1700F/927C, this process accelerates. The flow of the glass increases (though still not like water) and any remaining air bubbles rise to the surface. The glass can even appear to boil in the kiln. And if left undammed, the glass is even more likely to flow off the shelf.

There are a number of kilnforming processes that take place in the high temperature range. These include simple high fires, which are similar to ordinary fusing processes, except taken to a much higher temperature. Other processes include pot melts and wire melts, in which patterns are created by glass flowing from above and onto the kiln shelf. Perhaps most exciting of all the high temperature processes is combing, in which the artist reaches into the kiln at 1700F/927C and manipulates the molten glass.

High fire

In some ways, the process for creating a high fire piece is very similar to the process of fusing any piece of glass, with the important exception that the glass is fired to a higher temperature. However, there are certain guidelines that will help you achieve a more successful firing.

Detail from "Quantum IV" by Dick Ditore, showing the typical swirls and intermingled colors of a high fire piece. (Photo courtesy of the artist.)

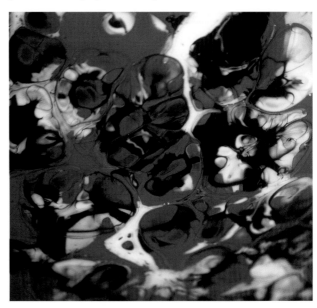

Detail from "Quantum VI" by Dick Ditore, . (Photo courtesy of the artist.)

Start with proper preparation of the kiln shelf. Don't use thinfire shelf paper; instead either use 1/8″ (3 mm) fiber paper or a ten to twelve coat application of kiln wash. Although high temperature kiln washes are available, any premium kiln wash (such as Bullseye's) will work well.

It's possible to fire pieces that are only two layers (1/4″/6 mm) thick. Pieces of this thickness can usually be fired without damming. However, two layer pieces aren't generally as successful as pieces made with three layers or more. So for best results plan on a thickness of at least 3/8″ (9 mm). A half inch thick may be even better. Plan also to dam the piece; not only will this keep the glass from flowing off the shelf, it will also encourage the mixing of the various colors used in the piece.

Think carefully about which colors to use. Although there are no absolutes (and all rules can sometimes be broken), some colors will work much better than others.

For the most part, avoid colors that react with each other. The reaction can create muddy brown areas that detract from the overall effect. Colors such as black should be used sparingly; they tend to flow more than other colors and can overwhelm the piece if too much is used.

The potential for compatibility shift is also a possibility with any high temperature firing. Pinks, cranberries, and some whites may be problematic. Aventurine green can be used, but only sparingly. And transparent reds and yellows often strike to opaque when fired, and may become incompatible as well.

It may sound daunting, but don't despair. Many colors work very well at high temperatures. Some colors will work fine in some firings, but be problematic in others. It's all part of the joy of learning to work with glass in a new way. Just keep in mind that since fusing glasses are not formulated for firing to 1700F/927C, a certain amount of experimentation and potential for failure is inevitable.

After selecting the colors, it's time to begin arranging them for the firing. One approach that works well is to begin with a layer of clear glass against the prepared kiln shelf. The clear botom layer can be any shape or thickness. Using an iridized glass irid side down against the shelf will help keep kiln wash from sticking to the glass.

Build a dam around the bottom layer using dense refractory material and fiber paper. (For more on damming, see Chapter 14.) The height of the dam walls isn't nearly as critical as with

141

a standard slab firing, so don't worry too much about precise cutting of the fiber paper lining the inside of the dam. Just make certain the paper is sufficient to keep the glass from sticking to the refractory material.

Once the base layer is ready and dammed, it's time to begin placing the colored glass you've selected. There are many placement variations, but the key to them all is arranging a fairly large number of smaller pieces to allow for movement between the stacked layers. Denser colors will tend to move down during the firing, while the movement of air toward the top of the piece will cause other colors to rise. A high percentage of clear glass pieces will yield a different result than using almost all colored glass. Here's where experimentation will pay the greatest dividends.

One method is to lay the pieces vertically, on top of each other, leaving gaps between the pieces to encourage trapped air and glass movement. But horizontal arrangements, with strips laid on edge, can also be used. The only real limit is your imagination.

For best results, add several layers of glass, keeping in mind that once the piece fires it will be considerably thinner than before the firing. It's sometimes difficult to estimate what the final thickness will be; if you're having trouble with this, one solution is to weigh the glass and use that information to estimate the final thickness. A 1/8" (3 mm) layer of glass that covers one square foot will weigh about 1.6 pounds (725 grams).

Once the glass is arranged, check to make certain the dam is still intact. Then begin the firing.

• Heat to 1100F/593C and hold for one hour

In most cases the glass used in a high fire consists of small scraps and single layer pieces, so it's possible to fire fairly quickly. A rate of 400 to 500F (222 to 278C) degrees per hour is conservative enough for almost all situations. Once the temperature reaches 1100F/593C, hold for about an hour. This hold will allow the pieces to slump onto each other, trapping air between the layers.

• Continue firing quickly to 1700F/927C

Since a successful high fire piece involves trapped air movement, it's best to fire without a bubble soak. After the hold at 1100F/593C, fire as quickly as your kiln allows to 1700F/927C. With many kilns this can take an hour or more, so patience is best.

• Hold at 1700F/927C

The longer the hold, the more glass movement will result. Holding for ten to fifteen minutes will yield a different look than a standard fuse firing, and a shorter time is enough for some colors (such as blacks) to begin to flow and move throughout the piece.

But for most colors and situations a hold of an hour or longer is best. That's enough time to allow most of the trapped air to rise to the surface of the piece. It will also allow for significant glass movement and for mingling of colors. It does take time for colors to move and for air bubbles to come to the surface and break.

• Begin the cooling process

After the hold at 1700F/927C, begin cooling the kiln. Flash venting by opening the kiln to speed up the cooling process is generally not recommended.

Some artists stop on the way down to the annealing range in order to allow the piece to smooth out a bit. This is especially helpful if air bubbles have significantly disturbed the top surface of the glass. A fifteen minute hold at around 1500F/816C is usually sufficient, but a quick peek at the piece at around this temperature can help determine if this hold is necessary.

• Cool to anneal

Never rush the annealing process with high temperature pieces. Anneal conservatively, allowing the glass plenty of time to recover from firing

Basic setup for the pot melt. The pot, which is filled with glass strips, should be supported several inches above the kiln shelf. Make certain that there is space between the supports to accommodate the hole in the bottom of the flower pot. (Photo by the author.)

and anneal without residual stress. For a half inch (12 mm) piece, a two hour hold at the appropriate annealing temperature should be sufficient. If you're at all uncertain of the thickness after the high fire step, then lengthen the anneal soak a bit to be on the safe side. After holding to anneal, cool at a rate of around 100F/56C per hour until the temperature inside the kiln drops to around 750F/400C. At that point it's generally safe to turn off the kiln and allow the kiln to cool naturally.

Of course these temperatures should be adjusted if your piece is thicker or if the glass you're using requires it.

- **Inspect and coldwork the piece**

Only rarely will high temperature pieces emerge from the kiln perfectly formed and ready to display. More often, pieces will need to cleaned, coldworked, and even re-fired.

Expect that the fiber paper or kiln wash used beneath the piece will only last a single firing. Kiln wash may be baked onto the glass, so a sandblaster or similar tool may be required to clean the surface of the piece. Also, a certain amount of devitrification is not unusual; sandblasting can help with that also.

One common technique used with high temperature pieces is to "flip and fire" the piece. First coldwork the edges, then flip the piece over and fire polish in the kiln. This works especially well for high temperature projects that were con-

structed on a clear base layer. Re-firing with the clear layer on top will give the final piece a extra depth and clarity.

Pot melts and wire melts

Pot melts, also known as aperture pours, are a very easy way to fire high temperature pieces. Damming isn't normally required, there are fewer coldworking demands than high fires, and it's also a great way to use scrap glass. In the basic pot melt, glass scraps are placed into a container with a hole in the bottom (a terra cotta flower pot is often used). The pot is suspended above the kiln shelf, then the kiln is fired to around 1700F/927C. Molten glass flows out of the hole in the bottom of the pot, creating a circular pattern of colors on the shelf below.

The wire melt, a close cousin of the pot melt, has many of the same virtues. The major difference between the two is that the pot melt uses a container to hold the glass prior to firing, while the wire melt uses wires or thick stainless steel mesh to suspend glass above the kiln floor.

- **Preparing to fire**

The basic setup for the pot melt requires that the pot be suspended at least 3 inches (7.5 cm) above the kiln shelf. A height of 6 inches (15 cm) or more is even better. You'll need two strips of refractory material (fiber board or kiln shelf material), each about 2 inches (5 cm) wide and as long as the kiln shelf is wide, kiln bricks or

143

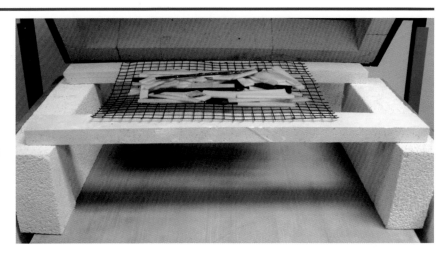

The setup for the wire melt is very similar to that for the pot melt. Use stainless steel wire mesh with approximately 1/2" (12 mm) holes. If the span between the supports is relatively small, as shown here, the mesh can sit directly on the supporting strips. Larger pieces of mesh may need to be tied to the strips with a high temperature wire such as nichrome. (Photo by the author.)

posts to support the ends of the strip, and one or more flower pots to hold the glass. The basic setup is shown at the top of the page to the left.

The kiln shelf should be throughly kiln washed or lined with fiber paper, just as for any high temperature project. Also, it's a good idea to kiln wash the floor of your kiln in case of an accident.

The pots should be prepared by creating a hole in the bottom of the pot that's at least 1/2" (12 mm) in diameter. It may be necessary to use a masonry drill bit, a hammer and chisel, or a file to make the hole larger. Holes can be round, slit-shaped, or any other shape you prefer. Multiple holes or extra holes in the sides of the pot are also a possibility. The shape and number of the holes will impact the final result.

Do not kiln wash the inside of the pot. Kiln wash can loosen and contaminate the glass. Instead, fill the pot with scrap glass. This can be done by simply dumping scraps into the pot, but you'll achieve far better results if some consideration is given to how to arrange the glass. Try cutting strips of glass, each roughly half an inch (12 mm) wide and the height of the pot. The cutting does not have to be precise; strips can be cut from glass scrap if desired.

Select up to three different colors of glass. Selecting more than three colors can create pot melts that are muddy brown in color. Use reactive colors with caution. Some colors, like black, will overwhelm other colors, so use them sparingly. Compatibility can also be an issue with pot melts, but these surface less often than with high fire pieces.

One way to determine the amount of glass to use to create a pot melt of a specific size is to weigh the glass and calculate the resulting size. A square foot (144 square in/929 square cm) of completed pot melt made with art glass weighs approximately 3.2 pounds. Remember to use a bit of extra glass to compensate for glass sticking to the pot. And keep records of your pot melts so that you'll know the exact amount of glass to use to create a certain size melt in your kiln.

One common method of loading the pot is to cluster strips of the same color together, up and down in the pot. This tends to result in more vibrant pot melts than a random distribution of strips. Fill the pot to the top, but be careful not to extend too much past the top or angle the strips so that as they melt they flow outside the pot, rather than inside and out through the holes.

Once the glass is loaded, place the pot on the supports. Make sure that there is enough space between the two supports; you don't want to block the hole at the bottom of the pot.

If you want to create a circular shape that's around 1/4" (6 mm) thick, no dam is needed. But if you want to create another shape or if you want a thicker melt, then you must build a dam on the shelf beneath the suspended pot. See Chapter 14 for more on building dams.

If you've elected to create a wire melt, rather than a pot melt, the key difference is that the glass is placed on top of wire mesh or high temperature wire that is supported above the kiln shelf. Stainless steel mesh or nichrome wire

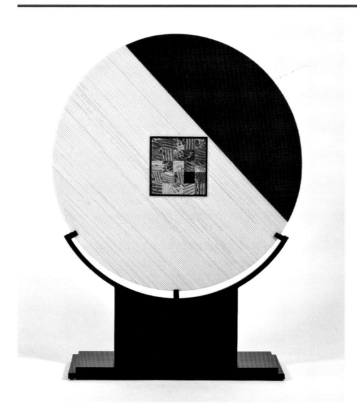

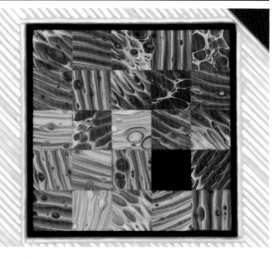

"Maris" by Steve Immerman. Strip cut and assembled, then fused and coldworked. The center area of the piece, detailed above, consists of a cut and reassembled high temperature melt. Page 36 has another view of this piece. (Photo courtesy of the artist.)

is essential. The firing schedule for a wire melt is basically the same as that for a pot melt.

• **Fire to 1700F/927C and hold**

Because of the small size of the pieces used for pot melts, firing can proceed very quickly. Fire to 1100F/593C at 600F/316C per hour, then hold for 15 minutes. Next fire as rapidly as your kiln allows to 1700F/927C. Hold at that temperature until all of the glass runs out of the bottom of the flower pot. Depending on the size and number of the holes in the bottom of the pot, this will take from fifteen minutes to an hour or more. Make certain you wear proper safety equipment if you open the kiln to peek at the progress of your melt.

• **Cool to 1500F/816C and hold 30 minutes**

After the glass flows from the pot and onto the kiln shelf, allow the kiln to cool naturally. Opening the kiln to speed up the cooling process is not usually necessary.

Holding at 1500F/816C allows the melt to even out at about 1/4″ (6 mm). It also helps smooth

out any bubbles or marks left from the flowing glass.

• **Cool to your annealing temperature and hold for one hour**

An hour is sufficient for pieces that were fired undammed. If your piece was dammed, you will probably need to lengthen the annealing soak. Thirty minutes per 1/4″ (6 mm) of thickness is a good rule of thumb. Because of the potential for compatibility shifting, a more conservative soak is recommended.

• **Finish the cooling process**

Cool at 100F/56C to 750F/399C, then turn the kiln off an allow it to cool naturally to room temperature.

• **Inspect and finish**

As with most high temperature pieces, it may be necessary to clean baked on kiln wash from the bottom of the piece. Grinding or cutting the piece, followed by fire polishing or re-fusing, may also be necessary.

145

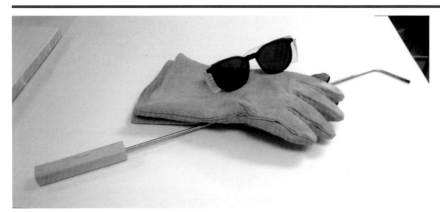

Commercial combing rod, along with gloves and safety glasses. (Photo by the author.)

Pot melts can be cut up and used as jewelry or as decorative elements in other pieces. They make excellent centerpieces for other pieces and can help add excitement to even the most humdrum design. Also, note that sometimes the bottom side of the melt is more interesting than the top, so be sure to check out both sides.

Combing

Combing, sometimes called raking, is the act of drawing a tool across molten glass. As with most high temperature firings, combing begins by heating an arrangement of glass to a temperature of around 1700F/927C. Once the kiln comes to temperature, it is opened and a wooden tool with a metal tip, called a combing rod, is drawn across the nearly molten glass to form patterns in the top surface of the piece.

As one of the hottest activities you can do with a kiln, it's essential to follow good safety procedures when combing. Unless you're experienced,

Closeup of the end of a homemade combing rod, showing the large metal hook which has been screwed into the tool. This wooden tool should be soaked in water for at least 24 hours prior to use. (Photo by the author.)

comb with the help of a friend. Wear clothes made of cotton, rather than synthetics such as rayon. Long sleeve shirts are best.

Wear a good pair of safety gloves. Common welding gloves will suffice, but if you have them available you can use gloves made of Kevlar or Zetex. Remove loose or dangling jewelry. And it's absolutely essential that you wear a pair of safety glasses to block infrared radiation. If you follow sensible safety procedures and proceed with care you'll soon see why combing can be one of the most exciting kiln glass processes.

• **Obtain the combing rod**

Combing rods can be purchased or can be made from simple household materials. Purchased rods should have a wooden handle and a metal end with a blunt tip. Some have a slight bend, but this isn't essential. Avoid rods that are metal from end to end, as these may conduct electricity if accidentally touched to hot kiln elements.

To make your own combing rod, start with a wooden rod that's at least three feet long. A broom handle or similar stick works well. Get a stainless steel or brass hook (not one made of aluminum or copper). The end of the hook should be blunt, rather than coming to a point like a nail. Screw the hook into one end of the broom and you'll have a combing tool that will work well and last a long time.

• **Prepare for combing**

If your combing rod has a long wooden handle, then soak it in a bucket of water for at least a day

A typical combed piece, as it emerges from the kiln. To create this kind of design, cut strips of glass 3/8″ (9 mm) wide, then turn them on edge and place them side by side on the kiln shelf. The combing process will do the rest. (Photo by the author, combed piece courtesy of Patty Gray and Tony Smith.)

prior to combing. The purpose of this soaking is to help ensure that the heat of the kiln doesn't cause the wooden part of the rod to catch fire. If your rod only has a short wooden handle (like the commercial rod pictured at left), soaking is not required, but it's still good practice to keep a bucket of fresh water close by for use during the combing operation.

There are a number of different ways to arrange the glass for combing. The most common is to simply cut strips of glass approximately 3/8″ (9 mm) wide, turn them on edge, stand them side by side on a prepared kiln shelf. Another option is to start with a base layer of clear glass and place smaller pieces of glass to form a second layer on top. This approach requires minimal preparation time and is a good way to utilize scraps of glass of any size.

Both precise patterns and random arrangements work well. The objective is to create an arrangement of glass that is 1/4″ to 3/8″ in total thickness (6 to 9 mm).

One very important key to good combing is to make sure you have enough glass. Always use at least 1/4″ (6 mm) thickness of glass, with 3/8″ (9 mm) being preferable. If you don't use

enough glass, then it's likely you will develop unwanted holes as the glass heats and flows.

Arrange the glass strips on the kiln shelf as for a normal firing. Glass will sometimes spread during a combing firing, so make certain to leave at least two inches between the edges of the glass and the sides of the kiln shelf. You want to avoid the disaster of glass flowing off the shelf and onto the floor of the kiln.

Fire on either fiber paper or kiln wash, but not thinfire shelf paper. If you kiln wash, use a slightly heavier application of kiln wash than normal and expect that you'll only get a single firing from the application. Thinfire shelf paper should never be used for combing.

- **Fire to 1700F/927C**

Once your glass is arranged in the kiln, begin the firing. With narrow strips the risk of thermal shock is very low so you can heat up as quickly as your kiln allows. No bubble squeeze is necessary. Keep increasing the temperature until it reaches 1700F/927C, then soak for a few minutes. At this temperature, the glass glows a very bright red.

- **Put on your safety gear and get ready**

Remember, it's best to wear a long-sleeved cotton shirt, safety glasses that shield your eyes from infrared radiation, and sturdy gloves that can withstand the heat. As always, avoid dangling jewelry and synthethic fabrics. Put on the safety equipment, then get ready to comb.

If your combing rod has been soaking in water, remove the tool and wipe the metal tip to remove excess moisture and possible contaminants.

- **Turn off the kiln**

Once the temperature reaches 1700F/927C, you should turn off the kiln. Never reach into a kiln with the power turned on, especially with a metal-tipped rod in hand. If metal touches the electrified elements, you could get a shock. So turn off the kiln, grab your combing rod, and open the kiln. Here's where it helps to have a friend to manage the door while you concentrate on combing.

Be prepared for the gust of extremely hot air that will flow from the kiln when it's initally opened. Wait just an instant before leaning forward to peer into the kiln and start the combing process.

- **Comb**

Reach into the kiln with the combing rod, taking care not to touch the sides or roof of the kiln with the tool. Draw the metal tip firmly across the glass. Imagine that you are combing about half of the way through the glass. You don't want to comb so hard that you go all the way through the glass and touch the kiln shelf.

The glass will be soft, but not watery, similar to molasses or stiff honey. You can either push the tool away from your body or reach and pull it toward yourself. Straight lines are easiest, but with experience you'll be comfortable with curved lines and more intricate patterns as well.

After several passes across the glass, you'll notice that some of the red color has faded and the edges closest to the opening of the kiln will be darker in appearance. This is a sign that the glass is beginning to cool. As it cools, it will become more difficult to comb. That's your cue to stop combing, close the kiln, and start heating the glass once more.

Depending on the particular pattern you're trying to create, it may be necessary to reheat the glass several times before you feel that the job is done. That's perfectly fine, just close the lid of the kiln, turn it back on, and reheat back to 1700F/927C. Allow the glass to soak for a few minutes at that temperature, then turn off the kiln and comb again.

Some people add frit or stringer to the glass while it is molten. This results in unique patterns, but be careful if you try this. Never reach into the kiln with a plastic container of frit or stringer; instead, use containers that can withstand the heat.

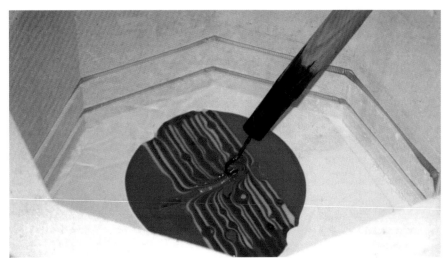

Using a combing rod to manipulate strips of glass in the kiln. Top loading kilns, such as the one shown here, are hotter to work in than front loading or clamshell designs. (Photo by the author.)

If you move too slowly or try to comb across the glass too many times, the metal tip may overheat and become stuck to the glass. Don't panic if this happens. Instead, just lift the stick a few inches up. Hesitate an instant to allow the glass to cool and harden a bit, then pull back and twist the rod sharply to one direction. This should break the metal tip loose from the glass. A helper can also assist by reaching in with a gloved hand and helping break the glass strand. Once loose, clean the tip with water and a soft cloth. Close the kiln, allow the glass to reheat to combing temperature, then try again.

• **Finish the firing cycle**

Once you're satisfied that the combing is done, allow the glass to heat one final time to smooth out the impressions left by the rod. You can do this by continuing the firing to 1500F/816C and holding for about ten minutes to allow the glass to level out. After this hold, allow the kiln to cool naturally. Stop to anneal as you would with any fused glass piece. For combing, as with many high temperature activities, a slightly longer than normal annealing process is recommended.

• **And clean the finished piece**

Sometimes you can complete the combing without picking up too much kiln wash, but at times the kiln wash will be caked onto the glass. If this happens, you'll need to sandblast or otherwise clean the kiln wash from the underside.

The vitrigraph kiln

Originally developed by Rudi Gritsch at Bullseye Glass Company, the vitrigraph kiln is a very effective way to quickly create abstract stringers and threads of glass that can be used as design elements on fused pieces.

The basic setup is fairly simple. Start with a small kiln, such as the Evenheat Hotbox or Olympic Hotsie (pictured on page 23). These kilns are approximately 8″ by 8″ by 6″ (20 by 20 by 15 cm)with a separate top, bottom, and middle.

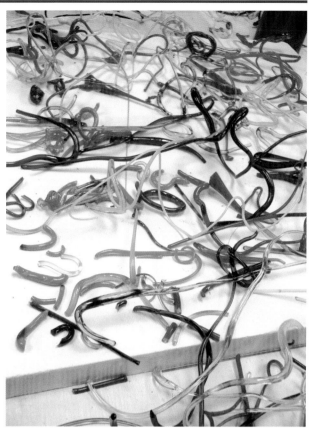

An assortment of vitrigraph stringers, fresh from the vitrograph kiln. (Photo by Jody Danner Walker.)

The middle contains the elements, the top and bottom are separate components that can be removed when required.

In addition to the kiln, you'll need a piece of 1″ thick (2.5 cm) fiber board approximately 12″ (30 cm) square. Cut a 2″ diameter (5 cm) hole in the center of the board. When prepared, the fiber board will replace the bottom segment of the kiln.

The next step is to mount the kiln assembly overhead, with the main body and top lid of the kiln centered on the fiber board bottom. The kiln should be mounted approximately six feet (1.8 meters) above the floor. This can be done by using brackets to mount the kiln to the wall or by supporting the kiln with a ladder or similar structure. The photo at the top of page 151 shows one approach, with the fiber board bottom supported by metal angle iron. Whichever mounting method is used, the key is to create a stable and safe platform to support the fiber board and kiln assembly.

"Dancing Grand Prismatic" by Jody Danner Walker. Kilnformed, with enamels and tack fused elements, including vitrigraph stringers. (Photo courtesy of the artist.)

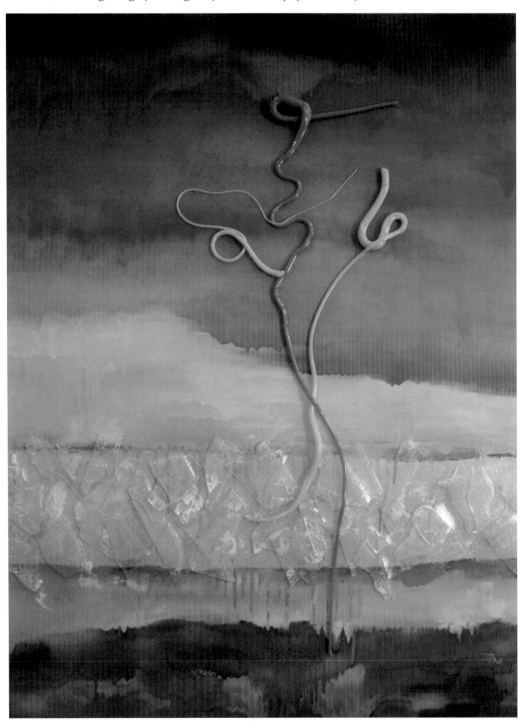

Making stringers with a vitrigraph kiln is both fun and exciting. Just be sure to wear proper safety equipment, such as gloves and glasses that shield the eyes from infrared radiation. (Photo by Jody Danner Walker.)

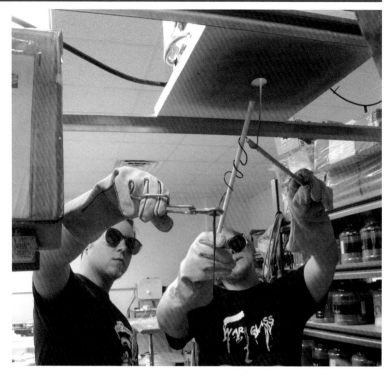

The final piece of equipment needed is a terra cotta flower pot. Use a pot that's free of cracks and that easily fits in the kiln. Fill the pot with scrap glass. Any color of glass can be used. It's possible to mix colors, but using a single color will usually create stringers with richer colors. Don't use pieces of glass that are smaller than coarse size frit. Don't kiln wash the pot.

Place the pot inside the kiln, with the hole in the bottom of the pot centered over the hole in the fiber board. Set the lid of the kiln in place and begin the firing.

Fire no faster than 500F/278C per hour from room temperature to approximately 1700F/927C and then hold the temperature steady. After a few moments, a bright trail of molten glass will come through the hole in the bottom of the kiln.

To manipulate the glass, you'll need a good pair of gloves and safety glasses that block infrared radiation. As with any high temperature activity, avoid synthetic materials and dangling jewelry.

For a distance of approximately two feet (61 cm), starting at the hole in the fiber board, the molten glass will be malleable. It's possible to shape the glass using tongs, metal pipes, graphite rods, even a gloved hand. You can even use a metal tray to catch the glass as it falls from the kiln.

Many people find that having a helper will make the process go smoother. Have one person manipulate the glass while a second person stands by to assist. A pair of glass shears (or even sturdy tin snips) can be used to cut the glass strands to size. A helper can also fine tune the temperature of the kiln, adjusting it higher or lower to help control the thickness of the vitrigraph stringers.

It's a good idea to place a metal sheet or square of tile on the floor beneath the kiln. The glass will still be hot for some time, so it's good to have a place to hold it while it cools.

When the pot empties, you can add more glass and continue the heating and pulling process. Just make certain to turn the power off before reaching into the kiln. Fill the pot very carefully, keeping glass away from the kiln elements and surrounding fire brick, which can be damaged by molten glass. Adding cold glass to a hot pot can also cause the glass to shatter and pop, so make sure to wear safety glasses and gloves.

If you change colors, there will be a period of mixed colors before the last of the old color runs out and the new begins.

151

Chapter 16

Bottles and recycled glass

Bottle slumping • Fusing and casting recycled glass • Making recycled glass tiles

Fusing with recycled glass isn't difficult. However, achieving satisfactory results requires an understanding of the basic concepts of glass fusing. Of special importance are the concepts of devitrification, incompatibility, and thermal shock.

Recycled glass has a much greater tendency to devitrify than glass specifically made for fusing. After firing, the glass will tend to lose its shine and take on a matte finish. It can also wrinkle slightly in places and become whitish as well. Use a devitrification spray to help prevent this problem.

In addition to the potential for devitrification, fusing recycled glass can lead to incompatibility issues. Because the manufacturer isn't making glass for use in a kiln, the glass made today may not be compatible with glass made days, weeks, or years ago. Consequently, haphazardly fusing two or more pieces of recycled glass together can lead to incompatibility cracks. To avoid this

A flattened glass bottle. This effect is fairly easy to achieve. (Photo by the author.)

problem, fuse together only pieces of glass that come from the same larger piece.

Thermal shock, the cracking of glass from being heated too quickly, can occur when fusing thicker pieces of glass, such as large wine bottles and thick glass insulators. Slow down the rate of heating to prevent thermal shock.

Bottle slumping

It's hard to understand the fascination that some people have with flattening glass bottles in a kiln. Perhaps it stems from the thought of creating something from an item that would be discarded or carted away. Or maybe there's a sense of wonder from changing the shape of something as basic as an empty wine bottle. In any case, flattening bottles (commonly called "bottle slumping") is by far the most common way to fuse with recycled glass.

The process of bottle slumping isn't nearly the same as slumping fused glass. Instead, bottle slumping involves heating a bottle in a kiln until it flattens out against the shelf. This takes place at around the standard fusing temperature of 1480F/804C.

Bottles can be slumped directly on a kiln shelf that's been prepared with kiln wash or a layer of fiber paper or thinfire. If a mold is used, it's only to create a shape other than just a flattened bottle against the shelf.

Also, note that bottles can vary greatly from color to color and manufacturer to manufacturer. Even two bottles that appear to be the same can actually perform quite differently in the kiln. As with many glass processes, experimentation and good notes are the keys to success.

• **Preparation**

The process of slumping bottles in a kiln starts with cleaning the bottle thoroughly. A dirty bottle is much more likely to devitrify than a clean one. Some people also apply a devit spray to the bottle to help prevent devitrification. This is recommended for most blue and amber bottles and is also helpful for other colors as well.

Some labels are actually sandblasted or fired permanently into the bottle with glass paint or enamels. If your bottle has this kind of label, count your blessings.

In most cases, the first part of the cleaning process is the removal of the label from the bottle. If your bottle has a sandblasted label or a label that has been fired permanently onto the bottle with glass paint or enamels, then the bottle can be fired with the label intact. But in most cases the label will need to be removed. The exact removal process depends on the type of label.

Paper labels will not survive the heat of the kiln. In most cases, the label is affixed to the bottle with glue, so removing the label is a matter of heating the glue slightly, so that the label slides off the bottle. This can be done with a heat gun, a hair dryer, or by placing the bottle in a microwave oven for a few moments. Once the label is removed, the area can be cleaned with mineral spirits, acetone, or a product like "Goo Gone."

If saving the label isn't a priority, the bottle can be soaked in warm water. After a few minutes, the label will come off and the bottle can be cleaned. Natural solvents such as "De-Solve-It" or "Undo" (U.S. brands) can also be used. Petroleum based solvents do not work as well as natural ones. These products are sprayed onto

the label. After about fifteen minutes, the label will slide off easily.

Once the label has been removed, clean the bottle with warm water and soap. Allow it to dry thoroughly before firing.

Place the bottle on a kiln shelf that has been covered with kiln wash, fiber paper, or thinfire shelf paper. Lay the bottle on its side. It's not essential, but some people place a piece of wire in the neck to form a wire loop which can be used to hang the bottle after slumping. Use high temperature nichrome wire or twisted copper. Around 20 gauge wire works well, although there may be a need to clean the wire after firing in some cases. If firing on a mold, rather than directly on the shelf, make certain that the mold has been coated with kiln wash before firing.

• **Firing schedule**

Fire the kiln to 1100F/593C and hold for 10 minutes. The rate of temperature increase should be no more than 500F/278C degrees per hour. Some people fire as fast as 800F/444C per hour, but be aware that the faster you fire the more likely the bottle is to crack from thermal shock.

Continue firing the kiln at 250F/139C per hour to 1300F/704C, then fire as fast as your kiln allows to 1480F/804C. Hold the temperature constant until the bottle has flattened to the degree you want. Usually this takes around 10 minutes.

After the bottle flattens, start the cooling and annealing process. For large pottery kilns, you can simply turn off the kiln and allow it for cool with the lid closed overnight. For kilns equipped with a controller, cool the kiln to 1030F/554C and hold the temperature there for about an hour. Then continue cooling at 100F/56C per hour until the temperature reaches 750F/399C. At that point it's generally safe to turn the kiln off and allow it to cool naturally to room temperature.

Modify this schedule by firing to a slightly higher or lower temperature (or holding for more or less time) if the bottles are not flattened the way you'd like them. Some bottles will capture large air bubbles just below the neck. Firing slower between 1100F/593C and 1300F/704C or adding a bubble soak at 1250F/677C may help minimize trapped air bubbles.

If kiln wash sticks to your bottle, try firing to a lower temperature and soaking longer. Or switch to a better brand of kiln wash. Larger and thicker than normal bottles will require slower firing rates and longer annealing cycles.

Fusing and casting recycled glass

The key to successfully fusing and casting recycled glass is to only use glass that comes from the same sheet or bottle. Trying to fuse together glass from different pieces or bottles, and especially glass with different colors, is almost certainly a recipe for a compatibility disaster.

Another significant issue with using recycled glass is that it devitrifies much more quickly than ordinary fusible art glass. This underscores the need to spend additional time cleaning the glass. Any impurities left on the glass act as "seeds" for devitrification, resulting in glass with a surface finish that may not be attractive. Also, note that devitrification will be more likely if you fire with a long soak at a high temperature. Heat from a kiln's top elements, as opposed to heat from side elements, also makes devitrification more likely.

When recycled glass is used in a casting, it will tend to become more matte in appearance. Some say it looks more like stone and less like glass. Devitrification can even make the glass look a bit like marble or limestone.

Generally, recycled glass will need to be fired to a slightly higher temperature than art glass. 1550F/843C works well. The annealing soak should take place between 1000F/538C and 1030F/554C. After three or four firings the glass has a tendency to stiffen and will not flow as well as it does during the first firing.

Note that the greenish tint in standard window glass may become more pronounced if the glass is used in a casting or thicker fused item.

Making recycled glass tiles

The process of making glass tiles from recycled glass begins with the glass. It's not enough to simply throw a random assortment of glass into the kiln and fire. Instead, try to use glass that has been sorted by color or type. Pay special attention to cleanliness; the cleaner the glass, the more likely you are to have success.

Experimentation is key. Try different colors and color combinations, as well as different types of glass. Vary the fusing temperature to find the one that works well with your glass. Keep notes to see which combinations work well and which don't. And remember, any time you switch glasses, you may need to start the experimentation again.

To make tiles, start with a simple square mold made from vitrious clay and one half to one inch (12 to 25 mm) deep. The mold, which can be textured if desired, must be coated with kiln wash. Use glass that has been broken into small pieces. Varying the piece size will change the look of the finished tile and may require a change in the desired firing temperature.

Load the mold with the glass pieces. Remember that, after firing, the glass will settle significantly (up to half the starting volume). Some people add water to the glass to keep glass dust down during the packing process.

After the mold is loaded, fire it in a kiln at 500F/260C per hour to 1100F/593C, then hold for 10 minutes. Continue firing 240F/139C per hour to 1300F/704C, followed by firing as fast as the kiln allows to 1600F/871C. This higher than normal temperature will quickly fuse bottle and related kinds of glass. Generally only a five minute soak is required, but there is ample room for varying the temperature and soak time until you achieve the desired results.

Cool and anneal as described in the section on bottle slumping. The finished piece will probably require sanding or sandblasting. It can be used with either side up; the side against the mold will be more matte in appearance.

Chapter 17

More about slumping

Key principles • The significance of depth • The concept of span • More difficult slumps • Drop rings • Floral formers

One of the most difficult things for the beginning fuser to learn is the right temperature for slumping. Slump too fast or at too high a temperature and the piece is liable to shift or distort. Slump too slow or too low and your patience wears thin before the piece is done. Finding the middle ground – the temperature and time that's Goldilocks right – is a big part of what separates the novice slumper from the expert.

Part of what makes slumping difficult is that the right temperature isn't as simple as just looking in a slumping "cookbook" and firing appropriately. The right slumping schedule depends on the size and shape of the mold being used, so a single schedule won't fit every situation. Moreover, since every kiln is different, the specific firing suggestions made in this chapter should only be considered as starting points. It's far more important to understand the basic principles of slumping than it is to slavishly follow a particular firing schedule or pre-programmed schedule.

Key principles

- **Make corrections to your piece before slumping, not after**

If your fused piece has dull patches, misshapen edges, or other imperfections, make corrections prior to slumping the piece, rather than after. It's far easier, for example, to grind and fire polish prior to slumping than to try to remove imperfections once the piece has taken on the shape of a bowl or platter.

- **Remember that slump firings usually need to be slower to avoid thermal shock**

Most slump firings involve pieces that have already been fused together. As a result, the pieces are thicker and must be fired slower from room temperature to 1100F/593C. Fire 1/4″ (6 mm) thick pieces at around 300F/167C per hour in this range. Fire even slower for pieces that are thicker, have metal inclusions, or are tack fused. Fire slower also in kilns with only side elements or if your mold is close to the elements.

- **Slump at as low a temperature as practical**

The higher the slumping temperature, the more likely the piece is to deform during the firing. It's far better to slump for half an hour at 1150F/621C, than it is to slump five minutes at 1250F/677C. So keep your top slumping temperature as low as possible. Never exceed 1300F/704C. In most situations, you shouldn't need to exceed 1250F/677C and there are artists who keep their top slumping temperature below 1200F/649C at all times.

- **Avoid trying to both fuse and slump in the same firing**

Since fusing generally takes place at temperatures above 1350F/732C and slumping is best at temperatures below 1300F/704C, attempting to do both in a single firing is usually a recipe for disaster.

- **Don't expect your piece to pick up a great deal of texture from the mold**

Some slumping molds are highly textured, with elaborate designs in the lower parts of the mold. Slumping temperatures are not high enough to pick up the texture from these designs, so the results will often be disappointing. Instead, fuse the piece flat on the textured surface of your choosing, then slump in a regular mold. In this way, the texture acquired during the fuse will remain after the slump.

- **Watch carefully and take good notes when using unfamiliar molds**

The first time you use an unfamiliar mold, it's critical to keep an eye on the firing to ensure that the piece slumps properly. Fire to 1100F/593C, then fire at a rate of 100F/56C per hour until the piece slumps about half way into the mold. Hold at that temperature until the slump completes. You may need to peek into the kiln during the hold period to check on the progress of the slump and verify that the piece has slumped completely. Note the temperature and the hold time required in your firing log for future use. That way, you'll have the information you need to fire the piece unattended in the future.

The significance of depth

The deeper the mold, the more difficult it is to slump. That's why the basic square slumper mold, which only requires a drop of an inch (25 mm) or less, is often recommended for beginners. But as your experience increases, it's normal to want to slump deeper, more difficult shapes.

The key to success with these deeper slumps is patience. Obviously, a deeper slump will take longer than a shallow one. It's possible to speed up the slump by firing to a higher temperature, but that will almost always result in a piece that slumps unevenly or stretches out of shape. Instead, accept that a deeper slump will take longer, and simply plan on a longer than normal hold. A hold of more than half an hour is not unusual. Some artists have been known to hold for three hours or more to allow a particularly deep slump to take place.

For really deep or difficult slumps, it's sometimes necessary to slump multiple times. This requires a different mold for each slump, starting with a fairly shallow mold and continuing with deeper molds until the final shape is acheived. A series of three molds is usually sufficient for going from a flat blank to a very deep finished piece. The firing schedule should also vary for each of these molds.

The concept of span

We all know what "depth" means – it's simply a measure of how far the glass has to drop in the mold. But the concept of "span" is a bit more complicated. By span, we mean the distance across the lowest parts of the mold. For a regular bowl shape, a mold with a 12″ diameter has a greater span than a mold with an 8″ diameter.

Smaller spans require higher slumping temperatures. A bowl that's twenty inches wide (50 cm), for instance, will slump easily at temperatures as low as 1100F/593C, while a smaller bowl (say, with a span of three inches) doesn't slump easily without a very long soak or a slumping temperature that approaches or exceeds 1300F/704C. The higher temperature makes uneven slumping more likely. As a result, smaller bowls are often more difficult to slump than larger ones.

If you put more than one mold in the kiln at the same time, take care that the spans of the individual pieces (as well as the depth being slumped) are close to the same. If you mix molds with different spans in the same firing, you risk over-firing some pieces and under-firing others.

More difficult slumps

Slumping deeper pieces or pieces with very small spans are not the only difficult slumps. Many other situations involve using molds with characteristics that require caution when slumping. Here are suggestions for a few of the most common situations.

- **Molds with steep drops and narrow or non-existent rims**

For molds that drop two inches (50 mm) or more, molds with a rim of at least 1/2″ (12.5 mm) tend to be easier to use than molds with little or no rim. That's because the glass has a greater tendency to slide down the sides of the mold when there's no rim for support. This can lead to uneven slumps or to the glass sliding down the edges of the mold.

The best way to fire this kind of mold is to slump at a fairly low temperature, in the range of 1200F/649C to 1225F/663C. Hold at the slumping temperature for an hour to an hour and a half, or even longer if necessary. This longer soak at a fairly low temperature will give the glass time to slump down into a mold with a minimum of distortion.

Square molds with fairly steep drops are also likely to be problematical. With a square mold, the glass will pull in more in the middle of the sides than it will in the corners, giving the molds a characteristic "dogbone" shape. This is difficult, if not impossible, to avoid entirely, but combining a longer slump at a lower temperature with a initial fused blank that is thicker than two layers will likely yield the best results.

- **Slumping over deep ceramic molds**

A general principle for slumping is that it's preferable to slump into ceramic molds and over molds made of stainless steel. A corollary of this principle is that it's difficult to slump over a ceramic mold that has steep sides like an upside down tumbler or mixing cup.

Molds that both slump and drape, such as this one, are a bit more difficult to use than molds that only do one thing. The narrow ledges on each side of the slumped area also complicate slumping and can cause a slight dogboning if not slumped carefully. (Photos by the author.)

There are two possible approaches to slumping over this kind of ceramic mold. The first is to cover the mold with fiber paper, so that the glass is kept from contracting tightly around the ceramic mold as it cools. The danger of this approach is that fiber paper changes the slumping characteristics of glass and often dictates a higher slumping temperature than desired.

A second approach is to create a slumping blank that is larger than would normally be required for the mold. For an upside down tumbler mold, the width of the blank can be the normal width, but the length should be around twice as long as normal. When this shape is slumped over the mold, the overlap will touch the kiln shelf on either side of the mold, allowing the glass to be easily removed when the firing is complete.

- **Molds that both slump and drape**

If these molds are well designed, they don't have to be difficult to use. But they more troublesome than a typical slumping mold. To fire them successfully, start by realizing that draping will occur first, followed by slumping into the depression in the mold. Fire slowly (around 100F/56C per hour) from 1100F/593C to your slumping temperature, then hold as long as necessary for the slumping to complete. This kind of mold generally requires a longer than normal hold time.

Drop ring mold, cut from Ceramaguard ceiling tile. After applying kiln wash, the mold will be ready to use. One advantage of Ceramaguard is that it the space around the hole, as well as the size and shape of the hole, mold can be customized as desired. (Photo by the author.)

• **Molds with multiple spans**

Complex molds that have more than one slumped area are often difficult to slump, especially when the various slumped areas have different spans. That's because the areas of the mold with narrow spans need a higher slumping temperature than areas with wider spans.

This type of mold should be avoided if possible, especially if the mold has a narrow or non-existent rim. But if you must use one then keep a close eye on the piece during the slumping portion of the firing. Because of the long time required to slump areas with a narrow span, it's easy to overfire the mold and cause distortions or excessive dogboning in the areas that slump first.

Drop rings

Firing the drop ring requires patience and careful observation, but the diversity of shapes that can be created often makes it worth the effort. Potential shapes range from simple bowls, vases, and sinks to more complex sculptural forms.

Most commercial drop ring molds are a simple ring of vitreous clay, around six to eight inches (15 to 20 cm) in diameter. These rings have a three to four inch (7.5 to 10 cm) hole in the center and a narrow rim, around two inches (5 cm) in width. To use the mold, prop it on kiln furniture at the desired height above the kiln shelf. When fired with a fused blank on top, the glass slumps through the mold and down to the kiln shelf.

Placing the mold directly on the kiln shelf, or propped up to a few inches above the shelf, will create a simple bowl or platter. Raising it higher is necessary for large bowls such as sinks or to create an elongated vase shape with a rim around it like a top hat.

• **Making a drop ring**

Hand made molds are more versatile than commercial ones and are surprisingly easy to make. These can be made from fiber board or vermiculite board, but the least expensive option is Ceramaguard ceiling tile.

Start with a piece of Ceramaguard of the desired size. The holes in a commercial mold are usually round, but they can be any shape you can imagine, so long as the hole is at least three inches (7.5 cm) across. Don't be afraid to try ovals, squares, or even elaborate kidney shapes. Use a Sharpie or similar pen to draw the desired hole shape onto the board, then carefully cut along the line with a craft knife or similar tool.

Once the hole is cut, pre-fire the Ceramaguard to 1300F/704C to burn out any binders and encourage the paint on one side of the tile to flake off. Since the paint will continue to flake off during the first few firings, it's best to use the mold with the painted side down. After pre-firing, the mold will need to be kiln washed prior to use.

• **Creating the blank**

Fuse a glass blank the appropriate size and thickness for your mold. Use any design you wish.

The size of the blank should be at least two inches (5 cm) larger than the hole in the mold. If the blank is too close to the edge of the hole, it can slip into the hole during the firing, ruining the piece.

Left: Two views of drop ring setup. The fused blank should be cented over the hole in the mold. As it fires, it drops through the mold until it touches the floor of the kiln. Careful observation is necessary to keep the piece from slumping too far.

Above: Finished drop ring piece. (Photos by the author.)

The thickness of the blank depends on the distance between the drop ring and the top surface of the kiln shelf. For drops up to four inches (10 cm), the fused blank should be at least 1/4" (6 mm) thick. An additional 1/8" (3 mm) of thickness is required for each additional two inches (5 cm) of drop. If the glass isn't thick enough, it will stretch too thin during the firing and won't be durable enough to use.

• **Preparing to fire**

Start with a kiln washed mold. Don't forget to apply wash to the inside edges of the hole in the tile. Allow time for the mold to dry before firing or fire the mold to 500F/260C to dry it quickly if needed.

Use kiln furniture or fire bricks to prop the drop ring at the desired height. Take care that the stilts don't block the hole in the center of the ring. Place the glass blank on top of the ring, then take a few moments to ensure that the hole is in the desired location beneath the glass. Make certain that there's at least an inch and a half (3.8 cm) of glass extending on all sides of the hole.

• **The basic firing schedule**

The firing schedule for a drop ring is similar to the schedule for any complex mold. Fire at about 300F/167C from room temperature to

1100F/593C to avoid thermal shock. When the temperature reaches 1100F, hold for ten minutes, then fire at 100F/56C until the temperature reaches 1250F to 1275F (677C to 691C). Hold until the glass slumps, then anneal and cool for the thickness of your glass.

The critical part of this firing is the slump, which must be monitored very closely. If you need to open the kiln to check the progress of the firing, do so briefly, so as to allow only a minimum of air to escape. Make certain to wear appropriate clothing and safety glasses that shield your eyes from infrared radiation.

Patience is extremely important. As the glass soaks at the slumping temperature, it will first bulge slightly through the hole in the ring. As the soak continues, more and more of the glass will poke through. It will probably take half an hour or more for the glass to droop far enough to touch the kiln shelf below. Once it touches, you will need to continue to monitor the glass until the base takes on the desired shape. Be careful not to over fire or the base of the glass will distort unacceptably.

Once you are happy with the appearance of the piece, stop the slump and then anneal and cool as normal. For particularly difficult slumps where the glass is moving more quickly, it may be necessary to carefully open the door or lid of your kiln to allow some heat to escape and reach annealing temperature more quickly.

Doug Randall, "El Camino Real." Fused, drop formed, cut and coldworked, hand polished. (Photo courtesy of the artist.)

With patience and careful observation, the drop ring mold can create unique shapes that aren't possible with any other kind of mold.

• **Tack fusing and slumping in one firing**

By monitoring a drop ring firing carefully, it's possible to fire so that the glass both tack fuses and slumps in a single firing. This novel approach requires a firing schedule that differs from the standard schedule in several respects.

Start with a single layer of glass. Choose any desired color. Cut the glass to size. This technique works best with rings that have a fairly small hole, rather than rings with a hole that is four inches (10 cm) or larger.

Place the ring in the the kiln, supported on posts or kiln brick. Place the glass on top of the ring. Then arrange smaller pieces of glass or frit on top of the base layer. These are the items that will be tack fused to the base.

Fire from room temperature to 1100F/593C. Because this is only one layer of glass, you can fire as fast as 500F/278C per hour. Once the glass reaches 1100F, hold for 10 minutes. Then fire as quickly as your kiln can fire to 1250F/677C.

Hold at 1250F for 45 minutes. This is lower than a normal tack fuse temperature, but the long soak time will help the small pieces of glass begin to stick to the base layer. After the 45 minute soak, begin increasing the temperature once again. Go as fast as your kiln allows to between 1330 and 1380F (721 to 749C). The precise temperature depends on the glass used and the size of the hole in the drop ring mold.

Now start watching the piece. The slump should take 10 to 30 minutes to complete. Watch carefully; at this temperature the glass can move fairly quickly. Once the piece has slumped the way you like, stop the slump and then cool and anneal as in any firing. Because of the prolonged time that the glass may spend above 1300F/704C, it may be a good idea to apply a devitrification spray to the top surface of the glass prior to firing.

• **Using coldworking techniques to create more sophisticated drop ring pieces**

Many glass artists find that the rim created during the drop ring firing detracts from the beauty of the piece that drops through the mold. The solution to this dilemma is simply to remove the rim with a tile saw or similar tool.

The setup for the floral former slump calls for the glass to be placed atop a stainless floral former mold. The mold can be kiln washed or thinfire shelf paper can be used to keep the glass from sticking to the mold. The finished floral former is shown to right. (Photos by the author.)

Once the rim is removed, the edge must be shaped and polished. This can be done with a variety of techniques, ranging from using diamond hand pads and grinders to more sophisticated machines such as wet belt sanders, lap wheels, and glass lathes. When the coldworking process is complete, the finished piece will have a deep bowl shape, with a pattern that can only be created by fusing.

See Chapter 18 for more on basic coldworking machinery and techniques.

Floral formers

The floral former is a stainless steel mold, shaped like a large tumbler or mixing cup. The mold is turned upside down and glass placed on top so that it hangs over the mold. After slumping, the glass folds and drapes around the mold, creating a unique "handkerchief vase" shape.

Before using the mold, it needs to be coated with kiln wash or boron nitride, so that the glass doesn't stick to the mold during the firing. Alternatively, a piece of thinfire shelf paper can be placed on top of the mold, beneath the glass blank. The thinfire should be slightly larger than the size of the glass used. Don't use fiber paper for this mold; it changes the draping characteris-

tics of the glass and requires a higher slumping temperature that can distort the final shape.

For a standard floral former height of around 9″ (23 cm), a circle with a diameter of 10″ (25 cm) or a square with 9″ (23 cm) sides will work well. More unusual shapes are also possible. A single 1/8″ (3 mm) layer can be used, but multiple layer pieces are also common.

After the blank is prepared, place it on top of the prepared floral former mold. Any edge coldworking or fire polishing should have already been done. The piece can be centered on the mold or placed slightly askew, which will create a more lopsided and random final piece.

Fire at 300F/167C from room temperature to 1100F/593C, then hold for ten minutes. Continue firing at 100F/56C per hour, keeping a close watch on the piece as it fires. It will begin folding, first in half like a taco, and then more dramatically on all four sides. When the temperatures reaches around 1250F/677C, hold until the piece drapes around the mold to the desired degree. Then cool and anneal. Because the folds of the glass create thicker areas in the finished piece, it's a good idea to anneal soak for twice as long as you would normally.

Note that if the tips of the glass fold down and touch the kiln shelf below the mold they can flatten out and lose their shine.

Chapter 18

Coldworking and finishing

When to coldwork • Basic coldworking process • Coldworking by hand • Coldworking machinery • Building a coldworking studio • Fire polishing • Polishing sprays and waxes • Drilling holes • Creating holes while fusing • Acid polishing • Signing your work • Displaying the piece

Coldworking refers to processes that take place outside the kiln, while the glass is at room temperature. This includes everything from basic grinding and cutting activities to more elaborate processes with specialized equipment.

This chapter can only serve as a basic introduction to coldworking machinery and techniques. For a more complete discussion, check out a more comprehensive work, such as Johnathon Schmuck's *The Joy of Coldworking*.

When to coldwork

Before a piece is placed in the kiln to be fused, the glass needs to be cut to shape using glass cutting tools, as discussed in Chapter 4. This basic process is sometimes augmented with the use of a grinder or similar small shaping tool.

These initial cutting and grinding steps are important, but coldworking really begins after a piece has been fused or cast. When a fused piece emerges from the kiln, it often has rough areas that need smoothing, dull patches in need of shining, or minor imperfections in need of correction. It may need to be carved or cut into smaller pieces. The edges may need shaping or smoothing. Holes may need drilling. Or the piece may need to be prepared for display.

All of these situations require coldworking. The time required may just be a few seconds to use a diamond hand pad to remove sharp needles from the edge of a fused piece to several hours to dramatically recontour a piece using a sandblaster or glass lathe. More than one coldworking process may be required before the work is finished.

For basic bowls and related slumped items, coldworking is an essential step that's required after fusing and before slumping. Misshapen edges won't look better after slumping. Blemishes and imperfections will not magically disappear during the slumping process. A good rule of thumb for pieces to be slumped is to spend time coldworking prior to slumping to make the slumped piece look as attractive as possible.

Remember, it often requires more equipment and specialized knowledge to coldwork a piece after it has been slumped, so get in the habit of examining each piece after the fuse to determine how you can make it better before you slump.

While it's possible to fuse and slump without investing heavily in the coldworking process, time spent coldworking is often time well spent. It can make the difference between glass pieces that look amateurish and those that have a finished, professional appearance.

Using a diamond hand pad to smooth out the top surface of a piece. (Photo by the author.)

Basic coldworking process

Before coldworking, make certain the piece is at room temperature. Pieces can crack if they're coldworked while still warm. This is especially critical for thicker pieces or for cast pieces, which can appear cool on the outside but still have significant heat within. With large pieces, it's a good idea to wait a full day for the piece to completely cool before starting the coldworking process.

A variety of different coldworking tools and machines are described in the next two sections of this chapter, but regardless of the tool used, there are several basic principles to keep in mind.

Any time a piece is cut with a saw or shaped with a grinder or similar tool, the shine is removed from the piece. It's possible to restore the shine by re-firing the piece (a process called "fire polishing") or by using coldworking tools. It's also possible to use coldworking techniques to create a smooth matte finish on the piece, rather than a bright shine.

Restoring a shine or creating a matte finish both require using a series of finer and finer abrasives to wear away the glass by scratching the surface until the scratches get so small they can't be seen. The abrasives used vary in size (called "grits),

with coarser ones being around 60 grit and finer ones being 400 grit or more. These abrasives are made of silicon carbide or of very fine diamonds, and are can be used loose or afffixed to pads, discs, or belts.

Regardless of the machine or medium used, the basic process is the same. Start with a coarse grit and finish with a fine one. Coarse grits, size 100 or less, are normally used for the initial pass on an edge or bottom surface. These remove a considerable amount of glass, but they also leave a very rough finish that will require further processing.

After using the coarse grit to even out the surface of the glass, continue with a finer one. With many pieces, the edge is already fairly smooth and the coarsest grits can be skipped. A medium grit, in the range of 100 to 200, will continue the smoothing process. It's often following with an even finer abrasive, with a grit of around 400 or 600. The key is to start with the coarser abrasives and finish with the finer ones. It's critical to allow each abrasive used to do its work before moving on to the next.

After the finest grit is used (400 to 600), the glass will not be clear or shiny. It will still appear whitish and a bit dull. More steps are required to make the glass shine. Or fire polishing can be

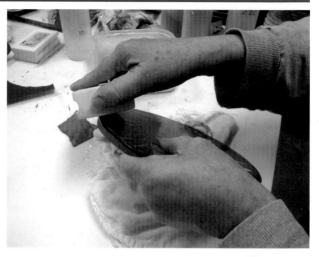

A diamond hand pad is an excellent tool for smoothing out the edges of glass. The edges of the piece to the left were finished by hand using a set of diamond hand pads. Above, a 400 grit pad is used to do some final smoothing on a piece getting ready to be slumped. It's good practice to create a small bevel on the edge to prevent chipping during any additional grinding operations.

Check out page 205 for a full view of the piece to the left. (Photo above by the author, photo to left by Jody Danner Walker.)

used to obtain a shine in the kiln. Fire polishing can also help a matte finish become smoother and more attractive to the eye.

Water is essential when coldworking. The purpose of the water is twofold: to keep the glass from overheating and cracking, and to wash loose glass particles away so that the abrasives can do their job. As a general rule of thumb, the more coarse the abrasive, the more water is required.

To achieve a full polish with coldworking equipment, polishing compounds such as pumice and cerium oxide are required. These are normally available in powder form. It's possible to purchase belts and discs that have been impregnated with the compounds, or they can be mixed with water to form a slurry about the thickness of paste. By holding the glass to a revolving belt or wheel, the piece can be made to shine. As with many coldworking activities, this requires considerable practice to do well.

Coldworking by hand

Since coldworking machinery can be quite expensive, learning to coldwork by hand is essential for those who don't have unlimited resources. There's also a great satisfaction that comes from using inexpensive hand tools and simple abrasives to create a desired finish.

- **Diamond hand pads**

Diamond hand pads, available for glass artists in grits from around 60 to 600, consist of a layer of industrial diamonds adhered to a firm backing pad. To extend the life of the diamonds, they should always be used wet. Pads are especially useful for smoothing edges of fused pieces or for removing small needles or other imperfections from the edge.

Diamond hand pads need to be kept wet during use. It's also good practice to keep the glass wet. Start with a coarse grit, then continue through a succession of finer and finer grits until the edge has been smoothed sufficiently. Rinse the glass well between grits. A 400 grit finish is very smooth to the touch. If desired, it can be fire polished to make it even smoother or to restore a shine to the edges.

Needles, small projections from the edges of fused glass, can also be removed with a 400 grit diamond hand pad. Simply wet the glass and the pad and then rub the rough spots until they become smooth. Done carefully, fire polishing will not also be required.

Manufacturers of the pads include 3M and Abrasive Technology (Crystalite). Wet/dry sandpaper can be used instead of diamond hand pads, but the finish isn't usually as smooth. Sandpaper also has a much shorter lifespan than diamond hand pads.

- **Hand lapping with loose abrasives**

Loose silicon carbide can also be used to smooth glass. Most often, this is done on a flat surface of the glass, but it's also possible for working straight edges.

In addition to the abrasives, hand lapping requires a flat piece of float glass and water. Mix the abrasive with a small amount with water to form a slurry in the center of the float glass. Place the piece to be coldworked on the slurry and rub it back and forth on top of the slurry. Adjust the water if needed; the piece should move smoothly across the surface of the float. As you move the piece, move it in small circles or figure-8's on top of the float glass. Move it around 100 times, then check your progress. After several minutes, the initial grind should be complete.

Another use for hand lapping is to flatten the bottom of a large bowl. Use a small bubble level to make certain the piece remains straight and move it in circles on the loose grit. It should only take a few moments to grind a flat spot on the bottom of the bowl.

As with most coldworking techniques, this process starts with a coarse grit and then moves through a progression of finer and finer grits

until the piece has been smoothed sufficiently. If the piece is very large or unwieldy, it's also possible to use wet/dry sandpaper and loose abrasive grit to bring the slurry to the piece.

- **Powered hand grinders**

Powered hand grinders are small tools that can be used to rapidly remove glass from a piece and complete the smoothing process. They were initially developing for the countertop fabrication industry, but have become very useful for the glass artist. They're available in both electric and pneumatic configurations, with electric tools being a bit heavier and pneumatic ones requiring a very powerful compressor. These tools also require a steady source of water and can be quite messy when used.

Hand grinders have a rotating head that can accommodate a small abrasive disc. This disc, which is available in various grits, rotates rapidly when the grinder is on. Because of the small size and relatively low weight of the grinder, it can be brought directly to the piece being coldworked.

Major brands are Alpha and Calibre, but these are also made by many major tool manufacturers, such as Makita and Bosch.

- **Hand engravers and flexible shaft rotary tools**

These tools are smaller and less powerful than the powered hand grinders discussed in the previous section. But they're still useful for grinding small areas, drilling holes, and for detailed engraving tasks, such as signing finished pieces. As with most coldworking tools, these need to be used with water to keep the glass from overheating and cracking.

The Dremel is the best known of this type of tool, but it's a bit underpowered for many glass activities. The Foredom tool, available in specialist woodworking shops, has much more power and excels at engraving and hole drilling tasks. Higher end tools are available from NSK and Lasco. Dental tools, which come with their own water supply, are best of all.

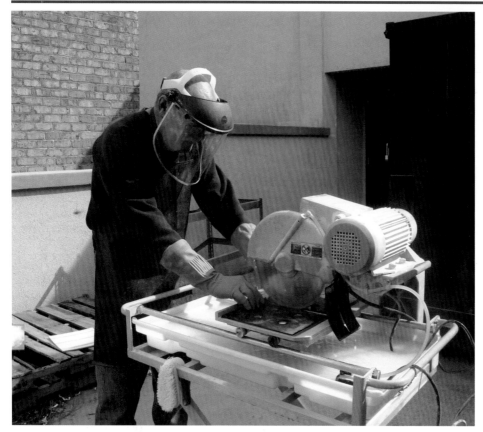

Using a large wet tile saw requires close attention to the work being cut. Wearing good safety equipment, such as this head gear, helps prevent potential injury from flying glass particles. (Photo of Lars Reuterdahl, by the author.)

Coldworking machinery

The variety of machines that can be used for coldworking is simply astounding. Many of these machines are quite expensive, however, and many have very specialized purposes. Here's a list of the most common kinds of equipment.

• **Saws**

Glass saws are used for two different purposes: cutting intricate shapes from glass and cutting glass that is too thick to be easily cut by hand. The cutting of intricate shapes is done with a ring saw, band saw, or similar saw that has a blade that is coated with small diamonds. By maneuvering a piece of glass through the blade, it's possible to cut very intricate shapes. These kinds of saws are generally used to cut glass to shape prior to fusing.

After fusing, most cutting is done with a tile saw, trim saw, or slab saw. These saws are mostly used to cut straight lines in thicker pieces of glass. When equipped with a blade made for cutting glass, these saws can trim an edge off of a fused piece and leave a finish that can be quickly cold-

worked using other machines or diamond hand pads. They're also very useful for cutting pattern bars and other thicker items.

Of all the major pieces of coldworking machinery, saws are probably the most useful. An inexpensive wet tile saw costs around $100 U.S., plus another $50 for a 7" (18 cm) blade made for cutting glass. Larger models with 10" (25 cm) blades start at around $400; premium brands can exceed $1000 in price.

Most glass saws for cutting intricate shapes cost around $400 US. These are small units that are not made for industrial use, but they can be useful for cutting intricate shapes for jewelry or decorative elements. Blades for these saws are fairly expensive, costing up to $100 US each.

• **Wet belt sanders**

The belt sander, known as a "linisher" in the Commonwealth regions, consists of a long belt that loops vertically between two sets of pulleys. A glass piece is ground by pressing it against the belt as it rotates. Since the belt is kept wet at all times, glass can be removed quickly and

166

Carol Beckett works the edge of her piece on a large wet belt sander. (Photo by the author.)

efficiently. The wet belt sander can be used for sanding down large curved areas, but it really excels at edge work. By resting the piece on a set of rollers in front of the belt, the artist can precisely control the pressure and angle of the piece against the belt.

The belts are available in a wide array of different grits, ranging from very coarse 40 grits to smooth 600 grit or finer. As with most coldworking equipment, the finishing process starts with the coarse grits and moves through a progression of grits to finish with the finest ones. A 400 grit finish is sufficient to fire polish in the kiln; it will also shine up slightly during most slumps. Cork

belts are also available for polishing glass on the wet belt sander.

A tabletop wet belt sander costs $500 to $900 US. Larger floor models exceed $2000, but with proper care will last for a lifetime. Silicon carbide belts are under $10 each. Small wet belt sanders are available from Covington; larger units from Somaca, CRL, and Bee.

• Lap wheels and rociprolaps

The lap wheel works like a record turntable, with the abrasive material on top where the record

Lap wheels are best for grinding flat surfaces, such as the bottom of a fused blank or the underside of a casting. (Photo by the author.)

would be. Glass is ground by pressing a piece against the abrasive material, which is either a wet slurry of silicon carbide or a diamond disc with a water feed mechanism to keep the glass cool as it is ground.

If wet belt sanders are best for edge work, then lap wheels are best for larger, flat surfaces, such as the bottom of a fused blank or underside of a paperweight. They also work well for grinding and smoothing a flat edge on a fused blank.

In addition to the normal progression of grits, lap wheels can also be used to polish glass using cerium oxide powder. Pieces polished on a lap wheel will generally have a brighter shine than pieces polished with cork on the wet belt sander.

The rociprolap, also called a "vibrolap," appears similar to a lap wheel that is equipped with a vibrating mechanism. A wet silicon carbide slurry is placed in a basin on top of the machine. The glass to be ground sits inside the basin and the device is turned on. After 12 to 36 hours of vibration, the piece has been ground enough to move on to the next grit. Rociprolaps can be very expensive, but they do have the advantage of doing the job with a minimum of attention.

Lap wheels vary in price from around $1000 US for units with an 8″ (20 cm) wheel to $4000 or more for larger 24″ (61 cm) models. In addition to the cost of the machine, diamond discs can easily cost over $100 each.

• **Sandblasters**

A sandblasting setup has three main components: a compressor that drives air and abrasive material through a nozzle, a closed cabinet where the work is done, and a vacuum system that removes unwanted particles from the cabinet. Sandblasting glass requires much stronger abrasives than sandblasting metal or painted walls; the most common abrasive materials are silicon carbide and aluminum oxide. Since it can be harmful if breathed, sand should never be used as an abrasive.

Sandblasting is a quick and reliable way to remove baked on kiln wash and other blemishes from glass. With a more powerful compressor, sandblasting can also be used to carve into the glass and create more intricate patterns and designs. It can even be used to blast holes in sinks or other glass pieces. An attractive matte finish can be achieved on bowls and other slumped items by blasting the underside of the piece evenly before slumping. It's also possible to fire polish blasted items to achieve either a matte finish or a brilliant shine, depending on the fired temperature. See the section on fire polishing below for more on this process.

Basic sandblasting setup, with vacuum, blasting cabinet, and compressor. (Photo by the author.)

The most expensive part of the sandblasting setup is probably the compressor. Small compressors, costing under $400 U.S., are adequate for surface blasting, but larger compressors, with a price tag of $1000 or more, are required for deeper blasting projects such as carving into a piece or blasting holes.

• **Glass lathes**

The term "lathe" refers to several different machines that have an arbor on which grinding wheels are attached. Glass is pressed against the wheel as it rotates; since water continuously drips on the wheel, glass can be ground and shaped without cracking.

In addition to being available in several grits, wheels also come in a wide variety of sizes and shapes. They can be used to carve into glass, to create unique patterns, and even to sculpt edges and rims of bowls. Wheels can be made of stone or various composite materials, but diamond wheels probably the most prevalent.

Lathes are expensive tools, but are among the most fun to use. A basic lathe setup will cost from $1200 US for a small unit to well over $3000 for a larger one. Diamond wheels are an added expense; it's not unusual to spend over $100 for each wheel.

Building a coldworking studio

Coldworking equipment can be very expensive. It's not unusual for a fused glass artist to have more money invested in coldworking equipment than in kilns. Not only can some individual pieces of equipment cost thousands of dollars, the accessory items, such as belts, discs, and wheels, can cost hundreds of dollars each. And it may be necessary to have half a dozen or more sets of belts, discs, or wheels. It's not a trivial investment.

Even though the equipment can be expensive, coldworking is an essential process for the glass artist. Often, the difference between a bowl that struggles to sell for $100 and one that sells for hundreds is the quality of the coldworked edge.

But don't despair. Coldworking studios do not have to be set up in one massive orgy of spending. It's possible to start with basic, smaller pieces of equipment and add more expensive items as your skills and needs develop. Moreover, different kinds of glass work require different kinds of equipment; if you start with a few basic tools, you'll soon learn which ones are most valuable for the kind of work you create. That will help you make more informed purchases of tools later on.

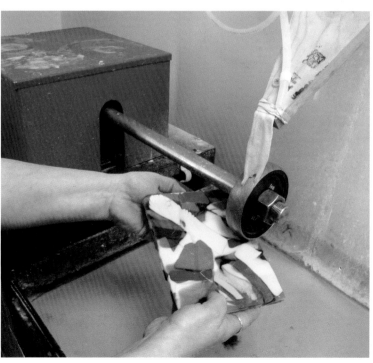

View of a glass lathe in operation. A wide variety of wheels are available, each of which makes a different mark on the glass. Lathes can be used to carve into glass, shape edges, and add texture to top and bottom surfaces. (Photo by the author.)

• Start with inexpensive manual tools

Many people will already have a small stained glass grinder. These tools are inexpensive to purchase and operate and greatly shorten the time required to shape glass and grind off minor inperfections. Grinding heads are also available for drilling holes, contouring interesting edges, and creating a channel for wire wrapping jewelry.

Aside from a grinder, the next most important piece of basic coldworking equipment is a set of diamond hand pads. These are invaluable for both touching up pieces and for edge working. Most basic coldworking activities can be performed with no more than a grinder and a set of diamond hand pads.

• Consider the purchase of a saw next

If your work requires cutting elaborate shapes in glass, then purchase a glass such such as the Taurus ring saw or a band saw from Gryphon or Diamond Tech.

Most people, however, will get more use out of a wet tile saw, which can quickly cut straight lines in thicker glass, such as fused slabs and pattern bars. Invest in a blade made specifically for cutting glass; the quality of the cut will more than offset the additional cost of the special blade.

The coldworking studio starts with a set of diamond hand pads. A 400 grit hand pads is invaluable for removing small needles from the edges of fused pieces. A full set of pads can be used to impart a beautiful matte finish to the edge of a finished piece. (Photo by the author.)

If your budget allows, spring for a saw with a 10″ (25.4 cm) overhead blade, rather than one with a 7″ (17.8 cm) blade that pokes through the cutting surface. Not only can the 10″ blade handle thicker pieces, the larger saw will cut quicker and last much longer than the 7″ version.

• Examine powered hand tools

Every studio should have a Dremel or similar tool for engraving or touching up small spots on glass surfaces. If you find that you're doing a lot of this kind of work, invest in a Foredom or larger flexible shaft rotary hand tool. This will also give you the ability to quickly drill holes.

If you already own a large compressor, give strong consideration to purchasing a pneumatic air grinder. These tools excel at quickly grinding glass. They're essential if your pieces are large or heavy enough that they're difficult to move or hold for long periods of time. An electric hand grinder is also useful for those who lack a large compressor.

• Sandblaster

If your pieces require extensive work to remove baked on kiln wash, or if you prefer a smoother or matte finish, then strongly consider investing in a sandblasting setup.

Many glass studios have a stained glass grinder. This model has both the standard grinding head (on top, on the white platform) and an additional small lap wheel (the disc below the platform) which is great for quickly straightening edges. (Photo by the author.)

The expense of the sandblaster is in the compressor, not the cabinet and vacuum. Basic cabinets can be purchase for under $200 U.S. An inexpensive shop vacuum can also be used if necessary.

If you only want to do surface blasting, a relatively inexpensive compressive that runs on regular household current (120v in the U.S.) will suffice. However, if your needs include a requirement to more deeply carve glass or to blast for more than a few minutes at a time, you'll need to obtain a compressor that runs on 240v. One advantage of purchasing a compressor is that it can be used power many other workshop tools.

• **Think hardest about the choice between a wet belt sander and a lap wheel**

Many people rush out and buy one of these two machines, or even both, without first considering the kind of work they make and which of the two will work best for them. Although the ideal studio would have both machines, it's possible to get along very well with only one or the other.

If your work centers on pieces that require more edge work, especially curved edges as in a bowl, then a wet belt sander is probably the machine of choice. On the other hand, if you create pieces that require grinding a flat surface or smoothing long straight edges, than a lap wheel may be preferable. Because of the high cost of diamond discs vs. silicon carbide belts, the ongoing maintenance cost of the lap wheel is generally higher than the ongoing cost for the wet belt sander.

Smaller versions of these machines, such as the Covington wet belt sander pictured on this page or the Crystalite lap pictured on page 167, are good starter machines. But if your work becomes larger, you'll want to trade up to larger (and more expensive) pieces of equipment.

• **Indulge in a lathe**

Of all the coldworking tools, the glass lathe is the only one that many people describe as "fun." It's more specialized than most of the other tools, but its ability to create unique textures and designs in glass is unparalleled.

A small wet belt sander, made by Covington. This is useful for grinding jewelry or edge working smaller fused items, but it won't be sufficient for large scale activities. (Photo by the author.)

Although it's important for all tools, it's especially critical to try a lathe before making a purchase. There are many different models and configurations, ranging from units adapted from bench grinders to ones specifically constructed for a lifetime of service.

Recognize also that in addition to the expense of the lathe, there will be a significant initial outlay for diamond wheels of various types to use on the lathe. Fortunately, the ongoing cost of the lathe is minimal.

Fire polishing

Although technically not coldworking -- after all, it does take place in a kiln -- fire polishing is an important tool in the glass artist's arsenal. It's most often used between fusing and slumping, to correct minor imperfections and re-shine

171

areas that have been ground, and as a final step to impart a specific finish to a flat slab.

The schedule for fire polishing should be adjusted for the thickness of the piece. It's critical not to thermal shock thick pieces by firing too quickly. It's also essential to anneal pieces properly after the fire polishing process completes.

The basic firing schedule should begin by firing from room temperature to 1100F/593C. A rate of 300F/167C per hour is sufficiently slow for most two layer pieces, but larger pieces should be fired more slowly.

After a ten minute hold at 1100F/593C, the real work of fire polishing begins by firing to the desired fire polishing temperature. The specific temperature required depends greatly on the glass used, the degree of finish on the glass prior to firing, and the kind of finish required, with the following guidelines:

• **Matte finish**

A typical fusible glass, such as Bullseye or System 96, will fire polish to a smooth, all over matte finish after around a one hour hold in the range from 1115F/602C to 1150F/621C. Float glass needs to be fire around 30F/17C higher. Some pieces can be slumped at the same time, allowing the two operations to be accomplished with a single firing.

Since each glass behaves a little differently and there is some variability in the finish prior to fire polishing, it will probably take a bit of experimentation to determine the precise holding temperature in your kiln. Use the ranges above as a starting place, then adjust as necessary.

• **Shiny finish**

Achieving a shiny finish requires a higher firing temperature and a shorter hold. For fusible glasses, try firing to somewhere in the range between 1350F/732C and 1375F/746C and hold for five to ten minutes. Float glass should be fired around 20F/11C higher.

Fire polishing at these temperatures is trickier, especially with thicker items. This is because the polishing temperature is high enough to distort the edges of the glass is the temperature is held for too long. So watch carefully to make certain that the piece doesn't distort in the heat of the kiln. Also, note that the longer the piece is held, the more likely it is to take on the texture of the kiln shelf.

Polishing sprays and waxes

There are two main types of polishing sprays: those that need to be fired in a kiln and those that do not. Each works quite differently.

Sprays that need to be fired are generally made of clear glass enamel or a similar product that matures at temperatures at or below the normal slumping range. Typically, these sprays are applied to the surface of the glass with a brush or sprayer, and then the item is fired to a designated maturation temperature and allowed to soak for 10 to 30 minutes. The specific temperature varies by product, but is generally in the range of 1100F/593C.

Some of these low-firing clear enamels (sometimes called "glass fluxes") are high in lead content, so they should not be used for surfaces that will come into contact with food. Note that some people claim that these products impart a slight haziness to the glass and do not polish as well as other polishing techniques.

A second type of polishing spray, which does not require heating in a kiln, is spray oil. These oils, which make the surface of the glass appear wet, will permanently change the look of the glass. They are applied by spraying an even coat on the glass. Fingerprints and smudges will be highlighted, so make certain that the glass is as clean as possible before applying. After spraying, wipe off any excess oil, paying special attention to areas of puddling. Allow at least half a day for the oil to thoroughly dry.

Any clear oil, even salad oil, can be used in this fashion, but commercial sprays, such as Varathane Natural Oil Finish #66 Clear are also available. Test on a piece of scrap clear glass to make certain that the oil dries clear and does not yellow.

Another kind of spray that works well but does not require firing is clear enamel or acrylic spray. These sprays, which are widely available in hardware or DIY stores, also impart a permanent, wet sheen. As with oil sprays, you should test for yellowing on a scrap of glass, then spray evenly on a clean, dry surface. Multiple coats may be used if necessary.

In addition to these sprays, items may be waxed to give a polished appearance. Carnauba wax, an exceptionally durable wax often used to polish cars, is a good choice to use on glass.

Drilling holes

In the ideal world, drilling holes in glass would be as simple as drilling in wood. Unfortunately, drilling in glass generates heat that must be dissipated by the use of water or a similar coolant. If the heat is permitted to build up, the glass will overheat and crack or shatter.

A number of different drilling techniques have been developed to cope with the dynamics of drilling glass. All have in common that the glass must be kept cool, either by placing it in a container with water or by creating a reservoir to hold water around the area to be drilled.

For drilling with a drill press or flexible shaft power tool, it's also critical to have the right kind of drill bit. Stay away from the inexpensive pointed bits available in hardware stores. Instead, use diamond core bits or triple ripple bits made specifically for use with glass. Both of these bits come in various sizes. They're diamond coated; used in the appropriate tool, then can drill a precise hole though glass in a matter of minutes.

• **Drilling holes with a grinder**

For those who've already invested in a small stained glass grinder, this is the easiest way to

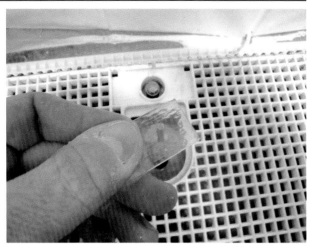

Using a grinder to drill holes in glass. (Photo by the author.)

drill a hole. Small grinding heads, generally about 1/4″ (6 mm) to 3/8″ (9 mm) in diameter, are available that fit on the shaft of the grinder. The glass is plunged onto the top of the head as it rotates and held in place until the desired hole is created.

To use this technique, start by drenching both the bit and the piece of glass with water from a damp sponge. Holding the piece firmly, press it to the top end of the bit. Grind slowly, taking care to add more water after every few seconds. It may go quicker if you have a second person use a squeeze bottle or similar device to keep the area being drilled cooled with water. As with most drilling processes, iIt will take several minutes to drill a single hole.

Using a grinder won't give you as many options for hole size as using a drill press or rotary tool, but the grinder heads usually last longer than most drill bits.

• **Drilling holes with a drill press**

The drill press, a device that holds the drill in one place and prevents irregularities caused by drill movement, will do a much better job of drilling holes than a simple hand drill. That's because it's difficult to hold a hand drill steady while drilling glass. Equipped with the proper bit, a drill press is one of the most reliable ways to drill holes in glass.

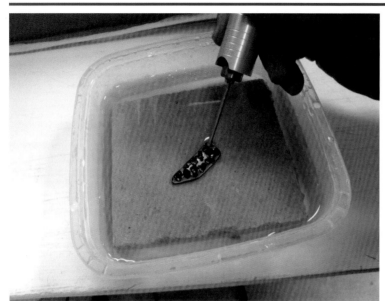

Using a flexible shaft rotary power tool to drill a hole. Note that the glass piece is placed in a pan of water on top of a scrap of wood or Ceramaguard that prevents accidently drilling through the bottom of the pan. The water keeps the piece cool as it is drilled. (Photo by the author.)

The key to successful drilling is to proceed slowly, rather than attempting to drill the hole in one go. Expect that it will take several minutes to drill a hole, even if you re using a drill bit made for glass. Move the bit into the glass, then back up slightly, so that fresh, cool water flows into the area being drilled. Then drill a bit more. Continue this process, alternately drilling and then easing up, until the hole is drilled completely through the glass. Be especially careful when the hole is almost complete; it's possible to chip the underside of the glass by drilling too quickly.

Sometimes it's possible to drill a portion of the way through the glass, then flip the piece and continue drilling from the other side. This approach, which is easiest for transparent glass, when the already drilled area can be easily seen, requires a more precise hand but will avoid chipping entirely.

Very large holes, such as for a glass sink, require a large diamond core bit. Many of these bits are available in sets which include both the appropriately sized cored bit and an additional countersink bit made for angling the top of the sink to create the drain area. Sink drilling also requires a larger drill press that can reach the center of the sink.

A drill press is available for the Dremel hand tool, but a small tabletop drill press is about the save price and will actually work better for drilling holes than a Dremel equipped with the drill press attachment.

- **Drilling holes with a flexible rotary shaft tool**

Equipped with the appropriate bit, most flexible rotary shaft tools are powerful enough to drill holes in glass. The process is not unlike the process of drilling with a drill press, in that it requires patience and a setup that will keep the glass wet at all times. The flexible shaft helps minimize the risk of shock by keeping water from the tool's motor.

Start the hole drilling process by holding the tool at a slight angle to the glass, rather than straight up and down. Gradually increase the speed of the tool, simultaneously straightening the tool so that the bit goes directly down into the glass. As with a drill press, expect that the drilling process will take several minutes. Drill slowly, with a careful hand, pausing if necessary to allow water to flow into the area being drilled. If a piece cracks during the drilling process, it's usually a sign that you're either going too fast or that the glass has become overheated.

- **Sandblasting holes**

Sandblasting is an easy way to make holes in glass. Just direct the abrasive stream toward the desired area of the glass piece and blast until a hole is formed. This approach requires a powerful compressor and creates the cleanest hole if the area around the area to be blasted is masked off to prevent a hole being created in the wrong place. Use a resist at least 9 mil thick if you plan to blast aggressively.

Creating holes while fusing

The techniques already discussed have centered on drilling or blasting holes after the glass has been fired. An alternative way to create a holes in fused glass is to form the hole during the fusing process. This technique, which is most appropriate for small jewelry pieces, works best when you wish the hole to run from side to side along the edge of a piece, rather than from top to bottom.

The hole making device can be made from fiber paper, from a mandrel or stainless steel rod, or from a bamboo rod or thick toothpick. For best results with fiber paper, use paper that has already been fired. Get the strip wet, then roll it on a flat surface to create a cylinder. You can just use water or you can roll the fiber paper it in a puddle of rigidizing solution (fiber mold hardener). Using the solution will help the fiber keep its shape better during the firing.

In order to keep glass from sticking, mandrels and bamboo rods need to be coated with bead release or kiln wash prior to use. After applying a thin coat of the release or wash, allow the coated rod to dry thoroughly before use. Note also that

The two layer method of creating a hole in fused glass jewelry is illustrated above. A coated stainless steel mandrel is placed between two layers of glass, then fired. The photo on the left shows the results after the firing. This layout *method tends to create a bulge above the hole. Instead of a coasted mandrel, it's possible to also use fiber paper, a coated bamboo rod or thick toothpick. (Photos by David Comstock, courtesy of Geri Comstock.)*

This more elaborate method of arranging the glass to create a hole in jewelry has the advantage that the finished piece has a flat top, rather than a bulge over where the hole was created. Start with a base layer, then add a layer of glass *to form a middle layer with a channel sized to fit the hole making device. Finish with a final layer of glass on top, then fuse. (Photos by David Comstock, courtesy of Geri Comstock.)*

steel mandrels may sink slightly into the piece during the fuse firing; to prevent this, support the ends of the mandrel with fiber paper on the sides of the glass pieces. This is illustrated in the top left photo on the next page.

In addition to the three different hole making devices, there are two different ways to layer the glass for firing. The basic method simply places the hole making device between two layers of glass and fires. This method is quick and easy, but it does leave a bulge on the top surface of the glass when the firing is done.

The second method of layering the glass is a bit more work, but it gives a neater finished appearance. This method, called the channel method, requires that a third layer of glass be placed between the top and bottom layers. This middle layer contains an open channel that has been sized to fit the fiber paper or rod. After firing, the top of the piece will be smoother, without a visible bulge.

Removing the fiber paper or rod is easier if the piece has totally cooled. Overfiring the piece will cause the area around the hole to be pinched in and may also require additional coldworking to remove needles around the hole making device.

Regardless of the particular method used, the best results will come from a multiple firing approach. Fire the jewelry with the hole making device in place, then remove the device, coldwork or grind, and fire again to fire polish the piece. The hole will close up slightly during this firing, so if you wish it to remain the same size it will be necessary to replace the fiber paper or mandrel during this second firing. The lower firing temperature required for fire polishing the piece should prevent further needling and distortion of the piece.

Acid polishing

Acid polishing, which uses potentially harmful chemicals such as sulfuric and hydrofluoric acid, should not be attempted by the novice. It requires extensive attention to proper safety procedures. Not only are acid burns a possibility, toxic fumes must also be dealt with and controlled. In addition, the acid bath works best when heated slightly, adding to the potential risk.

In the typical acid polishing process, the glass to be polished is dipped into an acid bath, then cleansed in water. In some cases a series of immersions is used rather than a single dipping. Only a very short immersion in the acid is necessary to produce a matte finish; longer periods of time in the acid bath will yield a more polished appearance.

Despite the effectiveness of acid polishing, its potential dangers outweigh the benefits for most glass artists. It should only be undertaken by those with the appropriate safety equipment and experience.

Signing your work

Although it's possible to sign a piece using an ordinary pen that's made for writing on glass, most of these markers are not good choices for signing artwork. The ink will wear off in time and can easily be removed with alcohol or detergent.

Far better to mark your pieces with something that lasts longer, such as an engraver or a pen with ink that needs to be fired permanently onto the glass.

Pens filled with glass enamels, available in a variety of colors, or precious inks, such as gold or silver, are a bit more difficult to use than ordinary ink pens. For most types, the barrel of the pen needs to be squeezed to encourage the enamel or ink to flow on the glass. After writing, the glass must be fired in the kiln to make the writing permanent. Fortunately, most of the enamels used mature at slumping temperatures, so an extra firing is not required.

Another option is the diamond tipped scribe, which is used to engrave into the glass, leaving a clean and easily visible signature. An electric engraver, which can be cordless or corded, will do the job faster than an ordinary diamond tipped scribe. Practice on a scrap piece of glass before attempting to sign a finished piece. Because they're

"Placesetting 2" from the "Objects of Desire" series by Geri Comstock. The photo to the right shows a detail of the goblet. (Photos by David Comstock, courtesy of Geri Comstock.)

more gentle on glass, rotary type engravers are preferable to impact engravers.

Once a piece has been engraved, a small amount of acrylic paint can be rubbed into the grooves to highlight the signature. Excess paint can easily be wiped away.

In addition to these pens and engravers, it's also possible to sign your name (or create a unique symbol) using millefiori, stringer, screen printing, or just about any technique that can leave a permanent impression. You can even fuse signature cane directly into your artwork.

Some artist also sign their works with a rubber stamp of their signature. To use this approach, dip the stamp into acid etch cream and apply it to the surface of the work.

Displaying the piece

Simple, inexpensive acrylic or wooden stands for holding plates and bowls are widely available. These work well for displaying relatively flat pieces and have the advantage of easy portability, but many pieces benefit from a more permanent display stand.

A carefully selected display stand, like the one shown below, can enhance and complement the final appearance of the work. These permanent stands can be fabricated from many different materials, but are most commonly made from either wood or metal.

Although making your own stand can require specialized tools and knowledge of such metal working techniques as cutting, grinding, bending, and welding, it's possible to make serviceable stands with minimal equipment and expense.

Metal stands are generally made of stainless steel, brass, copper, regular steel, or aluminum. Most of these metals are available in rods, tubes, and sheets of various dimensions and thicknesses. Display stand fabrication begins with these basic materials and then cuts and bends them to shape. Metal is attached to metal by welding, by soldering, or by using screws and bolts. Sandblasting and painting are two of the main techniques most commonly used to achieve a desirable final finish.

Some artists make their own display stands, but others rely on metal workers or others more experienced with welding and related techniques to fabricate their stands.

Top: Janet Kelman, "Blue Rose Sandal." Kiln cast in lead crystal using the lost wax process. (Photo by Leslie Patron, courtesy of the artist.)

Below: Terri Stanley, "On a Roll." Kiln cast Gaffer glass. (Photo by William Stanley, courtesy of the artist.)

Chapter 19

Kiln casting

Model creation • Mold manufacturing and preparation • Filling the mold with glass • Casting with glass frit or chunks • Using a crucible drip • Pate de verre • Firing the casting • Annealing and cooling • Removing and cleaning the casting

The term "kiln casting" refers to a variety of kiln-forming processes, but all have in common that they involve filling a mold with glass, then firing the glass in a kiln until the glass flows and takes on the shape of the mold. Kiln casting contains many of the elements of fusing and slumping, but it is generally more complicated and requires a solid understanding of kilnforming principles.

Although there are almost as many different way to kiln cast as there are artists, most kiln casting activities have six basic steps:

- **Model creation** --creating the specific design and shape desired in the final piece

- **Mold manufacturing and preparation** -- using the model to create a mold that will hold the glass for firing

- **Filling the mold with glass** -- the size, shape, color, and precise placement of the glass used determines the appearance of the final piece

- **Heating the glass and mold** -- here's where the kiln takes center stage

- **Annealing and cooling** -- absolutely critical for casting

- **Removing and cleaning the casting.**

Model creation

Kiln casting starts with a model of the item to be transformed into glass. The model can be a "found" item, such as a pine cone or a department store mannikin, or it can be an image that has been formed from wax, clay, or another substance. Some models require virtually no work before they can be used, while others require extensive forming and elaborate carving.

The most common substances for models are clay and wax. Both are relatively inexpensive, easily found, and can be used for both simple and elaborate items.

- **Working with clay**

The key criteria for using clay as a model material are that the clay is easily shaped and that it maintains its shape once worked. Use throwing or modeling clays rather than stoneware, porcelain, or oil-based clays, which tend to be less malleable.

Major techniques for working with clay include pinching the clay into shape with your hands, coiling (forming shapes with rope-like coils of clay), and slab working (rolling out thin slabs of clay). Special tools are also available to simplify and expedite the process of working with clay. Many ceramics books discuss these and other clayworking techniques.

One key characteristic to keep in mind when working with clay is that clay tends to shrink as it dries. The degree of shrinkage depends on the type of clay used, but it is not unusual for clay models to shrink five to ten per cent (and as much as fifteen to twenty per cent) as they dry. Another factor to consider is that if the clay model is extremely complicated or elaborate it may be difficult to remove the clay from the mold. For this reason clay is most often used for making a shallow or open faced object like a plaque or medallion.

• Working with wax

Wax is often used for more intricate or detailed pieces. This is because it can be heated and melted out of the mold, leaving a cavity that can be filled with glass particles and then fired in the kiln. This process is called "lost wax casting."

Like clay, wax can be sculpted if necessary. Moreover, wax can be use to quickly make replicas of a particular model by using an original form to create a master mold. This mold, which is often made of rubber or latex, can be used to create wax copies of the original. This greatly reduces the time required to create duplicates. It also allows the artist to create variations on a particular shape by starting with a wax copy of a master form that can be altered as desired.

• Other materials

In addition to wax and clay, models may be made from "found" items such as vegetables, paper mache, small tree branches, and other organic substances. The materials, like wax, can be burned or steamed out of the mold.

Other materials, such as glass, metal, or plastic, are more rigid and can be difficult to remove from the mold. In addition, undercuts (see the illustration below), can interfere with easy removal from the kiln.

Because of the difficulty of removing some model materials from the mold, it's common to make a copy of the original model out of a material that can easily be removed from the kiln.

Since the model is used to create a mold that will be filled with glass and fired in the kiln, it's critical that the model be made of a material that can easily be removed from the mold. Some materials, such as wax or many organic items, can simply be burned or steamed out of the mold. Materials such as clay must be pried loose from the mold without damaging it. And some materials, such as glass, metal, or plastic are very rigid and are difficult to remove from the mold. In addition, undercuts (see the bottom of this page) can interfere with easy removal from the mold.

Because of these problems, it's common to make copies of the original model for use in kiln casting. Products for making copies include various alginates (such as Hydrogel) rubbers (such as room temperature vulcanizing rubber and latex), and silicones. Each of these products is used a bit

Right: Undercuts make it difficult to remove the model from the mold. The lost wax process is often used with undercuts.

Far right: Sloped sides without undercuts can be more easily removed.

differently, but the common objective is to create a final version of the original model that can be used to create a mold for casting.

Mold manufacturing and preparation

Once the appropriate model is created, it is used to create a mold that can hold its shape while withstanding the heat of the kiln. Mold materials vary considerably, but most molds are composed of two different ingredients: a "binder" and a "refractory." These ingredients are combined to form an "investment," which is the common name for a mold mixture.

The purpose of the binder is to hold the components of the mold mixture together; it's what allows the mixture to be created. The most common binder material is plaster, which is made from ground gypsum stone. Gypsum can also be used to make various cements which can withstand the heat of the kiln.

Several steps were required to make the mold for Terri Stanley's "On a Roll" casting. The artist used a master model (pictured top right) to create a flexible rubber copy (below left). A final mold was created from the rubber copy using a commercially available investment (R&R Glass Cast 910). Creating a model that can be used to make a mold is one of the most challenging facets of the kiln casting process. See the completed piece on page 178. (Photos by William Stanley, courtesy of the artist.)

Because plaster alone is not strong enough to withstand the heat of the kiln, a second ingredient is needed. This is the refractory, which helps the mold withstand higher temperatures. Silica is the most common refractory material used, but non-silica refractories, such as alumina hydrate or zirconia, are also available.

Some mold formulations contain additional additives, such as fiberglass fibers or grog (ground up pre-fired clay). These ingredients change the properties of the investment by modifying the setting time, increasing strength, or making the mold more durable. They're used in smaller quantities and aren't used in all formulations.

The most basic investment formulation is a 50/50 mixture of very fine plaster (200 mesh or finer) and ground silica (sometimes called flint). This formulation is fairly inexpensive and works well for many basic casting processes. As molds become larger and more complex, additives such as fiberglass fibers can be added to give additional strength. Many commercial formulations are

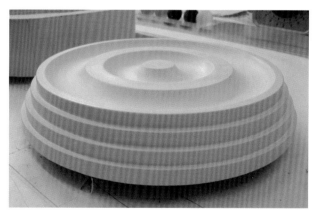

also available. Some of the more common are R&R Glass Cast, Castalot, and Mold Mix 6.

• Preparing a box for the mold

Before the mold can be created, it's important to create a box to hold the investment during the pouring and curing process. The box can be a simple plastic container or it can be constructed from cardboard, linoleum, or a similar inexpensive material. Although it is possible to construct a box from a refractory material such as vermiculite board, most constructed boxes are intended for only a single use.

For all but the smallest items, the box should be approximately one to two inches larger than the model on all sides. In most cases, the height of the box should be around one inch taller than the model. If the box is made from cardboard or a similar substance, it should be secured to a base material using hot glue, duct tape, or a combination of both. It's important that the box is tight enough so that the investment material won't leak out before it cures.

Some mold boxes require a thin coating of a release, such as cooking oil spray or oil soap, to keep the investment from sticking to the box after it dries. Don't overdue this release; use a very thin coating, rather than a thick layer than can contaminate the investment.

Constructing a mold box using cardboard, duct tape, and hot glue. Boxes constructed in this fashion should be built on a sturdy material, such as wood or plexiglass. (Photo by the author.)

• Mixing the investment

The process for making a mold from plaster/silica starts by mixing the two dry ingredients together. A 50/50 mixture works well. The ingredients can be measured by volume or weight. Additional silica up to 1.5 times the amount of plaster can be added if a softer mold is desired. Unlike molds made from plaster alone, plaster/silica molds often remain soft enough to carve for several weeks.

Once the bags are opened, both plaster and silica should be stored in airtight containers. This will prevent plaster from hardening from exposure to humid air. And since silica can cause silicosis and other lung problems if inhaled, storing it safely helps avoid exposure to spilled or loose particles.

Because of the potential for harm when handling ground silica, it's important to use a respirator when using plaster and silica. A respirator rated P100 is preferable, but at least an N95 mask should be used if no P100 is available.

Once the two dry ingredients have been combined, the next ingredient is water. Use clean, clear water at room temperature or cooler. Since the temperature of the water dictates how quickly the mixture will set, warm or hot water should almost always be avoided.

Always add the dry ingredients to the water, not vice versa. Place the desired quantity of water into a clean container. Using a container that has not been thoroughly cleaned may contaminate the mixture or cause it to set up more quickly than desired.

Some people prefer to mix by feel, while others prefer to measure ingredients prior to mixing. Either method will work, but even measuring precisely requires some fine tuning during the mixing process. The amounts of plaster and silica required can vary slightly based on brand, age of the ingredients, and over humidity level. A general rule of thumb is to use xx parts water for every xx parts of the plaster/silica mixture.

182

Investment mixture coming to a "peak." Note the small "islands" of investment floating at the top of the mixture. (Photo by the author.)

The container should be filled no more than half of the way with water. Adding the plaster/silica mixture will approximately double the level in the container.

Add the dry mixture a little at a time, rather than dumping it all in at once. Some people use a sifter to evenly spread the dry mixture on the surface of the water; others simply sprinkle the mixture by hand or with a small cup across the surface. Except for a final stirring at the end of the process, stirring the mixture isn't necessary.

Continue adding the investment until it "peaks." Peaking occurs when the mixture sinks slowly and dry investment islands appear in the container. If the ingredients were measured out prior to starting the mixing process, the mixture should "peak" just as you use the last of the dry ingredients. If it doesn't, just add a bit more of the plaster/silica mixture.

Once the investment peaks, give the mixture one complete stir to mix in all the dry ingredients. Take care not to agitate vigorously and create air bubbles in the mixture. After mixing, allow the mixture to sit undisturbed for five to ten minutes. This process, called "slaking," helps ensure that the investment particles become saturated with water.

An alternative to the model creation and mold preparation processes

Much of the difficulty of kiln casting stems from the elaborate model creation and mold preparation processes, which can require considerable skill and time. In recent years vitreous clay molds, such as those used for slumping glass, have emerged as an alternative to the traditional processes.

These molds, as shown below, are simply filled with glass, then fired to the appropriate temperature. Generally, a full fuse firing schedule is used. The mold can be filled with loose frit or chunks of glass or pate de verre processes can be used. The final pieces are usually suitable as jewelry, paperweights, or simple platters or plaques.

The advantage of this approach is its simplicity; the disadvantage is that designs are limited to what is commercially available. Using a manufactured casting mold can be a good way to create small, simple items, but it won't help you learn the fundamental model creation and mold making processes.

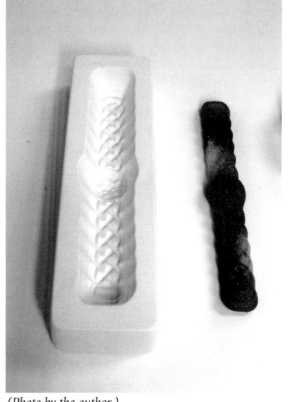

(Photo by the author.)

- **Pouring the mold**

After allowing the investment to slake, you'll notice a slight thickening. That's your cue to stir gently, then slowly pour the mixture into the box that surrounds your model. To minimize bubbles and distortion of the model, pour the investment along the edges of the box, rather than directly on the model. Do not pour leftover mixture down the sink, as it will harden and ruin your plumbing.

- **Removing the model**

After the mold has air-dried (this may take several days), you should be able to remove the model. Clay models can generally be worked loose with a stick or removed by hand. They can be difficult to remove from deep inside crevices, so are best used for more open molds.

Models made from wood, paper, or organic materials can be burned out, although it may be necessary to remove ashes and any other possible contaminants from the mold after firing.

Wax models will need to be steamed or melted out. Once this has been done, the remaining cav-ity can be filled with frit or cullet and then fired. This process, which is adapted from the jewelry-making field, is called "lost wax casting." See the box below for more on this process.

- **Curing the mold**

Only the smallest molds can be immediately filled with glass and fire in the kiln. Most molds will need to be air or kiln dried before they're completely cured and ready to use.

Air drying is relatively simple, but it can take several days, if not weeks. Make certain that the mold is away from traffic, so it doesn't get accidentally damaged while it is drying. A dry-ing box, a vented chamber which surrounds the mold and heats it slightly (usually with a simple light bulb), can speed the curing process if de-sired.

After air drying, it still may be necessary to com-plete the curing process by heating the mold in a kiln. This is especially recommended for larger or more complicated items. The key to success is to take it slow. The slower you heat, the stronger the finished mold will be. Fire the mold at a rate of 100F/56C per hour (even slower for larger, thicker molds). Soak the mold at 225F/107C and

---

The lost wax casting method

The lost wax casting method involves making a wax model, investing it in a mold, and then melt-ing the wax out of the mold to form a cavity into which a glass replica can be cast.

Wax models can be made in several ways, ranging from hand modelling with beeswax or a similar easily molded wax to casting from a latex or other master mold. Wax can be poured into a pan to form sheets which can then be cut and formed.

Regardless of the method used, the creation of the wax model is the first step to using the lost wax process. Once this model has been made, it should be encased in the investment material (usually a plaster/silica mixture) as with any other casting model.

Once the investment dries, the wax should be re-moved from the model by inverting the mold over a pan of water and heating it to about 225 F/107 C. The wax will drip out into the pan. Be careful not to heat much above this temperature and don't allow all of the water to evaporate. Since wax is flammable, it can catch fire if it is allowed to get too hot.

After the wax has been melted out, the mold is ready to be cured and fired as described in the main body of this chapter. As the glass pieces melt in the mold, they will fill the spaces once occupied by the wax, a process that gives this technique its name.

With careful reclaiming, the wax can be used again in a later project.

again at 350F/177C. This is to drive off remaining water and help stabilize the mold. Continue to heat until the temperature reaches about 1200F/650C. Some artists fill the mold with glass while it is at this temperature (both exciting and risky), but most allow the mold to cool slowly back to room temperature.

Cracks sometimes appear in the mold after curing; if these are small they won't present a problem, but large cracks may require repair or even starting over again. These cracks are more likely to occur if you fired too quickly or if the mold is large.

One interesting aspect of casting with molds is that you are far more likely to crack the molds than you are the glass. This is contrary to slumping, in which the glass is more at risk. In casting, the mold tends to protect the glass, but its tendency to crack requires that heating and cooling take place more slowly than when fusing or slumping glass.

Filling the mold with glass

Once the model has been removed from the mold and the mold has been cured, it's time for the next step in the kiln casting process, filling the mold with glass.

The first major consideration is to determine which size glass pieces to use. As was noted before, size can range from very small particles to large chunks. Small particles will tend to capture more air bubbles than larger ones, making the piece appear less clear. So if you want a clear casting with a minimum of bubbles use large pieces of glass, rather than small ones. Using a single piece of glass of the appropriate size is one way to ensure that the final piece will be virtually bubble free.

In addition to size, the type and color of glass are also important. Either use glass pieces from a single piece of glass or select compatible glass to ensure that the piece doesn't crack after casting. Also, select glasses that are not prone to devitrification. The longer soak times typically required for kiln casting make controlling devitrification

even more important than in fusing and slumping. If at all possible select a glass that has been tested compatible or that has been specially formulated for casting.

Many castings use transparent colors, rather than opaques. If transparency is your goal, remember that thick pieces will make even a very light glass appear dark and a darker glass can become almost opaque if the final piece is thick.

Note also that many "clear" glasses actually have a greenish tint; if this is not desirable, seek out a special "casting clear" (sometimes called "Colorless Clear" or "Crystal Clear") that has been formulated without the green tint.

Once you've determined the color, type, and size of the glass to be used, the next step is to decide the method to use to fill the mold with glass. There are three major alternatives, each of which results in a different final appearance.

• Filling the mold with frit or chunks

Probably the easiest approach to filling the casting, this method usually results in a relatively homogeneous casting that can vary from transparent to opaque depending on the glass used.

• Using a crucible drip.

Best for situations where you want the casting to be as clear as possible, this method requires a kiln with a relatively high clearance. It also requires a "crucible," a container to hold glass frit or chunks that can resist the heat of the kiln. A flower pot with an enlarged opening in the bottom can serve as a makeshift crucible.

• Making a paste of glass

Often known by its French name, *pate de verre*, using a paste of glass is probably the most technically challenging of the three methods. By mixing glass frit with a glue (sometimes called a "binder"), it is possible to precisely control the location of each color in the finished piece.

Casting with glass frit or chunks

The easiest way to kiln cast is to fill the mold with frit and then fire. Unfortunately, this is not as straightforward as it sounds. That's because frit compacts as it melts and settles down into the mold. How much it compacts depends on the size of the frit (or chunks) used. The smaller the individual pieces of glass, the less it will compact. A good general guideline is that it will compact to about two thirds of the original size.

There are several ways to deal with the settling of glass as it flows into the mold. One is to use an approach such as the one described in the box below to determine exactly how much glass you need. But even if you know the exact amount of glass required, you will still have to find a way to heap it on top of the mold.

If your casting allows it, it's possible to use very large chunks of glass that sit on top of the mold and drip into the mold as the temperature inside the kiln increases. Alternatively, a reservoir can be constructed at the top of the mold when it is made and used to hold glass until it melts and compacts into the mold.

Another option is to add more glass to the mold during the firing, after the settling has occurred. This approach requires that the kiln be opened during the hottest part of the firing. Obviously this has the potential to be an unsafe operation, so care must be taken to prevent burns or electric

A set of molds with glass frit and chunks of various sizes. Placing the molds on supports, rather than directly on a kiln shelf, helps ensure that moisture from the molds won't crack the shelf. (Photo by Jody Danner Walker.)

shocks. Always turn the kiln off before reaching inside and always wear appropriate glasses, gloves, and clothing. Use a metal tool, such as fireplace tongs or shovel, to top the mold with additional frit or chunks of glass.

If necessary, topping off a mold can be done several times. Frit is small enough that thermal shock will not be a problem, and even if individual pieces of glass crack, they will quickly melt inside the kiln. Add the glass, let the mold soak at casting temperature for another 15 to 30 minutes, then check to see if additional glass is needed. When the mold appears full, finish the soaking process and then begin the annealing and cooling process.

How to determine how much glass is required to fill a mold

If you plan to cast by filling a mold with frit or chunks of glass and have decided to use a single color or to mix colors indiscriminately, there is a simple process which can help determine precisely how much glass to use.

First, get a jar and fill it with water. On the outside of the jar, mark the top level of the the water inside the jar.

Second, pour water from the jar into the mold until the mold fills. Work quickly, before the water wicks away into the mold.

Third, fill the jar (which should still have some water remaining) with casting glass until the water level in the jar reaches the original mark made in step one. The amount of frit required is the amount needed to fill the mold cavity.

Allow the mold and glass to dry before firing.

This method can also be used to estimate the amount of glass needed for crucible casting, but it's a good idea to add some additional glass to compensate for the glass that will stick to the crucible.

A collection of flower pots setup to fill a mold using the crucible drip method. (Photo by Jody Danner Walker.)

Using a crucible drip

For situations that require an exceptionally detailed, clear kiln casting with as little distortion or demarcation lines as possible, consider using the crucible drip method of kiln casting. This approach, which requires a kiln with relatively high clearance, involves placing the glass to be melted into a crucible with a hole in the bottom.

Most crucibles are made out of clay or a similar material. You can buy crucibles, or you can use a terra cotta flower pot (which already has a hole in the bottom) as a crucible. In most cases, crucibles are not coated with kiln wash. This allows some glass to stick to the crucible, but it avoids contamination from the kiln wash.

Since not all of the glass will flow out of the crucible during the firing, use a bit more glass than it will take to just fill the mold. When loaded, suspend the crucible above the mold, so that as the glass melts it drips into the mold. The firing temperature for a crucible drip casting is generally higher than for most other kiln castings.

Pate de verre

Pate de verre involves making a paste of glass that is applied to the surface of the mold, then fired. The big advantage to pate de verre is that it allows for precise placement of specific glass colors in the mold. Other ways of filling the mold often result in some shifting of glass from where it has been placed prior to firing, but the pate de verre process helps to control this shifting.

In traditional French pate de verre, the artist mixed crushed glass with enamels or paint to form a paste that was carefully placed in a mold and then fired. Many of the pieces that were made using this technique were relatively small, elaborately decorated, and required more than one firing before they were complete.

The modern equivalent builds on this traditional foundation. Generally the pate de verre process involves creating a paste from frit (small particles of glass). Frit of any size may be used, but most artists use a mixture of frits of various sizes. This allows the frit to be packed more tightly than if frit of a single size were used. Because of the relatively small sized glass pieces used, pate de verre castings tend to be translucent (or even opaque).

Once the mold is thoroughly dry and the frit has been secured, the next step is to make the glass paste. In some cases, where the mold has gently sloping sides, the glass can simply be mixed with distilled water to form the paste. Most molds, however, will require that the glass be mixed with a glue (called a "binder") to form a paste. Specific pate de verre glues are available, but glues can also be made from CMC (carboxyl methyl cellulose) or gelatin mixed with distilled water. It's a good idea to wear a mask or respirator while mixing the paste to prevent inhaling small glass particles.

Delores Taylor, "Ocean Waves." Pate de verre from clay model using a plaster/silica mold. (Photo by Art Smith, courtesy of the artist.)

Debra Carr Young, "Self Preservation." Kiln cast glass, electroplated. (Photo courtesy of the artist.)

Use a brush or thin palette knife to apply the glass paste to the sides of the mold. Start with a relatively thin coating of about 1/16" (1.6 mm). Some artists fire this initial coating to tack fuse (about 1400F/760C), others let it air dry or use a heat gun to speed up the process. After the first layer dries, a second layer of paste should be added to bring the total thickness to around 1/8" (3 mm). Using a palette knife or other tool, gently pack the layer down as much as possible.

If the mold is hollow or slopes significantly, it will be necessary to find a method to prevent glass movement during the firing. There are several possible ways to achieve this. One of the simplest is to fire to a lower than normal temperature and hold for a long time. Another method is to create a second mold to fit inside or atop the first mold (called a "press mold"). Packing the mold with fiber blanket, talc, or a similar product can also help minimize shifting during the firing.

Differences in firing temperature and hold time can result in significantly different final appearances. Lower temperatures, for example, will result in a crystalline appearance, while higher firing temperatures can give the piece a more polished look.

Firing the casting

The precise schedule for firing a kiln casting varies significantly, depending on type of glass, finish desired, and complexity of mold. Nevertheless, the same basic procedures and steps used in fusing and slumping also apply to kiln casting, with the major caveat that the thickness of the glass and mold generally dictate slower heating and cooling times. It may also be necessary to adjust the firing to minimize the possibility of cracking or damaging the mold during the firing. A cracked mold can cause glass to leak out of the mold and leave a sharp projection on the

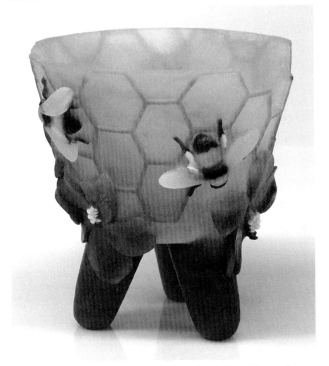

Ellen Abbott and Marc Leva, "Marsh Mallow Honey." Pate de verre with pre-cast inclusions using a two piece press mold. Lost wax casting process. (Photo courtesy of the artists.)

side of the finished piece, a phenomenon called "flashing."

A good rule of thumb for how fast to heat the mold and glass is to increase the temperature no more than 200F/111C per hour. Very small items, such as cast jewelry, can be fired a bit quicker than this (up to around 300F/167C per hour), but it never hurts to increase the temperature slowly. For castings larger than around 6 inches (15 cm) in any dimension, a rate of 100F/56C or less is suggested to avoid thermal shock.

For a mold that has not been totally cured, it's essential to pause during the heating process to drive water from the mold. Pause for an hour just below the boiling point, at 200F/93C, to drive water from the mold. Then heat slowly to 350F/177C and hold for another hour. This second soak will drive chemically bound water from the mold, completely the curing process.

Continue firing slowly until the temperature reaches 1250F/677C. Hold here for another hour, then fire rapidly to the desired casting temperature. In most situations this is approxi-

mately 1500F/816C. Hold at casting temperature until the glass has completely flowed into the mold. The length of time to hold depends on the specific mold and glass used. A small casting will be complete in around 30 minutes; larger, more complicated shapes can easier require several hours soak time. Once the casting is complete, begin the cooling and annealing process.

Note that these guidelines are for relatively small castings using fairly simple shapes. Larger cast items and more complicated shapes will require slower rates of temperature increase and longer hold times.

Annealing and cooling

Once the casting has been formed, the mold and glass should be cooled quickly (just as in fusing and slumping) to around 1200F/650C. Hold at this temperature for at least two hours (longer for larger pieces), then cool slowly the remainder of the way to the annealling temperature for your particular glass. The purpose of the hold at 1200F/650C, as well as for the slow decrease the rest of the way to the annealing temperature, is to ensure that the glass cools evenly during the critical stage when it is contracting as it cools. The long soak helps prevent "cavitation," irregularly shaped unwanted depressions in the glass (also called "suckers"). Cavitation is most likely with soda lime glasses such as Bullseye, Uroboros, and Spectrum; casting glasses with lead, such as Gaffer and Schott, are less likely to develop suckers. Darker glasses are also more likely to develop suckers than clear or lightly tinted glass.

Once the glass reaches the annealing temperature, it's time to begin the annealing process. Annealing and cooling cast items generally takes much longer than annealing and cooling slumped and fused items. The thickness of most kiln cast pieces is one reason for the additional time required for annealing and cooling. Another reason is that kiln cast items tend to be surrounded by a thick, fragile mold. Temperature variations with the casting and greater than in fused and slumped items, which are open to the air. Extra time is needed to account for the thick-

Dick Ditore, "Sculpture #4." Lost wax casting for chain and key. Handworked clay for padlock, raku fired. (Photo courtesy of the artist.)

ness of the mold and to allow the temperature of the cast glass to stabilize.

How long do you anneal and cool? It is not unusual for annealing of large items to take several days, or even weeks. Even small cast items will generally require several hours to anneal. When figuring the length of time, you must consider both the thickness of the casting and the thickness of the mold.

Bullseye, Spectrum, and Gaffer publish annealing schedules for thicker items on their websites. When consulting these schedules, estimate the thickness of your casting conservatively -- there's nothing worse than losing a casting during the annealing and cooling phase.

Removing and cleaning the casting

Even when your piece appears to have cooled to room temperature, it often a good idea to leave it to cool for an additional day or more before removing it from the mold. This is because the inside of the mold can still be hot even though the mold itself feels cool to the touch.

Once you are certain that the mold and glass inside are cool, carefully break the mold away from the glass. The mold will be much weaker than when it was placed into the kiln. Handle it with care. Proceed slowly, taking care not to break the glass. This can be easier said than done, but if you are careful you will eventually be able to remove the entire mold and free the glass. Sometimes the edges of the glass are sharp, so it may be necessary to wear gloves during this process. A respirator or mask is also advisable.

The surface of the casting will probably look ugly, not at all like the shimmering piece of glass you may have imagined. Often, there are small particles of investment material stuck to the glass. Use wooden tools to gently remove stuck on particles. Metal tools, such as dental instruments or picks, can also be used, but take care not to damage or scratch the piece. A stiff bristled nylon brush can also be used to remove investment.

Once the bulk of the investment has been removed from the piece, wash the casting in water. Scrubbing with vinegar or a product such as CLR or Limeaway can also help the cleaning process go more quickly.

Once the casting is clean, it may need to be coldworked to achieve the desired finish. Some pieces can be fire polished carefully or shined with wax, an acrylic or enamel spray, or a clear spray oil such as Varathane Natural Oil Finish #66 Clear. Many of these approaches will significantly change the piece's surface appearance.

Above all, remember that although kiln casting can be more rewarding and interesting than fusing and slumping, it is also more complicated. There are many more tricks and techniques, and most artists have developed their own approaches to kiln casting. This variety can be a source of frustration (there is, after all, no single "right way"), but it is also part of what gives kiln casting its charm and excitement.

Chapter 20

Making your own

Devitrification spray • Kiln wash • Frit • Stringer • Confetti

The formulas and techniques in this section have been derived from many different sources. Credit has been given where it is known, but in many cases the originator of the formula remains anonymous.

Please be very careful when handling or mixing chemicals and make every effort to follow proper safety procedures. Chapter 21, the Health and Safety chapter, has more information on these procedures.

Devitrification spray

This spray, which will prevent or minimize devitrification on glass, is inexpensive and easy to make. It works well on most kinds of glass, including fusing glasses and float glass, but won't stand up well to prolonged outdoor exposure.

To make the spray, mix one part borax with eight parts water. Heat the water until the two mix together well; you should not have to bring the mixture to a boil. Add a few drops of detergent (any dishwashing liquid) to the mixture; this will help keep the mixture from beading up when applied to glass.

To use the solution, clean the glass, then spray or brush the liquid on the top surface of glass before firing. Don't coat the kiln shelf or the bottom surface of the glass. Allow the spray to dry before firing. Slumping temperatures may not be hot enough to mature this spray, so use it for fuse firings only.

In the United States, borax is available as a laundry detergent under the brand name Twenty Mule Team Borax. Get the version that's pure borax, not the one that has soap added.

Kiln wash

Equal parts of kaolin and alumina hydrate can be used to make a basic kiln wash. Dry mix the two ingredients and store in an airtight container. When you're ready to use the powder, add four to five parts water to create the kiln wash solution. Use as you would use any kiln wash.

An alternative formula is to mix 80% alumina hydrate and 20% kaolin. This produces a kiln wash powder that is softer than the standard mixture. Only one coat is needed on the shelf, and you can apply by brush or spray. It's a single use formula; after each firing, remove with a damp paper towel (no scraping needed!) and then reapply. It's important to remove the kiln wash after each firing; if you leave it on, it can discolor the glass on future firings.

The two main chemicals in these kiln washes -- alumina hydrate and kaolin -- are commonly used in ceramics and can be found at most ceramics supply places. Make sure to specify a size of 120 mesh or finer.

Frit

The easiest way to obtain your own frit is to buy it already made. Tested compatible frit is available from Bullseye, Spectrum, Uroboros and other suppliers in a variety of different sizes, ranging from powder to chunks as large as 1/4" (6 mm).

If you want to make your own frit, you should also consider purchasing a set of screens in various mesh sizes to separate the frit by size. These are often available from pottery suppliers.

• Using a hammer

For this approach, place the glass to be used between several pieces of newspaper or inside a sealed plastic bag and strike with a hammer until the pieces reach the desired size. This method is crude, but effective. Make sure you wear eye protection and a mask or respirator.

• Pipe-crushing

Obtain two hollow pipes, one slightly larger in diameter than the other, so that one pipe fits inside the other. Close off one end of the smaller pipe, fill it with rocks or similar heavy items, then close off the other end.

Now place the larger pipe upright on a hard surface like cement and fill it part of the way with the glass you want to break. Slide the smaller, heavy pipe into the larger one, letting it drop full force onto the glass. You may need a second person to help you hold the larger pipe. Raise the smaller pipe and drop again and again until you are satisfied with the size of the particles.

If you use this technique, wear eye protection and a mask or respirator to protect you from the silica dust. You many need to use a magnet to extract any metal chips that may be caught in the frit.

If you don't want to make your own pipe crusher, commercial models are available.

• Tack fusing

Place the glass in the kiln. One arrangement that works well is to heap smaller chips of glass on a larger sheet. Heat until the glass tack fuses — around 1400 F/760 C. Once the glass has fused, turn off the kiln. Wearing gloves and eye protection, remove the glass from the kiln using large tongs, such as steel fireplace tongs. Immediately drop the glass into a metal container about two thirds full of cold water. The shock will crack the glass into many small pieces. Glass broken this way will be in relatively large chunks. If you want finer pieces, you can use the hammer technique described above to break it down some more.

• Melting in a crucible

This technique requires handling glass that is much hotter than the other techniques. Place glass pieces in a crucible, a ceramic container made for withstanding the heat of the kiln. Heat it to around 1700 F/825 C and soak to allow the glass to melt.

Then turn off the kiln and use tongs to remove the crucible. Wear gloves and eye protection and take special care. Slowly pour the molten glass into a bucket of cold water. The glass will break into finer particles than in the tack fuse approach discussed above. Make sure you return the crucible to the kiln and let it cool slowly to prevent thermal shocking the crucible.

• Frit-making machines

It is possible to buy frit-making machines, called "glass crushers" or "ball mills." Alternatively, you can rig up your own machine using a garbage disposal, heavy duty blender, or similar item.

Stringer

Although the resulting stringer will not be as straight and perfectly formed as commercially made stringer, making your own stringer has its own rewards. Handmade stringer is more interesting than store bought and the resulting shapes often vary in thickness and color in ways that aren't possible with commercial stringer.

- **Flameworking method**

Even if you aren't a skilled flameworker, you can easily make stringers in the torch. Begin by cutting a strip of glass about 1/4" (6 mm) wide and 10" (25 cm) long. Grab one end of the glass with a pair of pliers and heat the other end in your flame. Heat until the end becomes molten and starts to ball up. Then quickly grab the molten end with a second pair of pliers and stretch the glass to form the stringer.

This technique takes practice, but after a few attempts you should be able to form longer and longer threads. If you do not have access to a lampworking setup, use a relatively inexpensive propane torch, found at most hardware stores.

- **Crucible method**

A second technique involves the use of a kiln and a crucible. Place glass frit or chunks in the crucible and heat until molten. Be aware that this requires a temperature of approximately 2000F/1100C, which is hotter than most glass kilns fire, so you'll need access to a pottery or enameling kiln. This approach also works with a glass blower's glory hole as the heating chamber.

Once the glass is molten, turn the kiln off and use a metal rod to reach into the crucible and remove some glass. A 1/4" (6 mm) steel bar works well. With the glass on the end of the bar, marver the glass on a metal or graphite surface. (Marvering means to roll the glass until it becomes smoother and rounder.)

Once marvered, return the metal rod to the crucible and pick up some more glass. Marver a second time, rotating the rod to keep the glass from falling off the end. Now have a second person grab the molten glass with a pair of pliers and slowly walk away from where you are holding the rod. It may take some practice to learn the correct pace for walking away. Too slow and the stringer will be short and fat. Too fast and it will

be too brittle. But if you walk at the right pace the glass will stretch into a long stringer.

This process can be repeated as many times as necessary to use up the glass and form the desired stringer. One variation is to twist the glass as you pull, forming stringer "twisties."

- **Vitrigraph kiln method**

The vitrigraph kiln is ideally suited for making stringer. Using a gloved hand or a pair of tongs or hemostats, simply pull the glass to produce stringers of various thicknesses. The vitrigraph kiln is discussed in greater detail in Chapter 15.

Confetti

There are several ways to use your kiln to make confetti, but all are based on the concept of slumping glass until the stretched sides become very thin. To achieve the necessary thinness, it's generally necessary to suspend the glass high in the kiln and allow it to slump and stretch until it reaches the floor. When the glass cools, the thin sections of the glass can be broken into small pieces and used in future fusing projects.

The simplest way to make kiln-formed confetti is to use a drop ring. A square drop ring will work better than a round one. Try making your own from a square of Ceramaguard ceiling tile. Support the ring high in the kiln, place a single layer of glass on top, fire quickly to around 1350F/730C, and allow the glass to drop until the sizes stretch very thin. Cool the kiln, then break the glass into pieces for use as confetti.

Another approach is to stretch nichrome or other heat-resistant wires across a metal frame constructed in your kiln. Lay a sheet of glass across the wires and then fire as described above.

Although the colors of the confetti made in this fashion tend not be be as intense as the colors of commercially available confetti, starting with tested compatible glass virtually guarantees compatibility, so that confetti can be layered heavily if your design dictates.

Chapter 21

Health and safety

General precautions • Kiln safety • Eye protection • Hearing protection • Ventilation • Respirators and masks • Ceramic fiber products • Hazardous chemicals • Cuts and scrapes • Burns • Essential safety equipment

While working with glass in a kiln is not necessarily dangerous, there are opportunities for cuts, burns, and even more serious health and safety problems. As with any activity, a little time spent paying attention to safety procedures can help prevent problems before they occur.

It seems obvious that glass can cut and hot glass can burn, but many people don't realize that working with glass can be dangerous in other ways. If you're not careful, you can ruin your lungs, damage your eyes, and even burn your house to the ground.

The purpose of this discussion isn't to scare you away; rather, it's to make you aware of the potential warm glass health and safety pitfalls and to offer some suggestions to keep you on the right track.

General precautions

Many of these suggestions will seem like common sense. Unfortunately, they aren't always "commonly" used.

Don't go barefoot. Wear shoes with closed-in toes. If your hair is long, tie it back. Don't wear loose fitting clothes. Cotton or other natural fiber is best. Long sleeves help if you're reaching in the kiln, as will tying back long hair and

removing dangling jewelry. Wear gloves anytime you handle anything hot, respirators if around substances that can harm your lungs, and ear protection if the machinery you're using is loud.

Most of all, don't forgot to use your head. Most injuries can be prevented if you just think about what you're doing.

Kiln safety

Kilns are very safe pieces of equipment. It's extremely rare, if not unheard of, for one to catch fire, shoot sparks, or damage the surrounding area. Nevertheless, there are several safety precautions that should be followed.

Kiln safety starts with the location of the kiln, which should be on cement or other inflammable surface. If you must locate your kiln on a wooden floor, place ceramic tile or inflammable board under the legs. Keep kilns at least two feet from anything that can catch fire, and make sure flammable liquids and loose papers are secured even further away.

It's best to place your kiln on a stand that keeps it directly off the floor and allows for air circulation underneath. Keep an ABC fire extinguisher nearby (that's good for all kinds of fires) and learn how to use it should the need arise.

If your kiln requires a special electrical connection, spend the extra money and have a qualified electrician set it up. Make sure to have a separate circuit for the kiln and know the location of the switch or breaker that cuts off power to the kiln. It's obvious that the kiln will be hot on the inside when it's operating, but be aware that most kilns get hot on the *outside* as well. Even the handle can become too hot to touch. So make sure you wear gloves, if you need to open the kiln while it's hot.

Some kiln manuals advise not to open the kiln when it's hot, but that's not very practical advice. Many standard kilnforming operations, such as combing and topping off glass molds when casting, require access to the kiln while the glass is hot. If you must open the kiln, do it safely by wearing protective equipment (gloves, goggles, etc.) and by - this is critical - *cutting off power to the kiln before you open it*. By cutting off the power you minimize the risk of electrical burns and you make certain that touching "hot" elements won't deliver a potentially painful shock.

Eye protection

In addition to dealing with the heat and electrical components of the kiln, it's also essential to protect your eyes when you're working around the kiln. When the temperature climbs above 1100F/600C, glass will start to glow red and emit infrared radition. Prolonged exposure to infrared wavelengths can result in cataracts, a blurring of the vision that often occurs many years after repeated unprotected exposure.

The intensity of this infrared exposure increases as the glass gets hotter. You may get away with a short peek at the kiln from time to time, but it's good practice to wear glasses that shield the eyes from infrared radiation anytime you open the kiln when the temperature is above 1100F/600C.

You can block infrared rays by using the right kind of eyeglasses. The least expensive kind of glasses to use are welder's glasses, which are generally available in hardware and similar stores. These glasses, which block infrared light,

Three critical pieces of equipment for protecting the eyes. Both safety glasses with clear lenses and with lenses to block infrared radiation are essential. A large face shield for protection when using a tile saw or similar machine is also good to have on hand. (Photo by the author.)

are rated with a number that corresponds to how efficiently they block the rays. Shade 2 to 3 welder's glasses (the higher the number, the darker) are sufficient for kilnforming activities. Lamp-working glasses (which have didymium lenses) don't block infrared rays and shouldn't be used for kiln work.

Another source for glasses that protect from infrared radiation are glasses prescribed by doctors following cataract surgery. These glasses, which generally need to be worn for several weeks following surgery, are designed to block infrared radiation. They make great safety glasses for the studio.

In addition to protection from infrared radiation, eye protection is also required when grinding, sawing, or working with most glass machinery. In these situations standard clear safety glasses are appropriate. For some equipment, such as tile saws, a full face shield is preferable to simple safety glasses. Clear face shields, which are available from workworking supply shops and hardware stores, help protect the entire face, including the eyes, from flying debris.

195

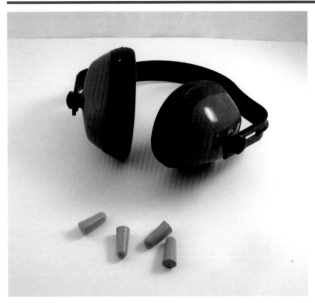

Hearing protection becomes more important when using coldworking equipment, which can be very noisy. Both ear plugs and ear muffs are shown here. (Photo by the author.)

Hearing protection

Most glass artists don't think about the need for hearing protection. However, many glass machines, such as sandblasters, wet belt sanders, grinders, and saws, are very loud and can lead to hearing problems after prolonged exposure. If you're working at a machine and have difficulty hearing someone talking to you from five feet away, then the noise level is probably too loud and you should take steps to protect your ears.

Ear plugs, which fit inside the ear, are inexpensive solutions to the noise problem. Some people prefer ear muffs, which fit over the ears and head like a pair of head phones. Either solution will go a long way to greatly reducing the sound level and will still allow for conversation if needed. Music head sets or iPod ear buds are not recommended; they just add to the noise level, rather than reduce it.

Ventilation

Normal kiln operations don't create enough noxious chemicals and gases to be a health hazard. Fumes from firing glass in a kiln normally come from burning off glues or from the binder in fiber products and thinfire. These fumes aren't generally harmful, but do have a smell that can be irritating to some people. If you're particularly sensitive, consider investing in a way to improve the ventilation in your studio.

The simplest ventilation system is to open a window or use a fan. In most situations, this is enough to do the job. But if your processes involve burning off or spraying potentially harmful contaminants, then you should consider a more elaborate system. Options range from installing a kiln vent, available from companies like Orton, to using a canopy hood to remove fumes and heat from the room.

Respirators and masks

Even with good ventilation, there are situations which require the wearing of a respirator or mask. Fine glass powder and ground silica shouldn't be inhaled. Many refractory materials, such as fiber paper, are either carcinogenic or sources of nuisance dust. So make it a practice to always wear an appropriate mask or respirator.

Masks and respirators come in several varieties, ranging from simple dust masks available in any hardware store to fullface respirators with cartridges to collect potentially harmful airborne particles. At a minimum, purchase several disposable masks with an N95 or better rating. Look for "NIOSH N95" on the package; the "N95" is an efficiency rating that means the mask blocks about 95 percent of particles that are 0.3 microns in size or larger. (The comparable European mask has a "P2" rating.)

For even better protection, look for a respirator with a "P100" rating. These are half face respirators. They're fairly comfortable and are reusable, with a disposable cartridge that can be discarded after a few months of use. A "NIOSH P100" rating means that the mask blocks over 99.97 percent of airborne particles. P100 masks are oil proof and can also be used to block chemicals that contain oil. (The comparable European mask has a "P3" rating.)

When selecting a respirator, it is essential that the respirator be the right size. One size does not fit

An N95 mask, pictured on the left, is useful for protecting the lungs when working with glass powders or other potentially hazardous items. A P100 respirator, shown at right, offers even better protection. (Photo by the author.)

all -- in order to prevent fumes from slipping in, an effective respirator should form a snug seal around the face. If you're not certain whether your respirator fits well or if you're uncertain about what kind of cartridge is best for your application, then it's a good idea to get advice from an informed expert.

Ceramic fiber products

It's nearly impossible to work with a kiln without being exposed to ceramic fiber products. Fiber paper is perhaps the most commonly used ceramic fiber product, but related products also include fiber blanket and fiber board. All of these should be treated with respect, as should silica dust. These items are potentially dangerous and can be carcinogenic, especially at high temperatures.

If you have decided to use ceramic fiber products in your work area, consider taking the following precautions to help minimize the dangers inherent in these materials.

• Wear a respirator in any situation where you are dealing with loose fibers or silica dust. Make sure you have the proper respirator for filtering out these particles -- it should have a purple/pink cartridge.

• Always use a HEPA filter in your vacuum, rather than the standard filter. HEPA filters only cost a few dollars more, but the do a much

better job of keeping ceramic fiber particals or other potential carcinogens out of the air.

• Even if you only use fiber paper occasionally, it's a good idea to use sweeping compound to help clean your work area. This substance is sprinkled around an area with loose fibers, then just swept and discarded.

• Wear latex or similar gloves when cutting or molding ceramic fiber products.

Hazardous chemicals

In addition to ceramic fiber products, many substances which are commonly used in glassworking can be hazardous. Glass itself can contain hazardous ingredients, but these are generally not a problem at kilnforming temperatures. Some substances, such as ground silica, silver nitrite, or muriatic acid, require the use of protective gloves or a respirator.

If in doubt about the safety of a particular material, ask the manufacturer for a copy of the Material Safety Data Sheet (MSDS) for the material. The MSDS contains important information about the substance and how it should be handled and used. Follow the guidelines recommended in the MSDS.

The key thing to remember is to always be on the lookout for hazardous chemicals and protect yourself accordingly.

197

Cuts and scrapes

Minor cuts and scrapes from working with glass are inevitable. Treatment is straightforward: wash the affected area. Apply an antibiotic ointment. Cover with an adhesive bandage. Seek a doctor's help for deep cuts or bleeding that doesn't stop.

If blood is on the table or floor, spray the area with a solution of 10% bleach (sodium hypochlorite). Bleach kills bloodborne pathogens such as Hepatitis and HIV on contact. The bleach solution should be used as soon as possible after the blood appears.

Burns

If you're lucky, you'll never burn yourself. If you're human, you probably will. Since kilns operate at much higher temperatures than a household oven, the potential for severe burns is always there. Most burns occur because you aren't using the right safety equipment or because your attention momentarily strays and you get careless. Proper treatment depends on the severity of the burn, but treating as soon as possible is essential for all burns.

For first degree burns, where the skin is red and painful, and second degree burns, which can blister or swell, immediately cool the burned area by placing it under cold running water. Then apply an ointment or protective dry bandage. Never pop blisters or peel back damaged skin.

It's not usually necessary to see a doctor for first or second degree burns, but third degree burns, in which the skin is charred and the damage extends below the surface, require immediate medical attention. Don't try to clean the burned area; instead, just cover the area, keep calm, and get trained help immediately.

Essential safety equipment

It is highly recommended that you invest in the following equipment to help keep the studio safe and make working with glass more enjoyable.

- **A fire extinguisher**. Pick one that's rated "ABC" for fires of any type, from electrical to paper. Keep it near the kiln, inspect it regularly, and know how to use it. You'll probably never need it, but you'll be eternally grateful if you do.

- **Simple first aid items**. Start with common items such as adhesive bandages, burn ointments, and aspirin or a similar painkiller.

- **Two kinds of safety glasses**. You'll need one pair of clear safety glasses for grinding and cold working glass and a second pair of shaded glasses for looking into the kiln.

- **Two kinds of gloves**. The first pair of gloves should be made for withstanding heat. The second should be made of latex or rubber and should be used for dealing with chemicals.

- **A respirator or mask**. Get the kind of mask or respirator that's rated for the kinds of work you do. At a minimum, keep a supply of N95 paper masks handy.

- **Bleach solution**. In a spray bottle, mix a solution of one part bleach with nine parts water. Spray this anywhere blood contaminates work surfaces or floors.

- **Ear protection**. Keep either ear plugs or ear muffs on hand for use with noisy machines.

These items should either be kept in a centrally located kit or be available next to the places where they are used.

Safety is something that most people don't think about, but it takes only a few extra moments to work safely. Not only is it time well spent, it will go a long way toward making sure your kiln-forming experiences are enjoyable, productive, and safe.

Chapter 22

Firing schedules made simple

Fusing • Slumping • Simple casting • Firing without a controller

In some ways, it's a misnomer to claim that firing schedules can be made simple. All kilns are different, all artist's want to achieve different things, and no two items being fired are the same. How could it be possible to make all this complexity simple?

The answer, of course, is that it's not possible. Instead, what's needed is a basic understanding of the principles behind firing schedules. Rather than blindly follow a "master" schedule or select a schedule from a pre-programmed controller, it's critical to learn to apply basic fusing and slumping principles to the project at hand. The focus should be on understanding what's happening in the kiln, not on memorizing the numbers in a specific firing schedule.

Toward that end, there are several key elements that must be considered before each and every firing.

• The kind of firing

Obviously, fuse firings are different from slump firings, but the differences don't stop there. There's a range of around 150F/84C between just barely tacking powder on top of a base layer of glass and fusing multiple layers of glass totally flat. Slumping a simple square slumper mold requires a much lower temperature than slumping a complicated mold with wavy edges and a deep drop. Casting a piece may require a different approach altogether.

Some firings will require a soak to minimize trapped air bubbles, some won't. Some can be started and left to fire unattended, others will need to be closely monitored. Some require a great deal of thought, others are similar to previous firings and can be started with certainty.

Every firing should be treated as though it is unique. Consider the difference between the next firing and all the ones you've fired before. Consult your firing log. Is this a basic firing? Or is it something that needs to be examined before starting the kiln?

• The specific kiln being used

Some kilns fire hot, some fire cool. Some fully fuse at 1480F/804C, others fully fuse the same piece at 1450F/788C or 1500F/816C. The actual numbers aren't as important as the ability of the kiln to fire consistently -- the same kiln should fire the same way day after day.

Kilns without top elements will fire differently than kilns with both top and side elements. Kilns with only top elements are different as well. The distance from the glass piece to the elements, wherever they're located, is another factor to consider. Firing close to the elements or with only side elements means you should fire slower during initial heating to prevent thermal shock.

It all boils down to one simple lesson. Know your kiln.

• **The type of glass**

Although many of the schedules in this book are oriented to using Bullseye glass, in almost all situations they'll also work well for System 96 glass or for glass from Uroboros. System 96 may need to be fired to a slightly lower fusing temperature than Bullseye glass, but the difference is slight.

Other kinds of glass, such as Wasser, float glass, borosilicate, and Effetre (Moretti), may require very different temperatures than the ones suggested in this book. But the logic of the schedules will be the same. Just use the suggested schedules as a starting point and adjust based on previous experience and on what actually happens in the kiln. Testing with scraps before firing an important piece makes a lot of sense.

In addition to brand of glass, the color of the glass is also a significant factor. Dark colors such as black tend to behave differently in the kiln than lighter colors such as white. Glasses that are hard to cut may not fire the same as glasses that cut more easily. And textured glasses will require more heat to flatten out than glasses with little or no texture.

• **The thickness of the piece**

The overall size of the piece is important, especially as it relates to the "cry factor" (see below), but when it comes to firing schedules, the thickness of the piece means much more.

Thicker pieces must be fired more slowly. That goes for the initial stages of a firing, when the piece is heated from room temperature to around 1100F/593C. It's also true for the cooling stages of the firing, starting with annealing and continuing all the way down to room temperature. It's even true that thicker pieces may require longer bubble squeezes or lengthier soaks at the fusing or casting temperature.

Thickness is not simply a matter of measuring the height of a piece on the kiln shelf. A stack of glass layers, each 1/8" (3 mm) thick, can be fired much faster ,if the layers haven't been previously fused together, than if they have. And a piece with highs and lows or sharp angles will need to be fired differently from a piece that's a perfectly shaped circle or slab.

• **Don't forget the "cry factor"**

The cry factor is perhaps the most important factor of all. When considering which firing schedule to use, ask yourself how painful it would be if the piece was lost due to being fired incorrectly. Is the cry factor high or low?

If the cry factor is high, then fire the piece more slowly. Heat a few degrees per hour slower than normal and anneal for a bit longer than normal. Don't take chances. It's far better to take a few hours longer to complete a piece than to spend days (or even weeks) starting the piece all over again from scratch.

• **If in doubt, test**

If your piece is very different from pieces you've fired before, or if you're using a complicated new mold for the first time, then it usually makes sense to do a test firing first, rather than just haphazardly fire to see what happens.

Don't underestimate the value of test tiles. If you're trying out new colors or textures, or want to experiment with a new inclusion or powder effect, then try it first on a small tile, rather than a large piece of glass. It will take less time to put it together, you'll get a first hand look at the effect, and then you can decide if it's worth committing to a larger project. The rewards of testing are much great than the cost of not testing. If you test first, the cost of failure won't be nearly so painful and the potential for creating a really wonderful final piece will be much greater.

Above all, keep good logs of your experiences, both successes and failures. In time you'll come up with your own firing schedules, optimized for your kiln, your work, and the way you like to fire your glass.

Fusing

A basic fusing schedule has five steps: initial heating, bubble squeeze, fusing, annealing, and final cooling. The rate of temperature change in each step, as well as the special firing temperatures, must be adjusted based on your kiln, your glass piece, and your desired final appearance. The first bold line of each step below, assumes a two or three layer piece that has not been previously fired, where each layer is 1/8" (3 mm) thick. Beneath each bold line are suggestions on how to modify your firing schedule for your specific situation.

1. **Initial heating: Fire at 400F/222C per hour to 1100F/593C, then hold 10 minutes**

- Smaller pieces, such as jewelry, can be fired faster, but firing at 400F/222C will not cause problems.

- Pieces that are already fused together need to be fired slower. How slow depends on the thickness of the piece. For two layers, try 300F/167C per hour. For three layers, try 250F/139C per hour. For four layers, try 200F/111C per hour. For eight layer pieces, 1" (25 mm) thick, try 100F/46C per hour.

- Fire slower if your kiln has side elements only or has a history of heating unevenly. A good rule of thumb is to fire at half the rate normally recommended.

- If the cry factor is high, then fire the piece more slowly.

2. **Bubble squeeze: Fire at 200F/111C per hour to 1240F/671C, then hold 30 minutes**

- If avoiding trapped air bubbles is not a concern, then it's possible, but not usually mandatory, to fire faster through this step and skip the hold.

- If your piece has more than two or three layers or if there is a greater than normal possibility of trapping unwanted air bubbles, then fire at a slower rate and hold for longer. Try a rate of 100F/56C per hour with an hour long hold at 1240F/671C.

3. **Fusing: Fire as quickly as your kiln allows to your fusing temperature, then hold 10 minutes.**

- A full fuse is generally in the range from 1450F/788C to 1500F/816C.

- A tack fuse is generally in the range from 1375F/746C to 1450F/788C.

- The 10 minute hold can be lengthened or shortened to achieve your desired final appearance.

4. **Annealing: Cool as quickly as your kiln allows to your annealing temperature, then hold.**

- The specific annealing temperature depends on the glass being used. Bullseye currently recommends 900F/482C, System 96 recommends 950F/510C, and Uroboros recommends 960F/516C. If the annealing temperature is unknown, use 960F/515C for art glass and 1000F/538C for float glass. The specific temperature is not as critical as making certain to include an annealing soak.

- For two to three layer pieces, the length of the hold at the annealing temperature should be 15 minutes per layer, plus another 15 minutes, if the piece incorporates tack fused elements or inclusions. A soak of one hour is conservative enough to work for nearly all two to three layer situations.

- For pieces that are 1/2" (12.7 mm) or thicker, up to two inches (50 mm), the hold at the annealing temperature should be 30 minutes per 1/8" (3 mm) layer.

- For pieces that are thicker than two inches (50 mm), follow the manufacturer's recommendations.

- It is not necessary (and generally not recommended) to open the kiln to cause the temperature to drop more rapidly from the fusing temperature to the annealing temperature.

- If the cry factor is high, then lengthen the annealing soak. A good rule of thumb for high cry factor situations is to anneal for a piece that is twice as thick as the actual thickness of the piece.

5. **Final cooling: Cool at 150F/83C per hour to 750F/399C, then turn off the kiln.**

- For pieces that are thicker than 3/8" (9 mm), follow the manufacturer's recommendations.

- For two to three layer pieces, Most kilns can be propped open about 1" (25 mm) at 300F/149C, 2" at 200F/93C, and fully when the temperature is below 150F/66C.

- If the cry factor is high, don't open the kiln until the temperature is below 100F/38C.

Slumping

A basic slumping schedule has four steps: initial heating, slumping, annealing, and final cooling. The rate of temperature change in each step, as well as the special firing temperatures, must be adjusted based on your kiln, your glass piece, and your desired final appearance. The first bold line of each step below, assumes a piece that is no more than 3/8" (9 mm) thick. Beneath each bold line are suggestions on how to modify your firing schedule for your specific situation.

1. **Initial heating: Fire at 300F/222C per hour to 1100F/593C, then hold 10 minutes**

- If desired, smaller pieces, such as jewelry, can be fired faster.

- Pieces that are thicker than 3/8" (9 mm) need to be fired slower. How slow depends on the thickness of the piece. For 1/2" (12 mm), try 200F/111C per hour. For eight layer pieces, 1" (25 mm) thick, try 100F/46C per hour.

- If the kiln has side elements only or has a history of heating unevenly, then fire slower. A good rule of thumb is to fire at half the rate normally recommended.

- If the cry factor is high, then fire the piece more slowly.

2. **Slumping: Fire at 100F/56C to your slumping temperature, then hold 30 minutes.**

- The precise slumping temperature depends on the glass and the specific mold being used. In general, large molds and shallow molds require a slumping temperature from 1100F/593C to 1150F/621C. Deeper molds, smaller molds, and molds with textured rims require a slumping temperature from 1250F/677C to 1275F/691C. Slumping above 1300F/704C is not recommended.

- A 30 minute hold is a good starting point, but it should be adjusted as necessary to achieve the desired effect in the mold. Longer holds at lower temperatures are generally preferable to shorter holds at a higher temperature.

3 and 4. Annealing and final cooling: Use the same recommendations as in the Fusing section.

Simple casting

Casting schedules are often more complicated than schedules for fusing and slumping. This is for two reasons. First, cast pieces tend to be thicker and more oddly shaped than fused and slumped pieces. Second, care must be taken not to crack or otherwise damage the mold during the firing. The schedule suggestions made below assume an open-faced casting no more than 1″ (25 mm) thick. They also assume a mold made of plaster/silica or a similar investment that requires additional time to finish the curing process as it heats. Larger or more complicated pieces will require a more conservative schedule than the one given here.

1. **Initial heating, part 1: Fire at 100F/111C per hour to 200F/93C, then hold one hour.**

2. **Initial heating, part 2: Fire at 100F/111C per hour to 350F/177C, then hold one hour.**

3. **Initial heating, part 3: Fire at 200F/111C per hour to 1250F/677C then hold one hour.**

4. **Casting: Fire as fast as the kiln allows to 1500F/816C, then hold 20 to 30 minutes.**

- The temperature and hold time may need to be adjusted, depending on the kiln, the type of glass used, and the complexity of the mold.

5. **Annealing, part 1: Cool as quickly as your kiln allows to your annealing temperature, then hold 4 hours.**

6. **Annealing, part 2: Cool at 40F/22C to 800F/527C, no hold required.**

7. **Final cooling: Cool at 80F/44C to 700F/371C, no hold required, then turn kiln off.**

Firing without a controller

It's possible to successfully fuse and slump without a kiln controller, but it is more difficult, especially as pieces become larger, thicker, and more complicated. If the kiln also lacks a pyrometer, which shows the temperature inside the kiln, then the degree of difficulty increases considerably for all but small jewelry-sized pieces.

Success starts by knowing your kiln. For a kiln that will only fire small pieces, no lengthy testing process is required. Just turn the kiln on, watch until your piece is done the way you want, then turn the kiln off and keep it closed until it cools back to room temperature. Successful results will depend on how closely you monitor your kiln.

The process is more elaborate for larger pieces. The basic schedule is to turn the kiln on and regulate it so that it takes two to three hours to reach 1100F/593C. After that temperature is reached, it's safe to turn the kiln to high and watch the piece until it finishes fusing or slumping. Then turn the kiln off and allow it to cool.

The key to making this schedule work is to learn how long it takes your kiln to fire from room temperature to 1100F/593C. To test to find out, place two pieces of scrap glass, one on top of the other, in a cool kiln. Turn the dial to medium heat (4 to 5 on many infinite switch dials) and time how long it takes for the kiln to reach 1100F/593C.

If your kiln lacks a pyrometer, watch until the glass start to glow red. If the time to reach this temperature is in the two to three hour range, Then you're ready to begin using your kiln to fuse and slump. If 1100F/593F is reached too quickly, redo the test with the dial set to a lower temperature. If it takes much longer than three hours to reach 1100F/593C, then try again with the dial set higher. Or start it on medium, then increase to medium high after the first hour. The key is to learn how to set your kiln so that it takes around three hours to reach 1100F.

Armed with that knowledge, you'll be able to fuse basic two to three layer pieces. Pieces that are thicker or more complicated will require better annealing than is possible without a controller to regulate the rate at which the kiln cools.

Left: Veruska Vagen, "Shakespeare After Cobbe, 1610," dot de verre. (Photo by Russell Johnson, courtesy of the artist.)

Below: Ellen Abbott and Marc Leva, "Hibiscus Box." Pate de verre lost wax casting. (Photo courtesy of the artists.)

References

Cummings, Keith. *A History of Glassforming.* London, England: A & C Black/Philadelphia, PA: University of Pennsylvania Press, 2002.

Cummings, Keith. *Techniques of Kiln-Formed Glass.* London, England: A & C Black/Philadelphia, PA: University of Pennsylvania Press, 1997.

Halem, Henry. *Glass Notes: A reference for the glass artist, Version 4.0.* Kent, OH: Franklin Mills Press, 2006.

Kervin, Jim and Fenton, Dan. *Pate de Verre and Kiln Casting of Glass.* Livermore, CA: GlassWear Studios, 1997.

Schmuck, Jonathon. *The Joy of Coldworking: A Guide to Grinding, Smoothing, and Polishing Blown and Fused Glass.* Clemmons, NC: Four Corners International, Inc., 2009.

Stone, Graham. *Firing Schedules for Glass: The Kiln Companion.* Melbourne, Australia: 2000.

Walker, Brad. *Contemporary Warm Glass: A Guide for Fusing, Slumping, and Related Kiln-forming Techniques.* Clemmons, NC: Four Corners International, Inc., 2000.

In addition to the published sources listed above, the Technotes and Tipsheets available on Bullseye Glass's website at *www.bullseyeglass.com* are an invaluable resource.

Other internet resources of note include the System 96 website at *www.system96. com*, the Uroboros Glass website at *www. uroboros.com,* the discussion on the Warm Glass bulletin board at *www.warmglass. com,* and articles contained at *www. warmtips.com.*

Resource Listing

An updated list of resources for the fused glass artist is available online at *www. warmglass.com.*

Right: "Undercover" by Jody Danner Walker. Enamels on glass. (Photo courtesy of the artist.)

Index

Photos of finished artwork indicated by **bold** page numbers.

Avery Anderson, "The Ancestors." Kiln-formed, laminated and coldworked. Cast glass and flameworked bird skulls. (Photo courtesy of the artist.)

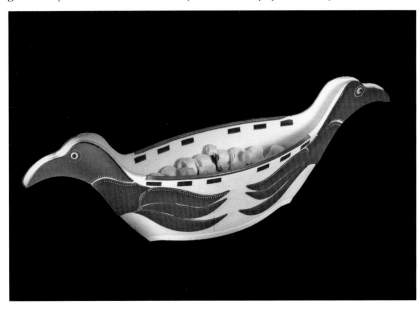

www.warmglass.com